LAND OF MANY BRIDGES

MY FATHER'S STORY

BELA RUTH SAMUEL TENENHOLTZ

CONTENTS

ISBN: 9789493231979 (ebook)

ISBN: 9789493231986 (paperback)

ISBN: 9789493231993 (hardcover)

Copyright © Bela Ruth Samuel Tenenholtz, 2022

Original Hebrew title: Eretz Gesharim Rabim (2019)

Dutch version: Land van vele Bruggen: Het verhaal van mijn vader (2020)

Publisher: Amsterdam Publishers, The Netherlands

info@amsterdampublishers.com

Land of Many Bridges is part of the series Holocaust Survivor True Stories WWII

Cover image: part of the family store's wrapping paper.

Dedicated to the memory of Cornelius and Hendrika Scheffer and in honor of their descendants. For over two years they kept my parents safe at a time when Jews were not safe anywhere. Our lives have been indelibly bound up ever since. Their heroism made it possible for me to be born, and thus, for my children, grandchildren, and great-grandchildren to come into the world.

And whoever saves a single soul, it is considered as if he saved an entire world.

Mishnah Sanhedrin 4:5; Yerushalmi Talmud 4:9, Babylonian Talmud Sanhedrin 37a.

So that all may know and honor them too.

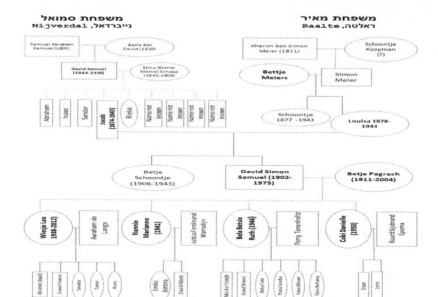

משפחת סמואל
Nijverdal , נייברדאל

משפחת מאיר
Raalte, ראלטה

Samuel Abraham Samuel (1801)

Bella Bat David (1810)

Aharon ben Simon Meier (1811)

Schoontje Koopman (?)

David Samuel (1844-1935)

Elina (Esther Malka) Schaap (1842-1906)

Bettje Meiers

Simon Meier

Abraham

Isaac

Sender

Jacob (1874-1943)

Rieka

Naam nog onbekend

Naam nog onbekend

Naam nog onbekend

Naam nog onbekend

Naam nog onbekend

Schoontje 1877 -1943

Louisa 1878-1943

Betje Schoontje (1906-1943)

David Simon Samuel (1902-1975)

Betje Pagrach (1911-2004)

Wiesje Lea 1938-2012

Avraham de Lange

Nannie Marianne (1941)

Justus Ferdinand Vilarradijn

Bela Betsie Ruth (1946)

Perry Tenenholtz

Cobi Danielle (1950)

Ruurd Sijsbrand Epema

Abanne Uiaud

Daniel Franve

Sender

Tamar

Arara

Emilie

Bettina

David Albert

Moshe Joseph

David Shimon

Batya Sara

Prana Sineba

Hava Mirum

Shira Nehama

Chaim

Leon

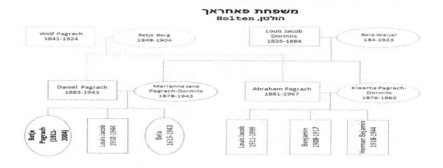

משפחת פאחראך
Holten, הולטן

Wolf Pagrach 1841-1924

Betje Berg 1848-1904

Louis Jacob Dormits 1835-1864

Bela Weijel 184-1923

Daniel Pagrach 1883-1943

Marianne Jane Pagrach-Dormits 1878-1943

Abraham Pagrach 1881-1967

Klaartje Pagrach-Dormits 1876-1965

Betje Pagrach (1911-2004)

Louis Jacob 1910-1944

Bela 1615-1943

Louis Jacob 1911-1996

Benjamin 1906-1917

Herman Bejamin 1918-1944

INTRODUCTION

Where does any story begin, and where does the story of my father and myself find its beginning? I thought that now, gray and filled with years, I finally held all the thinning threads of our lives in my hands, and that I had already succeeded in unraveling all the knots. The story was finished. I was ready to start the task of passing on our history to my children, just as a good Jew is commanded to pass down the laws of our religion and the story of the Exodus from Egypt. But the story of my father? To my chagrin I discovered almost immediately that I did not know a thing. There I was, on the cusp of understanding, falling again with a big bang into a vacuum between the naked truth and my compromised memories. Before I could honestly begin to tell my father's story as it had happened, I had to make a journey to the far bank of my life.

Often, the truth is much stranger than the imagination, and what happened next came as an answer to my intense prayer: a kind man by the name of Johan Alferink placed in my shaking hands the content of his archive from the village of my birth, Nijverdal, the Netherlands. It was a virtual avalanche of new data that spanned some 50 years, ending 10 years before my father's death. And there I was, unable to fully grasp the storm of papers, letters, and photographs, yet stubborn as always, I worked my way through the documents. Slowly, a new understanding grew about everything that had happened to my family during "The Terrible Times", as my mother used to call the years leading up to the persecution and murder of the Jews in occupied Europe – what we now call Shoah.

I respectfully removed the virtual dust from the documents, and slowly and gently as I laid them among the puzzle pieces of our life, the picture clarified in light of the new information. I saw the horrible suffering that my father had endured, and life, as I had dreamt it up, shifted. I saw how my father, in spite of all the horrors and difficulties, had found the courage to clear a new path for us, his children, so we could walk more lightly. He had cleared the boulders from our paths with all his strength and had lovingly paid the price for it. Perhaps he hoped that we would never know the details of everything he and my mother had been forced to live through.

For a moment the clouds shifted, and I clearly saw both my parents standing as they blocked the horrors with their bodies. I saw my father in the center, in a place of honor, high above his descendants, and I knew he was worthy to be given this place. He was the center of our family's history, there in the small village where we were born, and this is where he will remain. I stretch out my hands to my father, but it is all an illusion, just as the rainbow with its beautiful colors appears within reach but always remains beyond touch, so near and yet so far.

And yet, and yet... Judaism provides one with a special blessing to recite when one sees a rainbow, for it is a rare event, and now that I see my father in his shining new light, I also wish to say a blessing. It is a blessing inspired by that special bond between us, something sacred and without words.

A secret bond? Yes, a bond that had to be hidden to survive in our traumatized home: my little sister and I lived in that house with parents and two older sisters who had lived through the Shoah, but while they had survived, none of them were the same in 1945.

My mother never got over the unimaginable loss of her parents, siblings, uncles, aunts, and cousins. She lived a life of perpetual mourning and a search for someone to blame for their horrible deaths. And papa? He was also the only one of his immediate family "to return" – as the euphemism called the survival. Back to what, then? Back to his previous life? Perhaps a return from living a life in hiding, a life with no civil rights, no right to life at all. Perhaps, but my father was a man who was cursed with a strong sense of obligation and responsibility. He never denied mama's daily accusations, uttered in a shrill voice: "It is on your conscience. You could have saved them, but you didn't!" He never denied being guilty, and I, born in 1946, had no idea what they were talking about. What was my mother saying? Neither Danielle nor I knew anything about the persecution of the Jews. This was a topic that never came up in our household. We only heard our parents' arguments, and so, I got the notion from my mother that our father was a bad person and that we should avoid him. As a result, I was deadly afraid of him and sought my mother's protection, which she gave us as long as we took her side and accepted everything that she said about our father without question or criticism. I accepted that my father was the kind of man who enjoyed watching our mother's suffering and took pleasure in his cruelty toward her. It was obvious that he was guilty of whatever crimes my mother accused him of, but what exactly they were remained a dark, threatening secret.

"Don't talk to him," mama impressed upon us. "Say only what I say to him." And so, we did. After their loud arguments, my father retreated in painful silence and escaped to his sanctuary, the store. At that point, our mother sent one of us to follow him and shout out a few hurtful phrases, which were a verbatim repetition of our mother's words. We learned to call after him: "Why are you so cruel to our mama? Why aren't you nice to her?" We were a home of two camps, the good ones and the bad ones, with all four children in our mother's camp, while our father remained all alone in his. Aside from saying that he could not help any of it, he never defended himself against her horrible accusations, and so, we children did not know any better.

Life at home changed when I was seven years old.

When I was seven years old, something happened so that I wound up in the other camp: in my father's camp. However, the resulting bond remained one of few words. Few words, perhaps, but it was a connection that held fast over the coming 20 years of my life and did not disappear even after my father's death. The opposite is true! There is still a special, almost silent narrative possible between his world of the dead and our world of the living. It is an eternal connection, painless and clear; certainly, now that I finally know everything that was hidden from me. With the help of this book, I have passed on the story and hope that it will continue to resonate down the generations with a new sound. A better, almost holy one. The connection with my mother has also lightened and I can write about her without reproach. I can write with love. Mama do not worry, everything is good between us. It is all good.

PROLOGUE

Two years ago, in 2014, my daughter Hani who lives in Jerusalem came for a weekend to my home in Kiryat Shmuel on the Mediterranean. After dinner we curled up on the sofa talking lightly about this and that, but in the middle of a sentence, she suddenly asked me if I would go to the Netherlands with her.[1] "To learn about my roots, mama." Hani does not usually ask for things without careful thought, and so I promised that I would consider it. And there I was, without warning, stuck once again in the morass of our past in the eastern province of Overijssel, Twente, in Nijverdal.

Why should I go searching for something that was not even there? I asked for clarification. "Mama, I want to understand all those stories you tell a little bit better." Oh, yes, my stories. I did indeed tell my children some shreds of the past, mostly entertaining anecdotes about my father's store; stories I had brought with me from my youth, all neatly sterilized. I knew very little about my roots or ancestors. Actually, I knew nothing at all. After all, we really had no history anymore. We were simply this one tiny Jewish family, the Samuel Prins family, the only Jewish family in Nijverdal. Our history had started with us: Father and Mother – created from the ashes of their creators – two big sisters and two little ones. Before that time there had been no one, although, paradoxically, there were photos of grandmothers and grandfathers, young uncles and aunts, whose dreary portraits hung in the stairwell, giving me dirty looks. They terrorized me when I needed to go downstairs at night to use the toilet. I was afraid to go down the steps. Their eyes followed me everywhere, and I was never sure of their feelings toward me. Perhaps they were angry with me or possibly looked at me with pleasure. "Hani," I said with a sigh, "let's go someplace else, to a country where people have incredibly deep roots and lots of ancestors. Italy perhaps? Or even Scandinavia. But our ancestry in Nijverdal – there is nothing to talk about. I would be done in five minutes. Look, here is where I was born, and here I went to school, and there my parents are buried. That is the whole story. And then what? Drink coffee for the rest of the week?" But I could tell that Hani was not to be put off and understood that I had to return to both Nijverdal and Holten. I needed to learn my parents' roots. It was going to happen. The die was cast and the time to dig into the past had come. I was about to conjure up a lost world. So far, I possessed only shards and slivers of gas chambers, transports, murder, and concentration camps; things whispered about during my childhood, and which had become embedded in my DNA, but nothing was clear. The truth was hidden in fairy tales I had created for myself to explain what my parents whispered to each other in secret. I needed a key to a place in the past, to a door that I could enter without fear in order to understand what I had never dared to ask about. And, in order to answer Hani's question about the origin of the stories I told my children, I needed to delve into them.

That key I needed was not to open the door to the Shoah. No, I needed to find the key to a door to before that time: to the time when Nijverdal had a small Jewish community that lived its life to the fullest, did business, educated its children, and was considered an integral part of the village. That was my destination. My stories had to grow up, just as I had done, and they needed to be colored with different shades. This meant that our trip to the drizzly Netherlands and the hills of Overijssel would be a journey of discovery for me too.

We were going to the spring of my stories: a clear, purified well of sparkling water.

From that moment on, I did nothing but think about what I knew, what I did not know, and what I wanted to know. I was looking for a starting point. Suddenly, I thought about the story of my father's grandfather, David Samuel, who was known in the village as "The Old Prince," the prince of peddlers.

One evening, when the house was quiet and the dishes done, I pulled out my computer and surfed Google for a bit, looking for something to catch my eye. I landed on a website dedicated to Johanna van Buren, an early 20th-century local poet, and looked for the poem entitled *de ole prinse* – the old prince – which she had written in honor of my great-grandfather's 90th birthday. I did not find the poem there, so I left the copy I had on my computer on the webpage with a short message. Shortly after, I received a reply from Dinand Webbink, the site manager. He told me about his work in the archives of Deventer. I told him about the trip I was planning for Hani and myself, and I asked if he knew anything about Nijverdal and the Samuel Prins family. Dinand responded with a family tree that covered over 150 years of my ancestry, and which landed in my lap like the proverbial ripe apple. I read names that were new to me and saw places to which I had no inkling that we were connected. Dinand also passed on my requests to Johan Alferink, the man who managed the historical archives in Nijverdal, as well as to Anton Heijmerikx from the historical circle in Raalte. I had so many questions, but finally I also had a place where I could ask them! "Anton, do you have a Jewish cemetery in Raalte, and if so, could we visit it? Do you have an index of the graves? Do you know who is buried there?" Everything was falling into place. I already knew that Nijverdal had a tiny Jewish cemetery but had no idea who lay buried there, or if any of them were related to me.

Slowly but surely, a kind of geographical clarity emerged. The comment I had left on the Johanna van Buren website had given me a starting point. We had to get to Raalte first. This sleepy town is only about 12 kilometers from Nijverdal and lies on the train route to Zwolle, the provincial capital. I had seen its station countless times but had never been there. Papa disliked even mentioning the town's name. "I will never set foot there", he would say as Raalte station disappeared out of sight and the train moved west, but he explained nothing. And now, suddenly, with the help of Dinand and Johan's archives, I learned that my father's mother had been born in Raalte. With the assistance of the digital population registration, I even discovered that her mother had been one of twins, and that she had tragically died only three weeks after giving birth to my grandmother Louisa. Her final resting place was the Jewish cemetery of Raalte. This was the place to start our quest for roots. DNA that was directly connected to me had found an eternal resting place; great-grandmother Bethe had not been murdered in the gas chambers of Sobibor. She had not been worked to death in a concentration camp. Notwithstanding the sad circumstances of her life, she had lived it without anyone conspiring to take it away from her. She was the first key to our quest, and Hani and I set our compass for the sleepy town of Raalte.

For ancestors of my grandfather Jacob's side, I could simply stay in Nijverdal. My father had grown up there and I had heard stories of who his grandfather was. He was that old prince whose name my father had inherited, and the man who had died in 1935, at the age of 92, surrounded by children and grandchildren. He had been buried with all the honors due to him in the Jewish cemetery of Hellendoorn, adjacent to Nijverdal. His wife Elina had died many years before him, and I was sure that I would find her there as well. This was my bridgehead, which would assure us safe passage over the Shoah. Great-grandparents! We could look at people who had lived simple and normal lives, dreaming their simple, normal dreams. Those who had not been swept away in the orgy of the mass murder of six million innocent souls. And what would be our next step? Hani and I would find their headstones that marked their final resting place and reconnect. We would carry their memory with us into the present. For me, this meant that we would metaphorically carry them on our shoulders to the land of the Jews, to Israel. We would recreate our own exodus where Moses had taken Josef's bones for burial in the Promised Land.

This became the title of my first story even before we had packed our bags – how we took upon ourselves the phrase that is engraved on every Jewish headstone: "May their soul be tied up in the bundle of life."

A bundle is something tactile, something we could pass on, and it would be our sacred burden to do so.

---

1. The official name of the country is really the Netherlands, and although in English Holland is more commonly used, I have chosen to stick to its official name because in Dutch, Holland actually refers to two of the western provinces where the seat of government and power reside.

1

DAVID SIMON SAMUEL IS BORN: 1902

Usually, the home of Louisa and Jacob Samuel-Meier was so clean that you could eat off the floor, but since the day before yesterday, it resembled a house in the eye of the storm. Breakfast dishes were lying in the dairy washing-up tub, and the meat cutlery from the previous evening had been left on the counter unwashed. The bedroom was dusty and unaired. The window remained closed despite the warm weather. One of their big bath towels lay damp and neglected on the bathroom floor, discarded as a dirty floor rag. Everything Louisa had sewn over the past few weeks in preparation for the child in her womb had not been washed, and yet her due date was close. It was the end of June 1902, and summer was already in the air. The house was stifling with the stale humid air.

Louisa, a young woman, lay in her bed dressed in an old night gown that stretched tightly over her swollen belly. Her black curls hung carelessly around her face. Pale as a ghost and her pillow wet with tears, she refused to get out of bed. Jacob, her husband of not even two years, did not know what to do. Up to this point, he had been so happy about becoming a father that he had not even noticed how Louisa withdrew more and more into herself. In the store, he could not concentrate on his work. He had already given the wrong change twice, and had spilled the hot black coffee all over himself. When his wife refused to even talk to him and couldn't stop crying, he gave up his attempts at cheering her up. He wrote an urgent note to Schoontje, Louisa's older sister who lived down the street and was married to his own brother Shmuel-Sandor. He sent one of the neighbor's children to deliver it to her. Perhaps she could come over and talk some sense into his wife, but she had not arrived yet. Once more, Jacob climbed the stairs to the bedroom and left the clerk in the store by himself. Jacob Samuel was a good-looking man, he had wavy black hair that hung low over his forehead and blue eyes that were dark with worry and sympathy for his wife's anxiety. Under his gray-blue dustcoat he wore a dark suit. He sat down on the edge of his wife's bed and leaned over. "Louisa, girl," he said softly, his voice filled with tenderness and his hand close to hers but afraid to touch her. "Darling, do not be afraid of the delivery! These are different times. You will be just fine. I have paid for a midwife and a doctor to attend to you when your time comes." He repeated these words perhaps three times, but his wife responded with a furious look. "You are just like my father. You will never succeed in raising a child on your own. You simply don't have it in you, and my poor baby is going to be an orphan just like me and will be passed from hand to hand without a permanent caregiver. I don't know what to do!" And she turned her back toward him. Jacob saw how her body heaved with sobs.

He knew perfectly well what his wife was talking about. Her own mother had died of complications a few weeks after Louisa had been born. During the first months after their *Huppe* (marriage) she had been so afraid of pregnancy that it affected their intimacy. He had been patient and had simply continued to court her. He spoke softly about their marital obligations, "We are husband and wife now, and this kind of love is part of that covenant." And now Louisa was at the end of her pregnancy, and all of those suppressed fears had surfaced again. Jacob was known as a charming man, and women liked him. Sitting close to his wife, he reminisced a little, "Do you remember in the beginning, that first year after the *Huppe*, you were afraid to even sleep in the double bed with me, and often you preferred to sleep in your *niddah* bed, the single bed of your menstrual period. Remember?" Jacob sensed that his wife listened to him intently, and it gave him courage. "Your sister spoke to you about women's things and promised you that in this day and age having children was no longer dangerous. We have modern medicine now, she told you. That was just after her Elina had been born. She even placed her firstborn child in your arms. Then we truly became husband and wife. Remember?"

Louisa turned back to her husband and gave him a small fleeting smile. "Ah, Jacob, of course I remember all of that just as if it happened today. How you came to Raalte on the train from Nijverdal. In the beginning you simply accompanied your brother who was courting our Schoontje, but later you came for me."

Now it was Jacob's turn to smile, "You were like the Mona Lisa, so beautiful!" He sighed with pleasure. "Well, you were not exactly hard on the eyes either, you know," answered his wife, who a moment ago had been shedding all her tears on the pillow. Together they relived that sweet memory.

The talk helped. Although Louisa remained tense, she made an effort to overcome her anxiety. She got out of bed and cleaned the house, picked up the mess, washed the dishes, and did the laundry. Jacob kept an eye on her so she wouldn't overdo it. The house now waited with bated breath for the blessed child that it was ready to welcome. Nature finally took its course, and on a warm night in early July, a little boy came into this world. He was Jacob and Louisa's firstborn son. True to tradition, they decided to name the baby after his two grandfathers: David and Simon. In the village people made jokes about the child's date of birth, July 4th, and with a wink and a smile, they related how in America little David Simon's birth had been declared a national holiday, with flags and fireworks. The year was 1902, the very beginning of the 20th century, and the Hebrew date was 29 Sivan, 5663.

Days turned into weeks. Louisa recovered physically and rejoiced that

9

her baby was easy-going and cried very little. Slowly, the tension of the delivery slipped into the past, especially after the first three weeks had passed and Louisa felt no discomfort. Since the cursed event had not occurred, the *Pidyon* ceremony (the symbolic release of the first-born from service in the Temple) could be celebrated with pomp and circumstance. The entire family was present at the event, and Abraham, the Cohen, conducted the ceremony. Grandfather David glowed with pride as he looked at the healthy little boy that was placed in his arms for a minute. Life returned to normal.

To his parents' delight, baby David grew into a smiling and curious little boy. He was obviously intelligent. Louisa adored him. She neglected the housework and let the dust settle in previously pristine corners; Jacob cut his losses and hired a girl to clean the house. Louisa simply did not have time for her chores, but truth be told, neither did she care about them. Everything was about her son. "Look at that little darling," she said to Schoontje and Jacob. "Look how clever he is!" With her own two hands she sewed silk vests and embroidered them with birds and flowers. She knitted him numerous little sweaters. However, notwithstanding the successful delivery and her joy in her baby, Louisa was unable to forget that even though her own mother had had no post-partum problems after Schoontje was born, she died after her second delivery. Louisa was sure: she did not want any more children.

Of course, this situation created a barrier between husband and wife. Jacob saw how his brothers Abraham and Shmuel-Sandor were parents of several children already, all born close together, and he fondly remembered the large family of his childhood. He had big plans for his own life: many children, to work hard and build up the business. Also, he planned for his children to later continue what he had created, just as he had taken over his father's business. But there was only little David. Deep inside, he hoped that if he were patient and gave Louisa time to change her mind, it would all work out. However, the distance brought on by her fear of pregnancy resulted in a different kind of relationship. They lived side by side and were courteous to each other. Jacob kept his disappointment to himself. He left it to her Schoontje to convince Louisa that children bring their own blessing.

As a result, David Simon Samuel, son of Jacob, remained an only child, and this meant that all his milestones were marked with great celebration. David, like most boys born in the beginning of the 20th century, wore a dress until he became potty trained. This was mostly a practical decision, considering that dresses saved on dirty laundry. Plastic was unknown at the time, and each diaper change meant that the baby's entire outfit had to be changed. In a time when women washed everything by hand, a dress for an infant was the logical choice. When a little boy was finally out of diapers, his first pair of pants was celebrated with a party. For David, the *in de broek steken* (putting him in pants) ceremony took place when he was about three years old. Louisa served cakes and sweet drinks, and the child received a special present to mark the occasion: it was a model of the house where he was born. His father and grandfather had built it together. It was an amazing toy, everything could be taken apart. The roof came off so he could look inside the little house, like Gulliver in Lilliput, the windows and doors opened and the front door had a hook he could move up and down. It was beautiful. He barely managed to put his arms around the house and with his eyes shining he sat down to see what it could do. He even forgot the cake that his mother had baked for the occasion, and from that day onward, David slept with the house dozing next to his bed. During the day, he took the model house outside with him and sat on the stones in back of the house while his mother weeded their vegetable garden. Only when he was nearly six years old and ready to go to school was the house wrapped up and put in storage in order to make room for more educational toys. In spite of his tears, papa Jacob wrapped the house in a large piece of strong paper, tied it together with string, and put it inside a cardboard box for safekeeping. He then handed his son a package with a slate board in a wooden frame and a stylus so he could learn to write, as well as a box of wooden letters. His beloved house disappeared behind the wooden wall in the attic, and there it fell asleep.

In April 1943, the looters in their Dutch police uniforms entered the empty house where Louisa and Jacob had lived, and with their unwiped boots desecrated every room. They made a careful inventory of every item they found in the house to present to the Nazi occupiers. Eventually, they also climbed the steep wooden stairs that led to the attic. There they found a dirty rag, not neatly folded and thrown down in haste, a stool with a broken leg, and some goods from the store. Nothing was too small or worthless to be noted down. Nothing was forgotten. Nothing too expensive or worn out. The house suffered it all in silence. It creaked a little but remained waiting. The looters failed to notice the attic's walled-off section neatly built of wood, which was so beautifully crafted that it seemed part of the supporting structure. Jacob and his father, the *Ole Prinse* David, had built that wall. What was hidden there remained untouched. Jacob and Louisa were long gone. They were dust in the cold wind of Poland, which without mercy, had spread their ashes over the earth. But the little house that Jacob and David had built for the child remained hidden and safe.

It remained that way for at least two years. The walls whispered stories of children's voices once heard in that big house. There were stories of a family which no longer existed. Perhaps it was even a miracle that the Nazi authorities did not succeed in selling that house. Potential renters were turned away. Consequently, 101 Rijssensestraat remained empty.

After that horrible war, and after the incomprehensible murder of so many people, the little house still remained in its protective wrapping paper and box in the attic. It still waited for little fingers to lift it out of its cardboard prison, for a child to be allowed to play with it. It remained in stasis until one evening in 1945, when David Simon Samuel, who had only recently returned from his time in hiding from the Nazi persecution approached the silent home where his parents had lived. He was the man who had been that sweet curious little boy, who had lived in that house, and who was now married and the father of two children who were kept safe by brave and noble

Dutchmen. The four survivors were back in their home at number 82, and he approached number 101 in silence.

Carefully, oh so carefully, he pushed the key into the lock, took a deep breath, and shaking with fear of what he might find, he walked from room to room. He walked slowly, the way a man follows a coffin. Everything was empty. Most leftovers were broken pieces of furniture. Everything of any value had been stolen. The house itself was like a body not yet buried, waiting to be laid to rest. Eventually, David walked up the steep steps to the attic. He remembered the wooden wall and found the groove which enabled him to slide it open. His hands remembered. In that small space, he also saw the box in its wrapping paper, with the string still tied around the toy house from his early childhood. His father's handywork still existed. For a long minute David was unable to move, paying homage to what he saw in front of him. Then, bowing reverently over the abandoned treasure, he picked it up and clasped it to his breast. Carefully, oh so very carefully, he carried the impossibly heavy box downstairs, crossed the street to his home at number 82, and waited. Betje, his wife, did not see him, and neither did his little girls. They had finally drifted off to sleep. Now in his own home, David tiptoed upstairs, still holding the toy house. He pulled out the ladder and slid away the bolt to his attic. There, balancing the box between two beams under the roof, he gently put the toy house in its new resting place.

Seven more years passed, and that little toy model of a house still remained in the attic, until the family moved into a new house at number 30 of the Rijssensestraat, closer to the village center. David had not forgotten the toy house built for him by his father Jacob and Opa David. He did not entrust it to the boisterous movers but moved it by himself and pushed it deep inside the space under the eaves of their new home. And once again, time passed through the hourglass until one rainy winter day, I, Bela Betsie Margriet, a little girl of seven, that mischievous little girl with heavy names of murdered aunts weighing down upon her, climbed up to the attic in search of adventure. The little girl that I was, found the cardboard box and carefully brought it out into the open. I undid the flaps, pushed back the string, and unveiled the hidden treasure. Oh! It was real treasure! For more than 40 years not a single child's hand had caressed the little toy house, and I freed it from its exile. For an entire afternoon, that little girl made up stories about the house, and turned it into a game fit for a girl. I knew nothing of its history and was not afraid of the house. I touched it with curiosity to see how to open the windows and take off the roof. It was simply interesting. The year was 1953, just after the huge floods in Zeeland in the southwestern part of the Netherlands. It was cold in Nijverdal too and the attic had no heat, but I did not feel anything. The little wooden house filled my imagination and warmed the world around me.

2

DAVID SIMON SAMUEL: NIJVERDAL
1935-1941

In pastoral Overijssel, in the small Jewish community of Hellendoorn-Nijverdal, Hitler's political victory was received as any other piece of foreign news. There were articles in the newspaper, and the radio reported and speculated about the consequences, but it wasn't really much more than that. They all heard broadcasts of the man's screaming speeches, and Betje Pagrach, David Simon Samuel's girlfriend, immediately nicknamed him "der Schreier" in their colloquial Yiddish. Within a short time, the entire family had picked up the name, spoken with contempt and a shake of the head, as if they were trying to swallow something unpleasant. It was especially because of this scornful nickname, that the situation became less frightening. They all agreed, all those gesturing young men: Hitler was a screamer and that was all they were going to say about it. He was but a passing phenomenon who would soon be forgotten. The biggest question was how a country as rich in culture as Germany had given their highest post to such a lout. Jews and non-Jews all agreed: "We are lucky to live here and to be the subjects of a beloved queen and a strong government. The Netherlands believes in equal rights for all its citizens in the kingdom. What happened in Germany could never happen here, and even there, that Schreier will be replaced by a more deserving head of state very quickly!"

Nevertheless, heated arguments broke out, especially when the subject touched the Netherlands. Could there be a situation when war might break out in their rain-soaked little country?

Despite the geographical distance between the Jews in the province and the events in Germany, David remained tense. The change in the German government could not have come at a more inopportune time for him. He was busy making meaningful changes in his life, for he had finally found "the one" and was head over heels in love. After a two-year courtship he had asked for her hand in marriage. He was ready to be a husband. He was already more than 30 years old and could picture himself as the head of a family with a wife and children, many children. All his life he had lived like a miser in order to save up for this moment, and he was more than capable of setting up his own household. Slowly, he had become well-to-do, and the time to take the next step had arrived. And now this in Germany. It was like an omen. It made him pause and consider whether the Yiddish proverb of man trying and G-d laughing was applicable here? David was a cautious man by instinct, and he said to himself that perhaps this was not the right time to set up a Jewish household only 60 kilometers from the German border. Perhaps he should bide his time to see what happens. Hopefully that screamer in Berlin would soon be booted out of office. On the other hand, the girl was perfect for him, and he had already started building a home for them. The contractor had been paid, and he and his father had made an agreement to expand the business. Perhaps, more important than all of that, there was the fact that Betje was sewing her wedding gown and he could not disappoint her. After much soul searching, David decided that life must go on as always. Stick to the routine. And yet, a small voice in his heart whispered hoarsely that there was more to this Hitler, that Schreier, than met the eye. The man was dangerous! The last thing he wanted to do was postpone the *Huppe* even if he could not deny that something in the world had changed. Still weighing all the facts and still incapable of making a final decision, he pulled out a huge red farmer's handkerchief from his pocket and tied a knot in one of the corners, just as the farmers did.

The knot would remind him that he had definitely heard that inner whisper.

And so, normal life continued: Betje and David got engaged on May 21, 1935, Lag BaOmer, 5695 according to the Jewish calendar. The young couple were given a few euphoric weeks, but then frightening news arrived from Germany: Hitler published his racial laws. From this moment, German Jews were a group apart and were no longer an integral part of society. Jews could no longer serve in the army; they were forbidden from using public parks; Jews were banned from the cinema; swimming pools were closed to Jews. David heard it all and it was like a slap in the face. He felt his blood drain from his face, started to shake uncontrollably and remembered the knot in his handkerchief. Was the world then nothing but a house of cards for the Jewish People? Was their sense of security and belonging but a sham? He had to do something. "*Tatte*," he said to his father, using the Yiddish word, "I am so sorry, but I must go to Holten immediately to Betje, in order to see what is going on there."

He tried very hard to control his voice but felt a great sense of urgency and could not wait another second. He shook off his dustcoat, put on his suit jacket, pulled a scarf off the coat rack, and ran to the back of the house to get his bicycle. Jacob nodded in understanding and turned his face away. He too struggled with his emotions and hoped that at least Louisa had not listened to the radio.

David rode his bike with fury and took a shortcut through the hills. Now he was on his way to Holten, to his fiancée. He used the picturesque tourist road which had been constructed between the two villages through the heather and the forests only a few years ago. This was a project he had actively campaigned for in his capacity as secretary of the Tourist Bond. How proud he had been when the road had become reality! But now he saw nothing of the hilly landscape with its green hills. He only knew that it shortened the distance to his destination.

In the Pagrach home he found his fiancée, the most beautiful girl in the entire village, together with his future extended family: Ome

Bram and Tante Klaar with their sons Louis and Benjamin. Also, his soon-to-be brother-in-law, also named Louis, was present in their tiny living room together with his parents, Daniel and Marianne. Only Bela, the youngest daughter of the Pagrach family, was absent. She was busy with her nursing studies.

It seemed that they had all been waiting just for David. They wanted to hear what he had to say about the worsening situation of the German Jews. David thought to himself, well, here we go again. Just like the Dreyfus affair. He had often heard his father say that France had not been ashamed to condemn this courageous officer out of pure antisemitism. He had grown up with that story, and once again the hatred for the Jews was raising its ugly head. Germany had made antisemitism into law. How could that be? He actually knew the answer quite well. It was in every fiber of his being. Even in the Netherlands there were difficulties connected to being a Jew. They took it in their stride, and for the most part, life was good for the Jews of the Netherlands, especially in their pastoral corner of Overijssel and Gelderland. The tiny Jewish communities of Nijverdal and Holten were comfortable and felt at home among their hills and forests, which in their flat-as-a-pancake homeland were lovingly called mountains. They were proud to be Dutch. In honor of their queen's birthday, they displayed flags and sang the national anthem with emotion. Every Shabbat, in their small synagogues they respectfully recited the prayer for the wellbeing of the royal family and the Dutch government. They simply belonged to two peoples and felt no strife regarding their dual loyalty.

David looked around the room at the relatives who sat knee to knee in a space that was way too small to hold them. The atmosphere was choking, and not only because the windows were closed. The shock of the news from Germany clearly showed on their faces. Daniel's Louis was the first to speak. He almost shouted the words, "*Schande* (a shameful thing), how can this happen in this day and age!" Daniel added, "I expect a strong condemnation from the League of Nations."[1] Poor Daniel, David thought to himself. He is as naive as a child.

As soon as David walked into the room and someone moved a little to give him a place to sit, questions started. They fired their worries straight at him. "David, what do you think about all this? How is it going to end? Are we in danger?" Betje's mother Marianne had trouble breathing. She was truly afraid. "What are we going to do if that Schreier comes here as well?" With one hand in her lap, she rocked her chubby body back and forth mechanically. While she tried to control her fear, small sounds escaped her lips which she stifled by clamping her handkerchief over her mouth. Tears rolled down her cheeks.

In the end, Ome Bram, the head of the Pagrach family, was the second person to stand up in order to speak. He was a tall, heavily built man, impressive in his muscular strength, and in that small living room behind his brother Daniel's butcher shop, he filled the space with his large body. "I want to say a few words," he started in the Holten dialect. "I am very happy that our ancestors fled Germany to cross the border into our village so many years ago." He nodded to emphasize his words. "I am also certain that what is happening in Germany with the *Yidden* (Jews), could never happen here. Don't forget that in the last elections, the Dutch Nazi party got a good kick in the pants, and even if Hitler were to declare war on the Netherlands," here he paused a moment and shook his body as if he had to shake off that very idea, "even if that could happen, and even if he wanted to make those *rishes* (hateful) antisemitic laws here too, he could never succeed. I know this as sure as G-d is my witness. Our friends in the village would never let such a thing happen. Not here in Holten and also not in Nijverdal. Our neighbors would protect us. No one would cooperate with such laws. If Jews are not allowed to go to the cinema, well, then no one would go. This Hitler is nothing in my eyes. Let him try in our country and we will show him!" Ome Bram looked around to his wife, his sons, brother, and the rest of the family. He saw that they agreed with him. Heads nodded, people sighed with relief, but Ome Bram was not finished. "But we cannot be stupid. Let's think ahead and make sure that we are safe. Let's send a little money to Sol and Eva in Baltimore. You never know. They can put it aside for us, in case..." He let the words hang and sat down, pulled a large clump of chewing tobacco from his pocket, stuck it in his mouth and bit down on it with satisfaction.

Ome Bram was no orator and preferred to keep silent. He was a man of deeds, not words, and what he had just said was a long speech for him. David, who had listened intently to the man, reflected on what he had just heard. The room remained silent, and all eyes now turned to him. David, the newest addition to the Pagrach family, a successful businessman with connections as far away as Amsterdam, was expected to say what he thought of the recent developments. Was Hitler intent on starting a war? Could it happen that Holten would be conquered by this man? To give the impression that he was not worried, David remained seated. However, he barely managed to control his shaking hands and to prevent his tea from spilling. He cleared his throat and said, "I completely agree with Ome Bram that we have to remain calm and that we need to consider all of our options very carefully without panic. We are safe here, but we cannot sweep what is happening in Germany with our Yidden under the carpet. Perhaps we should consider crossing the English Channel and move there for the duration. Perhaps we should even consider emigrating to America. But we have time to make such plans. In the meantime, our prime minister is an army veteran and I trust that he will know what steps to take. Let us simply take the time to keep ourselves informed of everything that is happening in Germany. The time for extreme decisions has not yet come. That is how I feel. Regarding cash for a rainy day in America, that sounds like a great idea too. It can't hurt to have some money outside the country." He finally took a sip of the already cold tea. It was bitter and there was milk in it. He swallowed politely. He hated milk in his tea but did not complain. Now he leaned back in his chair and waited for a reaction from the assembled family. He was especially interested in hearing what the younger generation had to say.

In the sudden silence, everyone started talking at the same time. They gestured with their hands, shook their heads, and touched each other's shoulders. David couldn't make out any words in the cacophony, but slowly understood that they agreed on one thing: that life had to carry on as usual. Life in the village had been good to them. The Jews had rights just like everyone else. Holten and Nijverdal were far away from the capital Amsterdam and The Hague, the seat of government and the place where decisions were made, and even if the worst were to happen and Hitler declared war, what interest would he have to come all the way to them to make their lives miserable. There were simply too few Jews in the area. Would anyone really send a soldier to arrest the only Jew living in Markelo if he dared to take a walk in the park? Holten did not even have a swimming pool or a cinema, so problem solved. Everyone should just stay calm. It was *a mazzel* (fortunate) that they had settled in the east of the Netherlands far from the seat of power. Besides, Hitler claimed that he wanted peace, so why did we have to bring up the topic of war? More importantly, the Netherlands was neutral during the Great War and no doubt, that would remain the case in further conflicts. We are safe here, really. Let's just wait and see, for there will be plenty of time to pack up and flee.

A decision was made that the time for decisive action had not yet come. "Let's live our lives as if there is no Schreier in Berlin and focus on what is truly important: Betje's marriage to David!"

The sun was sinking beneath the horizon by the time David made his way back in the direction of Nijverdal. Betje rode along with him for a while. In the middle of the forest, at the Losse Huus Restaurant, they stopped for a cup of tea, and sat, holding hands, and sipping slowly. They whispered sweet ideas about their future together. David looked deep into his bride's eyes, those beautiful green-blue pools, and once again was deeply moved by how beautiful she truly was. Yes, Betje was indeed the most beautiful of all the girls! "I will push the contractor to hire some extra hands so that our home will be finished soon." He added that her parents needed a larger house, and that he would take care of that as well.

"Then they won't be so cramped anymore. They deserve that," he said with a smile. Finally, he embraced his beloved, reluctantly took his leave, and cycled back to the village, deep in thought. In the dark, he pushed his bike into the shed. He felt totally exhausted. He had not even noticed all the millions of stars twinkling above the hilly road. And yet, not so long ago, he had written enthusiastic articles in the newspaper when the Tourist Bond had to drum up support for building it. It felt as if all that had happened in a different era to someone else's life, and he was unable to push aside the nagging feeling in his gut that the family's decision to do nothing – not to be afraid, not to flee, nothing – was not really the right one. He worried about whether they were doing the right thing, and something told him that the Dutch Jews were no longer safe. In the past his instincts had always stood him in good stead: they had helped him build his father's business and had helped make him prosperous. "I have to talk to someone," he said out loud, there in the dark shed. And suddenly he also knew who that person should be. "I am going to call Mr. Sigmund Menko." He was still talking to himself, but this time, he lowered his voice and whispered his decision into the dark night.

Mr. Menko was the head of the largest Jewish community in the east of Overijssel. He was a rich industrialist whose factory produced fabrics. For a number of years there had been a kind of friendship between the two men in spite of their age difference. David saw Menko as a kind of mentor, and the latter viewed him as a protégé. While their connection was first of all based on business interests, the two men trusted each other, and David could not imagine anyone else who might know what was really going on under the surface. He thought that Menko might hear things that were not broadcast over the radio. After considering the situation for a while longer, he knew that he was going to make a phone call to Enschede. He did not have the patience to start a correspondence about the questions that were disturbing his equanimity. The big question was whether Menko would be just as worried about the news from Germany, and whether he had formulated a response to the new racial laws across the border. No doubt, David would give more weight to Menko's opinion than that of his family in Holten.

He had decided: the time for deeds had come. He entered his father's home, took the phone off the hook, and called the operator, "Good evening, this is number 361, Nijverdal." As soon as the operator told him she could hear him well and the connection was clear, David gave her Mr. Menko's home phone number and asked to be connected. In Enschede, the phone was answered on the second ring. "Menko." David quickly came to the point. He rushed to save the costs of the connection, but after two sentences, Menko interrupted him. "Dovid," he said with a Yiddish intonation, "Dovid, *Mammeloschen reden* (speak Yiddish)," and warned him to use that language only. "We can no longer say whatever we want with the situation as it is. Ears may already be listening in and there is a lot for us to discuss." David realized that Mr. Menko was not planning to sit with his hands in his lap, waiting for events to play out. "Come to me," Menko added, still in Yiddish, and the two men made a date to meet the next afternoon. David would take the train to Enschede, and then they could speak in private.

In time, it would become clear that his short telephone call had been virtually prophetic because from that moment on, a communication started between the men that was not connected to business. They very quickly concluded that together they might be able to take steps that would save human lives, but if they made the wrong decisions, G-d forbid, the opposite might happen. Mr. Menko insisted that between him and David a kind of code would come into existence, so that they would both know immediately that a meeting was essential. Menko was already busy with the growing stream of Jewish refugees from Germany who crossed the border at Glanerbrug, the border town close to Enschede. And the stories these bedraggled people told him! Menko did not hold back. Already at their first meeting, he told David, "Let's first of all come up with a suitable code word to initiate our meetings." David was not about to argue, knowing with certainty that the older man was the one to guide their actions. "Our code word must be connected to the possibility that at some point in the future the lives of Dutch Jewry, including those here in Overijssel, will be in danger." They pondered this reality in silence for a while. The word had to be one that would not come up in a casual conversation, yet not sound too outlandish. It had to fit in a regular sentence. In the end, they decided on the Hebrew word *Vayibrach*. The word was well-known to them from the Books of Moses and meant "to flee, to make yourself scarce." Its source was the story of Jacob who fled from Esau, but the Jews used the word colloquially when they were visiting someone and felt it was time to go home: "*We got Vayibrach*," they could say to each other, half in the local dialect and half in their familiar Yiddish and accompany their words with a meaningful movement of the eyes and head toward the door. Immediately the speaker's intention would be clear. Now the word was given a new task: the moment one of them needed to speak privately to the other, he only needed to pick up the phone and say a sentence with their code word *Vayibrach*. A meeting would take place as soon as the next train. David, the younger of the two, would do the traveling. And from now on, they would make it their business to know the train schedule. Their first rule was to avoid written documents. They did not want to create a paper trail. No letters. No postcards. Everything was kept under their hat. Mr. Menko promised David that he would convey every bit of news that came his way without censoring it. He had friends in high places and kept his ear to the ground. He might learn things that would be important information for the Jewish communities which they in a way represented. From now on, David Simon Samuel, the secretary of the Tourist Bond in Nijverdal, a man of words and creative ideas, would be Sigmund Menko's liaison in the municipality of Hellendoorn, which included the village of Nijverdal. He would also do the same for Holten because of his personal interest in that village. He took upon himself the responsibility of keeping "his" Jews abreast of whatever he found out and to advise them how to proceed if that became appropriate. Meanwhile, their *Vayibrach* discussions had to remain a secret – Menko insisted.

David was a discrete man by inclination and thus he told no one that he had had a long discussion with the factory owner in Enschede which had absolutely nothing to do with damask or corduroy. He told neither his parents nor his fiancée. And who knows whether this meeting of 1936 actually set the plans in motion which eventually resulted in the survival of 50 percent of the Jewish communities that the two men represented, 50 percent of the Jews of Enschede, Hellendoorn and Nijverdal, and part of the family in Holten.

The Terrible Times, the Shoah, was still far in the future, and the Schreier was still confined to Germany. And yet, the pact between Samuel and Menko shows that already very early on, there were Jews in the sleepy towns and villages of Overijssel who understood that the writing was on the wall, and that their future was filled with darkness, thunder clouds and danger.

And in Germany? Hitler was not satisfied with merely antisemitic oratory and ordinances, such as closing parks and cinemas to the German Jews. In Nijverdal and Holten, the family had scathingly called these rules David and Betje's engagement gift, but they were only the beginning.

Barely four more months passed, and suddenly, German Jewry found itself stateless. With one fell swoop they were ousted from the German nation. Nevertheless, the families chose to continue ignoring these developments, and in 1937, Betje and David married in the synagogue of Holten. Within the year they were also new parents to a little girl whom they gave three names: Louise in honor of David's mother, Marianne in honor of Betje's mother, and Beatrix in honor of the first-born daughter of Juliana, the crown princess of the House of Orange and her royal consort, Prince Bernard. The new parents felt that in this way they gave expression to their dual identity as good Jews and loyal Dutchmen even though the baby had been born under difficult circumstances: The Anschluss with Austria took place, and this bloodless invasion resulted in the same anti-Jewish laws and a storm of hatred against the Jews.

David was not able to return to his normal routine. He took the train to Enschede. "Mr. Menko," he said as soon as he entered the older man's office, "I have always seen our deep-seated integration in Dutch society as a blessing, and now, without warning, people in Germany have to sign an Aryan declaration. Jews are no longer allowed to teach non-Jews; they are simply pushed out. Jewish doctors and other scientists are forbidden to continue the research that placed them at the center of knowledge. Now their work is taken over by Aryans. Aside from the terrible implications, for me this is a personal insult and a heavy cowardly kick below the belt. No wonder Jews are fleeing Germany and you hear their stories day after day!" He remained standing. His face was flushed, and he was deeply upset. Menko pointed to a leather armchair and pushed a small glass of jenever in David's hands. He answered slowly that he had seen much of antisemitism and hatred during his life. "*Nu,* Dovid," he said with the hope that his Yiddish words and body language would calm his friend a little. "*Nu,* so that Schreier has the *hutzpah* to differentiate between Jew and non-Jew. What else is new? Has it ever been any different? You and I both know that much water will flow from the Ijssel into the sea, and we also know that there will always be people who hate us for what is really an accident of birth. You are a Jew, but did you choose this? Did you seek this identity actively? Of course not. It was simply a matter of fate, and just as a black man cannot decide that tomorrow his skin will be white, so also with the Jews. But what can we do about it? Human nature is difficult to change, and our task must be to try to minimize the damage of these new developments. Meanwhile we have to believe that things will work out in the end."

David shook his head, "But Mr. Menko, it is all too absurd and how can we fight absurdity? The only thing we can do is to turn away from such a situation and leave." The two men continued their conversation for a long time, and in the end they both realized that unfortunately, the world would most likely not go to bat for the German Jews. The big question now was whether similar things might be possible in the Netherlands. Neither of them had a satisfactory answer to that question, and because they simply did not know, they thought that the cautious way would be to assume that similar events could actually happen – even in the outlying areas of the Netherlands. Even in Enschede, and then certainly also in Nijverdal and the surrounding villages. With that possibility they thought it best to make concrete plans for the day the worst scenario might become a reality. If Dutch Jewry were to find itself surrounded by darkness, then the Jews themselves had to be prepared to prevent disaster. Concrete plans of action for the worst event in their lives. Well, both men believed that they still had time, but agreed that the time had come to include more like-minded partners who were in a position to help lay the groundwork for concrete action.

On the train back to Nijverdal, David went over his conversation with his business partner and wondered what would happen if his comrades in Nijverdal were suddenly faced with an Aryan declaration. Would they sign it? Would they protect him? He was no longer sure. Back in the village, he picked up his bike and slowly rode back to the Rijssensestraat, deep in thought, his head about to burst with worries, and deeply depressed about their future.

He realized very soon that he must not let anyone notice how he felt. HE was supposed to be the man of steel for both families, those in Nijverdal and those in Holten. Even more than that, he was a father now and he had to protect his baby girl. Wasn't that why he and Betje had chosen those three names for her?! In signing her birth certificate with those names hadn't they also signed a symbolic declaration of their right to a place in the society of all Dutchmen? That is how proud they were of their double identity which to him felt like one. He could not deny that also in Germany Jews had been part of mainstream society; they had served in the German army and were deeply patriotic, just like him and his fellow Dutch Jews. And yet, with one signature, der Schreier had erased a thousand years of Jewish existence there. "And that is the way it is," he mumbled to himself. "We can no longer take our lives here for granted."

In those days, women in the Netherlands gave birth at home and after the baby was born, the husband would go to city hall accompanied by two witnesses to declare the birth of the child, ask for the baby's name to be entered in the couple's marriage booklet, and request a birth certificate. When David stepped up to the clerk at the window, he carefully pronounced the three names he and Betje had chosen for their daughter, and after the official part was over, handed out cigars and jenever. Betje was still very weak, for it had only been one week since the delivery, but she was waiting for David when he returned home. The radio had just broadcast some new terrible news from Germany connected to the Jews. They had been ordered to add a typically Biblical name to their existing one. Sarah for the women and Israel for the men. This addition once more emphasized the government's revulsion with anything Jewish, and the extra name was intended to make Jews feel that being Jewish was a disgrace.

"David!" Betje was waiting for him at the door. "I can't take any more. I can't bear all this any longer. We have to get out of here. I don't care where we go. It does not matter. We just have to get as far away from Germany as possible."

She haunted him with those words day after day while he was in the store, the living room or upstairs in the bedroom. Her tears were real, but they also were meant to soften her husband's opposition to leaving and to get him to start the process of emigration. "David, you know perfectly well that I am not strong enough to withstand these *rishes* (evil). What if Hitler came here? What about our sweet little girl, your sick father, and my delicate mother? We have to get away from here. Away. Away!" David no longer knew what the best solution for his family was. There might be a war tomorrow and it could even affect the Netherlands. He kept turning over this notion in his head, but Betje had no patience to let him come to a decision in his regular manner, which was slowly, well thought out, and weighing all the options. She took over the lead in getting her family far away from the threatening noises the Schreier in Germany was making. She started by writing a letter to her cousin in Baltimore, U.S.A., asking her to sign affidavits for the entire family so that they could all emigrate together. Eva responded immediately and turned to her local authorities to sign the proper documents. The die was cast. Now Nijverdal simply had to respond by setting the process into action at their end. David did not object, but he was torn about it all. He did not see how he could leave his two prosperous stores behind. It was not that long ago when he had told his father, "Who knows, in the future we may even be able to start selling under our own label. I already have a name in mind: SAPRINI. It is an acronym for Samuel Prins Nijverdal." Their last name had slowly developed into a double one after the *ole prinse* had died at the age of 92, and Jacob, the son, had added his father's honorific to the store's name. The latter had after all been one of the founders of their Jewish community, and after his wife's untimely death had lived with Jacob and Louisa at 101, David Simon's childhood home. At the time, little David was only five years old, and by the time the younger man had established his own shop at Rijssensestraat 82, father and son had no longer simply been owners of a shop but ran what was fast becoming a blossoming firm. And so, this was the name written on the shop's window: Firma J. Samuel Prins. J. for Jacob, and Prins for the old Prince of peddlers, the head of the tribe and the grandfather of David Simon, husband of Betje and father of Louisie, her nickname.

David had no objections to the store's new name. He did not even mind that his own name was not overtly part of it because in the end, his name was deeply embedded in all the parts of the firm's logo. Furthermore, all the people in Nijverdal knew quite well that he, David, was the owner of both shops and the wind in the sails of their success. He had the instincts to find the right products, and his direct advertisements in the local papers had put him and his family firmly on the road to becoming financially secure. As a result, he found it difficult to pull up roots and simply leave. Added to this was his father's deteriorating health, and he was clearly anxious about the possibility of drastic changes in their lives. The same held true for Betje's parents who continued to say that they had time. "Nothing has happened yet, no?" Emigration meant having to learn a new language, and how at their age could they do that? All they had was their local dialect and Yiddish. English? Betje might as well have suggested they learn to fly. And how would they earn a living in that new country? No, the older generation believed that it was already too late for them to start an adventure in a new country. Let the younger ones go. But with that, the entire process stagnated, for neither Betje nor David could imagine leaving their parents in the Netherlands. While they continued to drag their feet, the thundering in Berlin did not stop and the Jews there had few options left. War seemed imminent and unavoidable.

Still, Betje kept trying new tactics. Each time she visited her parents, or her in-laws across the street, she sang the praises of America, the land of endless opportunity. She showed them photos of Eva and Sol's beautiful new home. She read them the letters from Baltimore and kept up her attempts to set off a spark of enthusiasm in her family to make them willing to emigrate. To the other side of the Atlantic Ocean. It seemed reasonably far enough to her. "Look at their home! And that garden of theirs! The streets are so wide that you can barely see the neighbors across the way. We can't stay here! *Moesje,* (mama) tell papa that I can't stay here with my David and our Louisie! You have to come with us. Eva has plenty of room and she will let us stay for a while. Over there we will no longer be in danger. David can start over in Baltimore. I can't bear it here even one more day!" She needs to feel safe and keep her little girl out of his claws. Get far away from Germany. Far from the radio even. Starting over with a new language. But she did not convince them.

At the end of her tether, she finally told her husband, "Let's wait before we have another baby. Let's wait and see how things work out in Germany. One child is manageable no matter where we have to run, but if I were pregnant and we wanted out, or we already had two children, it would just be too complicated. Louisie is still so young, let's wait till she is a bit older. Is that all right with you? I am still young enough and there is time before we make our family bigger again." As always, David did not argue with his wife. He thought that the best thing would be to do whatever he needed to keep her calm. Let her do what she needed. Perhaps then the feeling that the world was an insane place would diminish a little.

Two short months passed. Betje and David got used to the routine of having a baby in the house, and things settled down a little. They viewed their little girl with pride, and David had his father take a photo in their garden, he, smiling up at the camera, with his little daughter in his strong arms. And then, as if their pleasure in their child had tempted fate too much, at the end of the summer of 1938, Hitler annexed the Sudetenland, with the sanction of England, France, and Italy.[2]

No one left for Baltimore, for Eva and Sol's.

Was there any way to explain that this annexation was a good thing? That it ensured peace in Europe? Perhaps, but the explosion of hatred against the Jews that would be known as Kristallnacht (the Night of the Broken Glass) when synagogues all over Germany were set on fire, and hundreds, perhaps thousands of Jews were arrested and sent to the Buchenwald concentration camp, was not justifiable in any way. Nevertheless, in order not to anger Hitler, the Dutch government reacted in a subdued manner.

Prime Minister Hendrikus Colijn was determined to preserve the country's neutrality, and by December 15, 1938, the Dutch government reached the decision to close its borders with Germany in order to prevent Jewish refugees from entering, stamping them as undesirables. In the east of the Netherlands, Jewish refugees had been crossing the border at Grönau in Germany, entering via Glanerbrug, located near Enschede, Mr. Menko's town. David had met some of those bedraggled men and women and listened to their stories which seemed more suitable to the Middle Ages than the 20th century.

There was no way anyone could justify Kristallnacht with sober logic. It could only be explained as barbarism. For David this was the end of the age of innocence concerning the future of Dutch Jewry. That was all gone. If a regime could tolerate and perpetrate such crimes against innocent men, women, and children, that had to be the end of reason.

For Betje too, Kristallnacht was the turning point, and her fear of the future did not leave her husband unaffected. Her anxiety increased his own doubts. One evening, when he sat in his checkers club with his friends, he opened the discussion. "Perhaps my wife is right," he started, and moved one of the pawns on the board in front of him. "Perhaps I should worry less about earning a living, and instead pack our bags as fast as possible and simply disappear from here, get as far away from Germany as we can, and then start over." His friends stopped their games, turned away from the checkerboards and their black and white pawns on the tables, or held one of the stones without placing it anywhere, and looked at him without speaking. Checkers could wait. No one spoke for a while and then they turned back to the game at hand in silence. But David's words stayed with them. David was not only their comrade; he was the club's champion.

From that moment on, the elephant in the center of Jewish life in Nijverdal became visible, and whisperings about concrete *Vayibrach* escape options started between David and Mr. Menko. Should they flee, emigrate, and disappear from the Netherlands and/or Europe? However, this was not the only place where the elephant had become clearly visible; also in non-Jewish circles, whisperings had started about the unimaginable possibility that Jews might be persecuted in the Netherlands. Among the latter, there was a rocksteady belief that there cannot be a situation where one person or group has the right to single out any other person or group for persecution, humiliation, and perhaps death. The year was 1938, the post-Kristallnacht era, the day when the German hatred of Jews burst into flames, literally, but the Netherlands was yet a free and democratic monarchy. Nevertheless, not long after this event in Germany, the Samuel family of 82 Rijssensestraat, Nijverdal, had a surprising visitor. It was *Dominee* Hijmans, the pastor of the Dutch Reformed Church. He and David Simon were good friends, and for years he had been a regular visitor at the Samuel home, at first, when David still lived at number 101 with his parents, and now that he was married, at number 82.

David was the secretary of the local Tourist Bond and when they first met, he thought the pastor might be interested in joining some of the activities supported by the committee, such as plans to build a road through the Nijverdal hills all the way to Holten.

That meeting took place shortly after the *dominee* had been appointed to his new pulpit as pastor of the DRC and discovered that Nijverdal had a small Jewish community. He walked into Jacob Samuel's shop and asked to speak to the son, David. Although the latter was only 26 years old, he was already a well-known figure in Nijverdal and an active participant in the public life of the village. He was an important member of the Tourist Bond and in his capacity of secretary, worked tirelessly to make the village and its shopkeepers more prosperous. It was no wonder that he assumed the pastor wanted to find out about the Tourist Bond, but as it turned out, that was not the case. To break the ice a little, David asked the pastor about the origins of his very Jewish-sounding name. "I know a few Hijmanses, but none of them are pastors," he started the discussion in his typically direct manner.

"Oh yes, Mr. Samuel," came the answer, "I am of Jewish origin. My great-grandfather was a Jew, but while still a young boy, he became deadly ill and having dreamt that Jesus called him to save him, he simply followed the call. He recovered and eventually even wrote a book about his experience." David was a little relieved to find out that the pastor had not converted himself, but still remained a little suspicious. Was the pastor out to make more souls for his church? Hijmans, unaware of any problems with his interlocutor, continued, "My family has always been proud of the fact that our roots are Jewish, just as Jesus himself, who was a Jew too. I was even named after my Jewish ancestor, the first Abraham of our family." David nodded politely and waited for the pastor to tell him the reason for his visit. Clearly he had not come to purchase coveralls. When the man remained silent, he asked, "So, how can I help you, Mr. Hijmans?"

For a few moments, the preacher searched for the right words, and then responded to David's question, "I have read much about Judaism, but I have never really met any Jews. I would so much like to see how you and your fellow community members follow your religious precepts. I understand that there is a service here in your home every Sabbath, and that there you also celebrate the Jewish holidays. To make it simple, I would very much like to observe your traditions and learn about them." David was relieved that he had found the right words to address this man, and suddenly, it seemed that this person was quite an unusual soul. "What do you have in mind?" he asked simply. "Is it possible for me to be present during your prayer meetings? And could I sometimes be part of your way of life in your private home?" Pastor Hijmans gestured to indicate that he had finished what he wanted to say.

The small Jewish community of Nijverdal had no synagogue. Therefore, Jacob's house served as a house of prayer and there, a quorum met on Shabbat to celebrate the day of rest. It was only natural to invite Hijmans to join the family for the festive meal after the service. Over time, the pastor became a frequent visitor to 101. He always came on time for morning prayers, sat quietly and respectfully, a yarmulke on his head, listening in silence to the ancient melodies. With shining eyes, he saw how the men opened the scroll with the Books of Moses, handwritten with quill on parchment, and read the portion of the week in an amazing, melodic singsong. During the meal he became animated and asked endless questions about the traditions the family observed. The blessing of the wine, the ritual of pouring water over one's hands before breaking the bread dipped in salt. "You are truly the People of the Book," he said with amazement. He said it every time he visited, adding that now he was able to imagine how Jesus had lived and how he could follow in his footsteps in a more meaningful manner.

The two men developed a strong intimate bond of trust, and the Jews of Nijverdal understood that Hijmans was their friend. He had no ulterior motives. They greeted him with a smile whenever they saw him in the street, and now that they all knew about his background, felt relaxed enough to make jokes at his expense. "In profile you look more Jewish than me," David said with a smile, despite the fact that he too had been blessed with a royal nose.

So that was the story of this *dominee*, and now, some 10 years later, here he was at David's door. "A few words in private, David. Can I?"

"Of course, come in, come in." David tried to play the good host although it was becoming more and more difficult to act normally. "Betje is washing dishes and then she will go upstairs to give Louisie her bath, feed her and put her down for the night. So, we can speak without disturbance. What can I do for you?"

"David," Hijmans started in a serious tone of voice and without small talk, he took the bull by the horns. That was the way he always was, but this time, the expression on the man's face! So serious. "The whole world is going insane. I hope you know what is happening in Germany and I hope you realize it can happen here just as well. Hitler is not interested in peace. He wants war. He wants to recoup Germany's so-called lost honor and that is only possible with brute force. He wants to overturn the Treaty of Versailles."[3] Abraham stopped talking and David could only agree with him. He took up the thread of the conversation. "I see it the same way. Not only does he want war, but he also wants a big war with as much destruction as possible. The world is giving this dictator from Germany pieces of territory as long as he does not start shooting. England handed over the richest lands of Czechoslovakia and kept its government outside the negotiations. So now this warmonger has territory that will supply him with the raw materials which will serve him well in time of war. All this only clarifies for me the idea that no one will take up arms to defend the Jews." David stopped speaking abruptly, taken aback at the words that had fallen out of his mouth. So clearly! He had never said that to anyone. David Simon Samuel was a modern intelligent man of the 20th century. He had grown up with the notion that a man must keep his emotions to himself. He was a man! The less said the better, and he had had absolutely no intention of letting those words escape his lips. Especially now he had to keep himself in check. That was his task. For one moment he was incapable of doing so. "Abraham, we had visas for America and we let them lapse. I was too afraid to abandon my parents and sister here even though they insisted that we leave for Louisie's sake."

At that moment, it became clear what made Hijmans such a good shepherd. He stood up, approached David, and put his arms around him. This gesture completely overwhelmed David, and he could not hold back a sob that came from deep inside him. He felt ashamed, but Hijmans remained where he was and still without speaking, produced a snow-white handkerchief from his pocket and handed it to David. "David, let yourself be, just for a minute. I do not understand how you are capable of pretending that you have no worries, but today I did not simply show up on your doorstep to wipe away your tears." Here David smiled in spite of himself. "And so," Hijmans continued, "I need to tell you what is in my heart. I want to say, no, I must say, that you are not alone. I am here to offer you my help and I pray to G-d that you will never need it, but if... but if you do, then my church and I will stand with you. With you and all the Jews, and we will do whatever is needed to keep you safe. In a situation where the lives of the Dutch Jews are no longer equal to that of all Dutch citizens, we will all be Jews."

David had no words. "Abraham, Abraham," he repeated again and again, but the pastor was not yet finished. "Time will teach us everything. Perhaps you should try to renew your visa. Perhaps you can explain to the American ambassador that Louisie's birth pushed everything else aside."

And David? He pushed the threatening sounds from Germany aside, and not a single soul in the small Jewish community of Nijverdal emigrated to faraway places, far from Germany.

Louisie grew, and Betsie – her aunt, papa David's sister – helped her sister-in-law with caring for the little girl. In this manner, she was able to imagine that she was also a little bit of a mother, and this comforted her somewhat in her unmarried state. Days flew by, and David Samson from Enschede – David Samuel's first cousin – met

Irma, a refugee from Germany. They wanted to get married. David Samson listened in horror as Irma told him hair-raising tales of what was happening in Germany, and he became convinced that Hitler was an arch-liar who should not be believed no matter what he said. "He will murder every Jew he can get his hands on," he said time and again. Holten saw another wedding: Louis, son of Ome Bram and Tante Klaar, was about to marry Rina from Arnhem, and he had the same opinion as David from Enschede. Even Bela, the youngest member of the Pagrach family, found love. Her suitor was Levi Cohen, a prosperous businessman, but they were in no rush because Bela was studying to be a nurse and insisted on finishing her education. Meanwhile, she was working as a student nurse in the TB sanitorium in Hellendoorn, not far from her sister Betje's home, and she too was one of Louisie's beloved aunts.

Time did not stand still. It swallowed the days with frightening speed. No one had the power to stop it. Hitler certainly did not rest on his laurels, but kept on with his secret plans, and when he was ready, he unleashed his soldiers in a Blitzkrieg against Poland. Europe saw Germany's might, the speed with which he reached his goal, and feared the future. The pragmatic David was almost too afraid to listen to the radio so as not to hear more terrifying news, yet he was also afraid to turn it off, and just like everyone else followed with inner quaking the developments in Poland. For just a little while longer, Jewish Overijssel clung to the hope that the Netherlands would remain neutral in any future conflict. The same was true for all of the Jews and non-Jews in the country. Meanwhile, the Netherlands reacted carefully to the German invasion of Poland and did not declare war on Germany as England did. In most households, sincere prayers were offered to beg for help in keeping their little rainy country outside the conflict. But the fact remained that Europe was once again at war, and the tension rose higher and higher. Dutch cinemas screened films to show how their army was mobilizing and the civilian population received instructions concerning blackout curtains to protect their homes against air raids. Fear hung in the air as a thickening fog, and David, who was not normally a very religious man, kept up a mumbled prayer to the G-d of Israel to "make it pass us over, make it pass us over."

He and Betje made attempts to cheer each other up a little regarding their future in the Netherlands. At the same time, they also waited impatiently to hear from the American embassy concerning the renewal of the emigration visas so that they could leave. David had decided that this time no one would keep him from packing up, neither his parents nor Betje's. His wife agreed completely. Their decision was final, for even if all the other family members insisted on remaining in the Netherlands, they wanted out. For Louisie's sake. But the embassy remained silent. And then it was May. May 1940.

It was the morning of the 10th. Betje got out of bed, put fresh coffee beans in the wall mounted grinder, poured the ground beans into the percolator, and put it on a low flame for David. She went back up to bed. The little one was still asleep.

David walked downstairs, poured himself the first cup of the day and turned on the news. It was nearly 8 o'clock, but instead of the normal jingle before the newscast, the sound of church bells came on. It was a somber tolling sound that seemed to go on and on. He had just enough time to wonder why there would be church bells at eight in the morning, but then the voice of the newscaster came on above the bells. "Good morning, ladies and gentlemen. This is Hilversum. We ask for your attention for the ANP"[4] and another male voice came on who began to read a proclamation from Queen Wilhemina. "My people," the man read. The coffee cup fell from David's hand and broke into a hundred pieces on the stone kitchen floor. Hot coffee stained his clothes and scorched him, but he felt nothing. He heard something about "neutrality" and then very quickly something about the Wehrmacht (the German army) and last night. And something else which he did not really hear but simply knew. An invasion had taken place. The country had been attacked. The Netherlands was at war. Hitler was at their door. This he knew to be a fact, for he had no illusions about their poorly trained army succeeding in turning back Hitler's Blitzkrieg. The radio continued to mumble, but it was beyond him. His ears were filled with noise, a hurricane in his head. "Betje, come down," he yelled, but regretted this immediately. Let her sleep another minute. From now on they would never sleep again. Let her retain the illusion of safety for another minute. David could feel the strong walls of his house closing in on him. He was caught in that net. The hater of the Jews had arrived with his hordes. The man who had orchestrated Kristallnacht was in the Netherlands. How could this have happened! The queen's letter to her subjects squashed all hope for Dutch Jewry, including the Jews of Overijssel, even in Nijverdal. It was all lost. This David knew for a fact: all lost from the moment of the reading of the proclamation. The border closed. And Betje did not get her period.

David's non-Jewish friends were in shock as well, and the first days after the Netherlands capitulated following a five-day war, most people remained indoors, hiding behind locked and bolted doors. When someone had to go out to buy bread or take a sick child to the doctor, he walked sideways, pressing himself against the walls of the houses, and rushed to minimize the time outside and return to the presumed safety of the home. People kept their eyes on the pavement, avoiding each other. How different this was from that other village life when people exchanged pleasantries in the street! Quite a few of the families had been hoarding food for some time now in fear of coming events, and now that the war, as well as the defeat and the invasion, were a fact, their main goal was to have as much food as possible in the house. Unfortunately, the war brought about an immediate breach in the delivery of goods and the result was that the grocery shelves quickly became empty.

Nevertheless, the occupier was interested in winning the local's trust. Order was quickly restored. The German propaganda played an important role in doing so. The population had to get the impression that the occupation was not so bad.

Newspapers published photos with captions that pointed out the civil and disciplined character of the German soldier. They were shown speaking to Dutchmen. The message was that the Dutch had nothing to fear. In general, the behavior of the German soldiers was correct and friendly. For a while, the presence of soldiers in uniform was the only indication of the German occupation for the majority of the Dutch population.

But David knew better and was already convinced that the people were being manipulated with lies. What was that expression again? That every word from Hitler's mouth was a lie?

Betje was nauseous. She could not hold down her breakfast. Looking after Louisie was almost too much for her, but her monthly flow did not come. She tried to convince herself that she couldn't be... no way she might be pregnant. They had been careful. But the nausea remained, and the smell of food made her ill. She did not get her period.

The Germans controlled the radio, and aside from Hitler's screams and music, the only other broadcast was about warnings to the population to adjust and to accept the German regime. More lies, David thought to himself. So, the radio no longer had anything to offer.

He insisted that neither his wife nor his sister Betsie show themselves in the street. No more walks with the child. To stay at home. They had a garden, after all, and she could play there. He could not bear the thought that Betje or his sister might be out there without his protection, and so he took over the task of shopping. Better safe than sorry!

David tried to put a good face on things and thereby show the world that he had the situation under control. His store remained open. He sold what people needed, but one did not have to be a genius to understand that the Germans would do their best to control every aspect of the populations' daily lives. Cooperate with the occupation. That was the message. Then it would all end well. But if not, Hitler would show his iron fist. The Dutch police remained at their post, but the force was enlarged by German police in green uniforms, known as the *Grüne Polizei*. Other regulations followed quickly: ration booklets with stamps[5] which gave the occupation power over the civilian population, and which were needed to purchase all necessaries, such as clothing, candies, food, and cigarettes. It was all distributed based on family size. To get the stamps, people had to present themselves at the civil registration authority, later known as the Ration Board. They registered all their family members, and with time, the Jews would no longer be entitled to these stamps, so that lending them a helping hand would also become much more complicated. Meanwhile, the first consequence of the stamps was that long lines formed in front of the stores, and shopping became frustrating and time consuming.

So, with all of the Netherlands trapped in the German vice, this was doubly the case for the Jewish Samuel family. Two weeks after the invasion, Betje told her husband that she was pregnant. She saw her own panic reflected in his eyes, although she realized he had become suspicious of her feeling so unwell. It was not a flu or upset stomach. He heard her every morning. She was pale and thin. For David, it was now clear that their fantastic ideas about fleeing across Europe, through France and then to walk across the Pyrenees to

Spain with a pregnant wife and a baby not yet two years old was out of the question. It would have been a difficult journey for even the most physically fit, but now circumstances would never allow them to complete such a journey. It was all too late. Too late. They had waited too long. They had not taken the chance when they had it.

Betje saw all this in a flash. David was speechless. She had to have her say in a rush. She stepped close to him, and facing him squarely, gently caressed his chest. Only two years ago they had been excited about starting a family and having many children, but now everything was different. Their lives had taken a whole new turn. "David, I simply cannot bring a child into this world. We had talked about it and we both wanted to wait. But we have to face the facts. Even with one child, fleeing would be complicated. Reaching a neutral country means an arduous and dangerous journey. Still, we can only try to get out if I am not pregnant. Louisie will have to be carried in our arms. How can I take on such a gamble? I am simply not strong enough to do all that and carry a new baby inside me." She stepped away from him. David remained silent, but of course he understood what her plan was. He experienced this as a physical pain and hugged himself, as if his crossed arms could protect him against an attack on his own body. "We don't do such things! To us, life is sacred. All life." That is what he wanted to say, but he did not dare and kept his words inside. He could not make things worse for his wife. Well, these are women's affairs, he thought. Betje had to make the decision for herself. And so, all he said was, "Do we have any other choice?" And when it was his wife's turn to keep silent, he turned away from her so as not to see her pain and to save her from his.

---

1. https://www.history.com/topics/world-war-i/league-of-nations.
2. In the early hours of Sept. 30, 1938, leaders of Nazi Germany, Great Britain, France, and Italy signed an agreement that allowed the Nazis to annex the Sudetenland, a region of Czechoslovakia that was home to many ethnic Germans. Adolf Hitler had threatened to take the Sudetenland by force.
3. https://www.history.com/topics/world-war-i/treaty-of-versailles-1.
4. ANP: the Dutch news service (like Reuters).
5. I have used both 'coupons' and 'stamps' to discuss the rationing of goods.

3

BETJE SAMUEL PAGRACH: 1940

"I know what I have to do," I say softly to my horrified David. "That is all you need to know." I walk into the living room to the phone sitting next to the radio and lift the horn. "Hello central, this is number 530, Nijverdal," and ask to be connected to Doctor Bakker. He is our family doctor and I need to know how soon I can see him. I am lucky. Tomorrow morning the clinic is open and I can come. I gently put the horn back. Deep in thought about what I am about to do, I touch my flat stomach. What normally would have been a protective gesture for the child in my womb is now a form of asking this unborn baby to forgive me. I have only enough strength to protect our living daughter and ourselves. That is it. "You will get your turn later," I whisper to the tiny life under my heart, but I do not really believe it. There will be no more good moments. I no longer see any future for the Jewish communities here and in Holten, or anywhere that Hitler has won the battle against human values and decency. But I must stay calm. There is no room for feelings at this moment. There is only room for decisions I could never have taken in a sane universe. "I am lucky that Dr. Bakker is in tomorrow," I tell myself. I simply have to get through this. It must be over with this pregnancy before I have the time to consider the moral implications of aborting my child. I also do not know how I can possibly convince our conservative, deeply religious doctor to help me in killing this new life inside me, but perhaps he will be capable of understanding how the new political realities here have changed everything for us.

All night long I toss and turn in a restless, broken sleep. Even David who usually sleeps like the dead, wakes up from it. My thoughts give me no peace. All of a sudden everything has become so urgent. Everything is a threat, including the streets of the village, which just a short time ago were friendly, familiar, and smiling. Since the occupation I am afraid to walk outside, for I fear the way people look at me. I rush back and forth, returning home as quickly as possible. As soon as I enter, out of breath, heart pounding, I lock and bolt the door. I feel persecuted. Since I realized that I am definitely pregnant, these feelings have only intensified. I even believe that my neighbors all know my plans to murder an innocent baby.

When I leave the house to go to the doctor, I carefully open the door, slip out, and take my bike from the shed. Louisie is with Betsie, her beloved and familiar auntie. Of course, Betsie wanted to know where I was going, but I told her some ruse. I cannot tell her what I am about to do because it is much too horrible and much too difficult to share with anyone. Only now, since the Netherlands has become an occupied country, and the Schreier of Berlin is busy with thinking up new *rishes* against the Jews, now something has shifted. Hitler wants us to be gone. He wants my sweet little Louisie! Suddenly I know this for a fact as clearly as I know that I am expecting another baby. Just as no one has to tell me this, I know for sure that Hitler is after my little daughter, and not because he wants to be kind to her. This war is a war against our daughter. I will make a deal with that devil Hitler, and I will give him my unborn child, but my living one? No, her I will keep out of his talons. I will save her. I will save her!

It is chilly outside, but I am wearing only a thin dress covered with a shawl Tante Klaar crocheted for me. I have hidden my hair under a scarf tied under my chin, the way the old women of the village do when they are in mourning. I push the pedals of the bike and move along.

Dr. Bakker's clinic is reached by the side entrance of his big, beautiful villa. The waiting room is full already with all kinds of people, old men and women, and also women with infants. There are even a few little boys with soiled casts on their arm. All are waiting for the doctor. A village doctor is a healer who can do almost anything and take care of his patients from cradle to grave. The men and women sit in silence, hunched into their coats, for the stove is off. Everyone is tense and perhaps a little nervous, waiting silently to be called by the doctor's assistant. Even the children are affected by the oppressive atmosphere and sit close to their mother, sometimes whispering in her ear. The clinic's wall is decorated with some fading posters advertising vitamins, green vegetables, fresh fruits, and instructions concerning personal hygiene and inoculations. There are also some prints and still lifes, which were apparently not nice enough to hang inside the villa's living quarters and had been delegated to the clinic walls. The printed damask curtains are drawn, leaving the room in semi-darkness. In the center of the room stands a small, round table with some dog-eared magazines and newspapers, and in front of them a wooden stand with a metal shaft that holds the numbered tokens. Each time someone enters, he or she first takes a number. When there are no more tokens on the needle, the clinic is full, and the doctor will not be able to see any more patients that day. Lucky for me, the needle is not empty. I slide off a token, take it into my hand and find a seat. For a moment, the villagers turn their eyes toward me and then they turn away. "Ah," I think to myself, "It has already begun. I am someone else now. Everyone wonders how things will turn out for the Jews." To pretend that I am busy with other things, I pull an old newspaper from within the pile and try to read it. It is all about the war. Much about the bombardment of Rotterdam. There are even photos that show the fires and the destruction of that city. Many dead. Many wounded. Sure, Hitler is not afraid to kill civilians. I have the feeling that as of yet, we have seen nothing and that the worst is still to come. I do not really succeed in reading. I simply hold that newspaper in front of me and let myself hide behind the wildly dancing lines. I empty my mind. I try to let it all go. I want to be hollow. I must be hollow. In all senses of that terrible word. I must not think about anything too deeply. One foot in front of the other. That is all.

The doctor's assistant, a blonde girl with a long braid framing her face, calls my number. I stand up and follow her white coat to the anteroom where she asks me to sit until the doctor buzzes her to show me in. Meanwhile she finds my file in the drawer, fills in a few details, and the doctor's signal comes through. He is ready for me. The girl accompanies me all the way into his office and announces me.

"How are you, Mrs. Samuel," the doctor starts politely, but then he sees my face, resolutely closes the door to the anteroom and points to the chair, meaning that I should sit down. He remains standing opposite me while leaning against the examination table. I notice the clean sheet.

"Betje, you need not be afraid, really! Nothing has happened as yet. That Hitler will surely not dare do here what he is doing to the German Jews! We are not Germany. You should know that, and also that you are neither a German refugee nor a Polish one. You are Dutch and you are in the Netherlands!"

I had so promised myself that I would not cry. I would not cry, not in front of my poor, tortured husband and certainly not in front of our doctor. I start to talk but then I hesitate and look down. He touches my shoulder, and when I raise my eyes, he nods encouragingly. He wants me to go on. For a second, he smiles at me. I focus on a point just above his head and start over, taking the bull by the horns. Saying it straight out. Not mincing my words. All those silly expressions that mean nothing now. "Dr. Bakker, I am expecting a baby and I cannot bring a new child into this world. I am already desperate about Louisie's future. I am so terribly afraid of everything that is happening around us. What kind of life can I possibly offer a new child? There is war all around us. It is swallowing all my hopes for the future. No one knows what lies in store for us, but it cannot be good. Especially for us. I need all my strength to keep my little girl safe. She isn't even two years old. I must not have one more. Not now.

46

I beg you, please, to help me. I have to have an abortion. Under normal circumstances such a thing would never even have entered my mind, but I also never thought that our lives could reach this terrible moment. This situation. We are in the middle of an earthquake and the ground is giving way under my feet." I have no words left, lower my eyes, and once more I put my hands over my womb. I have to ask this baby to forgive me for what I am about to do. I am so sorry that I am taking away your life, I say through my entwined hands. But it is the only option left to us. Please believe me. I know for myself without a doubt that Hitler has won already. He has succeeded in taking away some of my humanity. He has made me capable of scraping my unborn child out of my body. A life that David and I created together.

The doctor is also silent. He is a G-d-fearing man, conservative and honest. He has been the doctor of the entire Samuel tribe since he opened his practice in Nijverdal. Now he pushes himself upright and leans close to where I am sitting. He is a tall, slender man. His white coat hangs open to reveal a well-cut, expensive suit, a silk tie half hidden beneath his stethoscope. His hair has been combed carefully and parted ramrod straight. He is freshly shaved and smells of Old Spice. His eyes bore into mine and I look down, blushing and confused, but he remains standing, one leg slightly before the other, and then he lets his head drop onto his chin. I cannot bear the tension and open my mouth, searching for something to say, but the doctor holds up his hand and motions with his index finger – I must be silent. He is trying to organize his thoughts and starts to pace back and forth in the small office. Back and forth he goes, back and forth. The ticking of the clock thunders in my ears, and then the assistant calls over the intercom asking whether she may send in the next patient, but Dr. Bakker answers abruptly that she is not to disturb him again and must wait for his signal. He keeps up his restless pacing and seems to have forgotten that I am even in the room.

All this takes a minute, or perhaps an hour. I sit. I do not know how much time has passed, but it could well be an eternity. I had been afraid that the doctor would be angry with me and tell me that I was committing a terrible sin, but no, and finally, when he stops his nervous pacing and sits down, he turns to me, and pulls himself together. "Betje, I see how your conscience plagues you and how difficult it was to keep this appointment today, but I cannot do what you ask of me. My conscience would never allow such a thing. I am a healer; I save lives. I do not take lives. Child, you are still but a bride, almost still a newlywed, and suddenly, in your eyes, you believe that your whole world has been blown to smithereens. But please, do not give in so easily. I understand what you are going through, I truly do, but I want to suggest something else." For a second, he stops talking, but quickly takes up the thread again. "Who knows, you may not even be pregnant. That I can check for you. Perhaps this is simply a false alarm brought on by all the tension?" How can I tell this doctor that there is no doubt, that I am certain, and even know exactly when it happened? How can I explain to this kind man that David and I keep the Jewish laws of purity in marriage, that only after I have been to the *mikve* (the ritual bath) am I allowed to be with my husband, return to the double bed, and that I can put the exact date on the day that I became pregnant?! "Doctor," I say in despair, "This is an emergency," but Dr. Bakker is talking to me again. "I can do everything in my power to keep you healthy. I can do all that I am capable of to look after you and your unborn child. If you are indeed pregnant, I will attend the birth, no matter what happens in the meantime." Of course, the doctor means that he may not be allowed to take care of me because I am Jewish, just as it happened in Germany. "Betje, life is sacred in my eyes, and that includes all life, also that of your unborn child, and your life and this baby's life are under my care. I cannot perform an abortion for you, but I promise you with everything that is dear to me, that I am responsible for this new life and that I will take care of it if there ever comes a time when you need help to ensure the child's safety. Then you will come to me. From this moment on, the life of this baby is under my protection. It is a sacred promise from me to you."

I no longer understand what the doctor is saying, and I ask him, "What do you mean? Do you mean to tell me that you would adopt my baby?" For a fleeting moment, there is a smile on the doctor's face. "Well, no, nothing like that. I simply mean to say that if there is any danger for the Jews," he stops as if to look for better words, "If this child is in danger, then you must come to me with that child. I will then find a solution to keep her or him safe. I swear this by all that is holy." He repeats this oath, emphasizing his words with his right fist hitting the palm of his left hand. Then he swats away his dark words. "Perhaps this is all empty talk. Let me have a look," and he points to the table with its pristine, white sheet.

Well, the examination shows what I already knew. A new life is growing inside of me. I remain silent. I get dressed and as I head for the door, the doctor stops me, "Not that way! I will teach you another route to my office. It is a little more private. Come, we will go out through the house." And then he takes me behind a screen that hides a door. From there we reach the kitchen and then the entrance hall with a marble floor in a checker pattern, and then one more door to the outside. "This is how you will come to me from now on. You simply ring my bell; my wife will let you in and you can wait here on this bench," he says, pointing to an antique wooden bench with beautiful wood carvings placed against the back wall of the vestibule. "And there is no need to make an appointment,"

Much, much later do I finally understand that the good doctor made a prophetic gesture and already prepared his practice for the day when he would no longer be allowed to see Jewish patients. That day he laid the groundwork which enabled him to continue looking after the Jews of the village. He opens the front door and holds it wide open. "Keep up your courage, Betje. You are G-d's People. He will not abandon you." For a moment he places an arm on my shoulder, and then the door closes behind me.

To my surprise, I still know how to ride my bike. I can do the instinctive pushing on the pedals without falling off. At the railroad crossing, the barrier is down and I can hear a train coming. Soon I see the smoke belching from the black locomotive, and we all wait patiently until it passes and the guard cranks open the barrier to let us through. I think to myself that I am doing all right and now that I remember the crossing, I also have the option of throwing myself under the train. Nevertheless, for today I ride on carefully back to my home, to David and Louisie.

From that day on, neither David nor I mention the pregnancy, as if we had agreed to keep silent on the topic. We also hold back on telling our parents. I wear dresses that hide my stomach and purposely eat very little so that I won't gain weight. The only one who does speak about this coming child is Dr. Bakker. "A child born in such difficult times will bring joy," he says every time I come for my checkups, but just as my stomach does grow and harden, life for the Jews hardens as well. Everything is like Germany now. Everyone follows the new regulations which make our lives smaller and more impossible. Everyone who can, signs the Aryan declaration. Almost everyone, and all the Jews present themselves at the occupation's civil registration offices and allow themselves to be registered as Jews.[1] No one refuses. We all think that if we feed the monster little tidbits and take the edge off his hunger, he may leave us alone. Let us live.

The baby starts to kick inside my body. What was an amazing experience when I was pregnant with Louisie, now brings only greater fear for the future and I cannot put into words what I see lying ahead. Meanwhile the gentle fluttering is almost unbearable.

Once a month I pay a visit to the doctor, always entering through his living quarters, the first the vestibule with its checkered marble floor, then the kitchen, and the clinic on the other side of the screen. The doctor's wife always lets me in, invites me to wait on the antique bench, and lets the doctor know that I have arrived.

Shortly before the baby's birth I finally tell David what Dr. Bakker swore to do for this coming child. David embraces me for a long time and then he tells me what Pastor Hijmans and his church have promised him.

---

1. http://ellenlandweber.com/rescuers/book/Strobos/Conditions.Holland.html.

4

BETJE SCHOONTJE (BETSIE) SAMUEL: 1906-1943

On the day of the festivities in honor of David Simon Samuel's first pair of pants, the entire family arrived to celebrate. Jacob and Louisa had spared no expense for their only child, and coffee, cake, jenever and wine were aplenty, and everyone was in a good mood. For the women there were tiny glasses with yellow *advocaat* (a kind of eggnog) and whipped cream, a typical lady's treat. They ate the alcoholic concoction with tiny silver spoons. The drinks, and the fact that David was already three and out of diapers, created a festive atmosphere, and all were loose and happy. Louisa too felt relaxed and beamed with pride at the success of this memorable celebration. It was all for her little David! How wonderful to see him growing so quickly! She felt proud of her small family. "Look at that little boy of mine," she said to her sister, nudging her with her elbow and pointing at the toddler. "He is already a little man! You'll see how he will make all the girls crazy for him. He is so handsome! That smile! And those eyes! Blue like a piece of heaven. Who could resist him!" Schoontje agreed with her sister and smiled without speaking, but she hoped that the time would come for Louisa to relax enough to put her nervous fears of childbirth aside. She said, however, "Yes, you did hit the jackpot with that little boy," and for a moment placed her arm around Louisa's shoulder in a meaningful embrace. "And his haircut!" she added, just for emphasis. The two sisters sat together with their arms around each other and observed with pride their children playing with each other. Schoontje's little girls, Louisa's little boy, Ome Abraham's sons and Tante Riek's son Daviedje from Enschede were there as well. All the cousins playing together. What more could a person ask for!

Louisa's good mood did not dissipate after the guests had left, and for a moment she even forgot her fears of a second delivery, went upstairs together with her husband Jacob holding on to his hand, and a few weeks later realized that she was expecting again. She accepted this news with equanimity and a little surprised at her lack of panic. And so, in 1906, a short while after David's fourth birthday, his parents presented him with a little sister. A daughter was born at 101 Rijssensestraat, and Louisa and Jacob became parents for the second time. They named the child Betje Schoontje in honor of the grandmother who had not even lived long enough to know her own child, and in honor of Schoontje, who had mothered her younger sister for as long as Louisa could remember. Using the two names together was, therefore, highly symbolic, and from the day the child was born she was called Betsie, merging both names so that she would bear her ancestry with love and pride.

5

BETSIE: MAY, 1943

"*Mamme,*" I called down to my mother. "Have you finished packing?" I did not hear an answer, so I went over the list from the German regional headquarters in Arnhem once more. "Did you put your medicine in the suitcase?" I lifted my parents' two small bags without effort, and hoisting my own backpack, carried everything downstairs. *Tatte* was standing at the window facing away from me. I saw that he had put on the shirt that I had fixed for him a few days ago. I had turned the collar inside out so that it did not look too frayed. He had his pipe in his hand although he had not had tobacco for more than a year. He twirled the empty pipe slowly around through his fingers just as the nuns did when they said the rosary. And just like them, his lips moved silently. I observed him carefully. These past years he had aged so terribly. His back was bent, and defeated by our lives, pale and thin, he stared unseeingly outside. *Tatte* needed new glasses, but there was no Jewish eye doctor anywhere and Dutch eye doctors were not allowed to treat us. Besides, we no longer had any money. He did his best to decipher the tiny letters in the Jewish newspaper, but he could not really read whatever it said there. It did not really matter. There never was any good news anyway. In the end, the only good use we had for the paper was to start a fire in the range whenever we had some coal or wood, and had managed to scrounge a few potatoes, carrots, or beets from *mamme*'s vegetable patch. Since last year, when he had been forced to close down the store, *tatte* was a broken man. I think this was the reason why he had refused to listen to David when he came to us with plans to go into hiding. Every day he came to sit in our kitchen to try to convince at least me to disappear, but I could not consider leaving our parents. Of course, I did not want to be sent to our uncertain future somewhere in Eastern Europe, but I would not let Hitler separate me from *mamme* and *tatte*.

David refused to give up. I knew that he had sent an official letter to the mayor with a special request to allow our father to stay in the house after April 9, the day when all the Jews of Overijssel had to leave their homes, but he only received a cold refusal riddled with official stamps and a threat that after this date, any remaining Jew would do so at his own peril.

Still, David wrote again, this time asking to send an ambulance to transport our father to Vught, our destination in the Netherlands, for our father was too frail to walk all the way to the train station on his own. He signed the letter with his official title as representative of the Jewish Council in Amsterdam. This request was denied too. The mayor wrote that the German headquarters would never allow such a thing. "Let the other Jews help," was his advice, because we were all supposed to leave together on that horrible April 9th. What was the mayor thinking? Who could help my poor father? Ome Abraham or Ome Shmuel-Sandor? They were nearly as old and frail as he. All three had knee pains, stiff joints, backaches, and poor eyesight. That is why I told David, "I can't abandon them." He got so angry. "How dare you sacrifice yourself. You can't. You mustn't! You have to be *Vayibrach*. The sooner, the better." But I gave him my best reasoning, "I heard, and I read in the Jewish paper that Vught is supposed to be a permanent work camp. I heard that they have special barracks for the elderly and infirm. And I have also heard that they need textile workers. And we are! Vught is not a holding camp. People who are sent there will remain." David had heard the same rumors and had read them too, and even some of his contacts in the Jewish Council believed this. But he did not. "Betsie, those are all lies. Nothing they say is true. Nothing. Only lies. To placate us. We must trust no one any longer. Only ourselves and people willing to help us. All of us must go into hiding. We have to go into hiding. *Onderduiken!* And we have to do so before April 9th. All you are doing is looking for excuses to justify that you are throwing away your life." For a moment I was afraid that he might take hold of me and shake me out of my complacency, but he stepped away. I felt insulted and hurt, and for a few days we did not speak and avoided each other's eyes. However, soon enough David came back with new arguments, but I did not want to hear what he had to say. David had accused me of throwing away my life. Well, he was right, really, in a way. In the end we agreed that I would merely accompany our parents as far as Vught, that I would look around, and that I would come back to Nijverdal if I saw that they were being taken care of.

Mamme also tried to convince me to go into hiding. There was no need to accompany them, she said, because David has asked Herman Flim, the baker's son, to help *tatte* on his journey. Herman had said yes! So, I could go with Betje and David to make *Vayibrach* without worry. But I was unable to do so. I could not abandon my parents to their fate. I had looked after them for so long already and I had to see it through. That is how I felt. To the family I said, "All right, then. I will stay with them as far as Vught and then I will come back to Nijverdal with Herman and then I will go into hiding. Really. I only need to see that *mamme* and *tatte* arrive in one piece, and that they are treated well. Then I will go to *dominee* Hijmans at the church, or Herman will help me to disappear." I knew I was taking a huge risk because who knew what awaited us now and I did not even know if I could simply turn around to take the train back to Nijverdal. My papers were only one-way. Deep in my heart I also knew that David's *Vayibrach* was a fearful step, but the idea that I might abandon our parents to their fate was too much for me.

I walked through the house one last time. It was clean. I had scrubbed and washed everything, and all the rooms were neat, especially my own. The sheets were freshly laundered, although I had no idea why that was necessary. But, well, I was used to keeping everything tidy and I wanted our house to look its best. I did not want the strangers, who would no doubt enter our home, to think that we lived in filth. I caressed the books on my shelf and straightened them a little. There were books from my youth. Stories of girls, novels, and that framed print with the Menorah from the Temple from the stories in the Bible, and in the background the walls of Jerusalem. Someone had imagined this place and painted it. Perhaps he had even seen it! I let it hang there. For a moment I wondered what Palestine looked like. Perhaps we should have tried to get certificates.[1] And perhaps we should have agreed to emigrate to Baltimore, to Eva and Sol.

I shake my head to clear it and return to the here and now, the bitter reality of our existence. The day we feared has arrived. "*Ach*, perhaps it won't be so terrible," I mumble to myself and standing up straight, as if I am filled with confidence, I take the stairs down.

"Are we ever going to come back here?" *mamme* asks, and her voice breaks a little, and then, whispering so *tatte* won't hear, she says, "Betsie, go across the street now. Just do it. Go with David and Betje. Disappear with them. I will explain it to *tatte*. Now we have Herman, so we are all right." I force a smile and answer resolutely that I can't. "*Samen uit, samen thuis* (Leave together and return together)" and I touch her shoulder with all the love I have in me. "Yes," she sighs and repeats the old Dutch proverb. Maybe if we believe it, I think. Maybe if we really do our best to get through all of this unknown. Perhaps the war will be over soon. Perhaps we will then see the little girls again. Our David's sweet children. Once again, I shake off this mood and return to what we have to do. We have to leave.

For over a year now, Herman Flim has been our savior. During that entire time, he regularly smuggles bread to our home and also supplies the other Samuel families in the village, so we won't starve. Today is no exception. Herman enters through the back door and immediately begins to help me with the few measly items we are allowed to take with us. Herman never worried about not being allowed to come to us. I am so grateful to him. He helps me with my backpack and hands me the two small valises. *Tatte* sits down behind

Herman and, considering that even that is very hard for him, it is clear that he could not have walked those 20 minutes it takes to get to the train station. Herman rides off on his bike, choosing the side streets rather than the main road, the Grotestraat. He is rightly careful to want to avoid curious eyes. On this day, the day of our Exodus from Nijverdal, it is not smart to upset the police or even a civilian. Anyone could easily betray him to the authorities and accuse him of helping Jews. On this day he will be extra careful. *Mamme* and I go outside together.

From the corner of my eyes, I see that at number 82, David and Betje's home, the curtains are drawn. They have also been ordered out today, but their destination is Amsterdam, not Vught. David had been ordered to present himself there together with the contents of his house. I know he has other plans, but do not know the details. I also know that the girls are no longer in Nijverdal, but I was not allowed to ask him what he had done with them. Knowing too much is dangerous. I pass their house quickly. I do not want to draw attention to it.

Mamme, tatte and I, together with all the uncles, aunts and their families have to go to Vught. At the train station we are to hand in the key to our home and then a travel permit will be inserted in their *Ausweis* (ID) which will allow us to take the train. At the corner of number 30 Rijssensestraat, where Tante Schoontje and Ome Shmuel-Sandor live, we wait until they too come outside. They too have small valises. Just like us. *Ach*, I think, look how pale and bent over they have grown. Worse even than *mamme*, which is understandable because all their children have already gone. They have disappeared in the fog of German *risches* (evil). Schoontje and *mamme* walk arm-in-arm. Once more we stop, this time for Ome Abraham and Tante Lewia. Their sons come outside with them, but the little girl, Truusje, is not with them. We understand immediately what that means: She has gone *Vayibrach*. Tante Lewia and Ome Abraham finally listened to David, but they have stayed. She approaches me because she sees the question in my eyes. Standing close, she whispers, "We are in G-d's hands now. If we are allowed to live, so be it. Should we not be given life, then we must make our peace with that. But Truusje was still so young. I was afraid to take her on this difficult journey and the boys refused to leave us." I understand very well. "Your boys are strong, just like me. We can make it and we have enough strength to help our parents a little along the way." Jacob, my cousin, takes one of the small suitcases from me and his brother David takes the other one. Now my hands are free, and they signal me with their eyes and heads, that I should go to the back of our small, sad group, and disappear – try to disappear. But how can I do that with all the locals along the way or behind their lace curtains? All staring at us?

Our progress is slow. We walk in the gutter, for Jews are not allowed on the sidewalk. Someone yells a curse at us, calling us *Jörre* (dirty Jew). Someone throws something that smells like dog poop or worse. Then, suddenly, someone pulls my arm. I look up. It is Nentjes, the fish monger. We are just about near his house, and he is pulling me into the direction of his back gate. Nentjes! He is opening a gate into life. The train station is a gate into something that is only fearful and horrifying. Life or death? In a flash I choose Nentjes' path, but as I take one step in that direction, someone at the side of the road sticks out his leg to trip *mamme* who stumbles and falls. She falls hard and painfully on her face and hands; her nose starts bleeding, and she has trouble getting up. She is not even allowed to sit down on the curb to recover a little. In that second everything changed again for me: what happened to my mother is the norm now. How did I forget! A woman of nearly 70 can be accosted and made to fall. She can be hurt, and no one will lift a finger to help her. Schoontje and Lewia pull her up, and slowly and with difficulty she continues walking, supported by the other two old women. Nentjes and his glimpse of rescue disappears in the shadows of my despair.

When finally we arrived in Vught, Herman tried to talk to the police on guard. The man silently raised his gun, clearly threatening Herman. Then *tatte* tried. He started to say something about his medical problems, his pains, and other difficulties he had, such as walking, but the guard hit him in the stomach with the butt of his gun. My poor father doubled over in agony and fell. We were not even allowed to help him get up. The uniform simply waved his gun in our direction, and we understood. *Tatte* finally managed to get to his feet. That is how we entered the concentration camp of Vught: both parents injured, and I? I entered understanding how helpless I had allowed myself to become.

When the gates closed behind us and were locked, and when the people in the outside world could no longer see what was happening to us, the destruction of our entire lives could begin. Everything we had once believed in was turned upside down. *Mamme* and I were pushed to one side, sometimes with blows of a stick, sometimes with curses, and *tatte*, still groaning, was pushed in a different direction together with the uncles and cousins. Somewhere, we were pushed through a door. The building was dirty and unaired. So, this is where we were supposed to live? The beds were actually planks, double-deckers, triple-deckers, and there was room only on the top tier. No way *mamme* could make it there. I walked through the sleazy barracks until I found a young woman who had a spot on the lower tier, and who was willing to change places with us. I lay down next to my mother. Somewhere in that place Tante Schoontje and Tante Lewia had also found a spot. *Mamme* was too overwhelmed to speak. She cried silently and mumbled to herself.

On Sunday, the men were allowed to visit us, but *tatte* did not come. I sought out the uncles, and Ome Abraham told me that because *tatte* was in such pain, he simply could not walk to our barracks. I did not know how to tell my mother this, nor did I know whom I might ask for permission to see him. Ome Abraham swore to me that he would do his best to look after his brother and that he would stay close to him. It was the best we could hope for.

The next week, *mamme* and I worked with textile in the camp. We cut and sewed. I found *mamme* a place to sit, but I had to manage on my feet. We still hoped to be allowed to stay in Vught. We were still in the Netherlands, and around us people spoke Dutch and Yiddish which meant that we could understand each other.

Passover came a good week after we had arrived in Vught, and the miracle was that we received a few matzos. The Jewish Council in Amsterdam had sent them to us. It had been two years since we last saw matzos. Well, we all told each other, perhaps it won't be so terrible. Perhaps we can manage in this place. We even held a Passover seder with the story of Moses and the Exodus to the Promised Land. It was bittersweet because I suddenly understood that we too were in exile and had become slaves. True, men and women were separated, but they let us conduct a Passover seder and the women did their utmost to remember how it was done. We all took a tiny bite of the few matzos we had and for a few moments, life returned to normal. Passover, seder, matzos. Yes, we really wanted to remain in Vught and held fast to the hope that this might happen.

The Sunday after that, *tatte* finally came, still pale and walking with difficulty. He told us that in the men's section there had also been a seder with matzos. A week later, *tatte* came to visit again. We were so happy to see him. Happy in that terrible place. We tried to adjust.

Then Passover was over, and everything changed. *Mamme* was told to report to the train station and learned that she would be transferred to Westerbork. I had to remain in Vught by myself.

After that second visit, I never saw *tatte* again, and *mamme* disappeared together with most of the elderly. They were all sent on to Westerbork. We were not told why, and together with the old people, the children also disappeared from our camp. There was even a newborn on that transport. They placed the infant in a basket and pushed it into the train to Westerbork. I tried to console the mother, but what could I say to her? All of us who were left behind in Vught fell into deep mourning. Deep inside I consoled myself with the idea that I would never know the pain of losing a child. My thoughts went to our little Louisie and baby Marianne, and the fact that in the camp there were children just as small as them. Many were ill, suffering from the terrible lack of food and sanitation throughout the camp. Yes, David had been right: every word uttered by the Germans was a lie and the reason was that they simply wanted to catch us. They wanted us caught in their trap. To make us believe those lies until it was too late. And then? I was not yet 100 percent sure, but I really thought they wanted us dead. We were on the road to our deaths. I finally understood this when I saw how they pushed the old people and the small children into the already overcrowded train, and I knew that, without a doubt, my turn would come too. Our home at number 101 Rijssensestraat disappeared together with my life before this place. All I could do now would be to pray that at least for David and Betje the *Vayibrach* plans had worked out well. I would pray for their safety. And then they called my name.

The train ride from Vught to Westerbork was long and difficult. We just about traversed half the country, and it took hours. Everyone stood the whole time, including me. On the way to the platform, we were beaten. It had to be done *schnell* (fast) and we tried, but people had already been weakened by the camp. All of us were afraid. I no longer had normal clothes since everything had been taken away. Under my thin dress, which flew up in the wind, I was naked. The soldiers and the Dutch policemen gawked at me and leered at the women as the wind exposed our bodies. They pointed and laughed at us. We had to stand there on that platform and there was nothing we could do about it.

In Westerbork I searched for my parents, but no one knew where they were; no one had seen them there. One of the women thought that *mamme* and *tatte* had already gone and that the train from Vught had gone east without stopping. Yes, I understood. Also, that the sick and dying children, sometimes together with their young mothers, and also those old people, had been "sent away". I understood and tore my dress as a sign of mourning. I no longer had parents. And they were so old already! They would not have had long to live! Why couldn't they have been allowed to stay in Nijverdal, die there when their time came and be laid to eternal rest next to my Oma and Opa? Why did they have to be deported, be made ill, be thrown, and pushed into a train? I did not understand. Who benefited from that murder? And then I understood that too: Hitler just wanted to see us dead. There was no other explanation and I had walked into the cruel trap together with all the Jews in Vught, Westerbork and throughout Europe. I was caught. I could not escape. Perhaps now they would also move us here and there, pushing us into trains until we died. Just like that, standing on top of each other, dying. No one would even know about it. No one would say kaddish for us, the prayer for the dead. So, I said kaddish for my dead parents and all those poor children. I said kaddish in Westerbork every day, caught in that horrible place together with all those other Jews. But I was still alive, and I could say that prayer in honor of the dead even though I was only a woman. But who would say kaddish for me? I asked the people in Westerbork, where exactly they send all those people. They just shrugged their shoulders and turned away from me. I was too afraid to press for an answer.

My hands can still work and they keep busy. That pleases me. It gives me less time to think. In Westerbork, I found many children who had ended up there without their parents and someone had to look after them. The Germans did not want so much crying and especially wanted to avoid panic. The children were confined to their own barracks and were not allowed outside very often. If my heart had not already been broken by the loss of *mamme, tatte* and those poor children in Vught, it would have broken now by those poor orphans caught in Westerbork. They were so small and innocent. They barely had clothes to cover their skinny bodies. Many of them were toddlers who were so young that they did not even know their own name. The Germans had caught them because they had been betrayed in their hiding place or had been rounded up in one of the razzias, the violent invasion of Jewish homes. This I heard from someone who had come to Westerbork from Amsterdam. What is it with those Germans? What could these small children possibly contribute to the war effort? What threat could they possibly pose? And again, I could not get my head around this impossible situation, but it was real. I saw it. Lived it. And again, I knew. We will all be put to death. Young and old. All Jews. We must be murdered. That is Hitler's true war: the war against the *Yidden*. So, one day passed. And another. Maybe a week or more. Maybe even a month. Not two months. I had lost my sense of time.

And now I am on that train leaving from Westerbork. I know that it is summer, the beginning of July, I think. Then, incongruously, I realize it is around David's birthday. What does that have to do with anything? Birthdays are a million miles away from the place I find myself in. I push all thoughts of the outside away. It is hot. I am in the train, standing, and this is not a train for human beings. It is a cattle train. In a flash I saw a sign on the platform at Westerbork: Westerbork-Auschwitz, and on the opposite platform: Auschwitz-Westerbork. For a second, I tried to hold on to that hope, but in truth, I know that sign is only one more lie. No trains from abroad arrive at this station. Well, I have no idea where Auschwitz is, what it is and why we are going there. I am hot and many people are nauseous. I hear them, but we have no space to move away. We are pushed together like sardines. The air in the wagon deteriorates by the minute and the journey is endless. Day and night this train pushes along. We are metamorphosing into cattle. Slowly but surely. Only our bodily instincts are still intact, but our brain is closing down. I find it harder to think coherently, but I refuse to have that taken away from me too because I know without a doubt that this is my final journey. This train is my coffin. I need to hold on to my humanity for as long as possible even if I believe that our destination is not another work camp. We are like cattle on our way to slaughter. Why am I forced to be here? I have let my entire life pass me by, let it slip through my fingers like sand in the egg timer in *mamme's* kitchen. I have achieved nothing. I have not left any stamp on this world. Suddenly I can't control myself any longer. "They are going to murder us!" I scream, and someone elbows me painfully in the ribs. "Keep quiet, woman! There are children here." I bite my lip, for I think of Louisie and Marianne, those little girls, almost babies still. Louisie not even five-years-old, and her little sister two-and-a-half. Betje kept them dressed in sweet outfits that she made herself and she always put a big bow in their hair. How I loved to brush their hair! I sewed for them as well. Betje and I embroidered the clothes with flowers and butterflies, made intricate patterns and sewed satin belts onto their *Shabbos* clothes. What kind of a monster would throw such children into this train!

And I? Again, I sink into my self-pity because my entire life has been one fiasco. I have left nothing behind. There will be no memory of me. I never married because I was afraid. *Mamme* and her stories about her mother and growing up without her. *Mamme* who warned me of the dangers of pregnancy. That women died in childbirth. Well, I was not ready for that. Yes, boys came courting and sometimes I agreed to go out with one of them. "You have such beautiful hair," one of them said to me. "You have nice eyes," said another. "Nice that you blush when I compliment you." It was wonderful to hear those things, but I was afraid of marriage, and each time I broke off the relationship. I was not ready to suffer. I did not ever want to be sad. Like Tante Schoontje who had children, and everything was fine, but her suffering came when Elina, her oldest, died. Elina was only a little older than me. I was 18 at the time. We played together, grew up together, lived in the same street. "You are like sisters," people said to us, and we giggled and hugged each other. I liked the idea of a sister, for I only had David, my brother. Then Elina sickened and died. She died. I did not go to her *levoye* (funeral). I could not bear the idea that they were burying her. My beloved cousin! I felt as if death was lying in wait for all of us and from that moment, I knew that I could never deal with death. And then I was 30, and men no longer came calling. All my friends from school and my cousins got married and had children. No one died giving birth and the children were all healthy.

The fact that David did marry and built his home across the street from us saved me from feeling like an old spinster. The two children that he and Betje had were also a little bit mine, and I came whenever Betje needed me. I pushed the girls on their swing, played with them in the garden and baked sand cookies in the sand box near the shed. All the love I had in me I gave to those two little girls. But then the war came and brought suffering. All our happiness was overshadowed by Hitler and his plans for the Jews. *Mamme* and *tatte* grew old and bent before their time. They grew thinner and sickened. The only thing I could do for them was not to abandon them. We saved food from our mouths to feed the little girls, of course. Poor David, my big brother. He wanted to save everyone, rushing from one to the other and making plans for our *Vayibrach*, but how could I believe that Hitler wanted to kill all of us? I could not understand that anyone in cultured Germany could be so evil.

Now I am locked inside this rocking train and try not to stumble and fall with its harsh movements. Around me people fall against me and each other and keeping myself upright is getting harder all the time. I need to relieve myself but there is no toilet, and slowly but surely my sphincters give in; like everyone around me, I am left standing in my own secretions. Just like those cows, my brain says. If only I had paper – a sliver of wood – I could write down something, throw the note outside through a gap between the slats. "I am caught in the death train. All roads lead to death. There is no work camp. Good *Yidden,* friends, brothers, and sisters, I had no ink. I wrote this note in my own blood. Flee! Flee! Flee! I did not believe this could happen either!"

I don't know how it is possible, but I dozed off for a while. I am like a horse sleeping on its legs, leaning on the woman next to me while she leaned against me. The brakes of the locomotive awaken us roughly. The train is slowing down. Slower, slower and then it stands still. Where are we now? Above the screeching of the brakes, I hear dogs barking. Suddenly, the doors are pulled open. German soldiers enter, and people carrying whips and sticks scream that we have to get out. "I was a good daughter!" I yell at them. "Why like this? Why do I deserve this? Is this the hand of the G-d we trusted? Into whose hands we committed ourselves?" My brain shuts down, I cannot think any more and the human river pushes me ahead. Screams and curses accompany us. Men and women are separated. I press my body into the throng of women and try to stand in one place, but the feet of the others push me onward. I am but an animal without language and without thoughts. I shuffle along. Some women are screaming but even they are walking. Even if I wanted to, it would be impossible to stand still. Further and further we go. What is this place? What is that smell? What is that smoke in the air and the smell of things burning? What do they manufacture here?

The women ahead of me are descending now. Someone stumbles on the steps and the others trample her and move along. We cannot stop. We will stop only when we are told to do so.

"*Auskleiden*," a male voice shouts. Why do we need to undress? When we hesitate, a whip swishes through the air, so we take off our clothes and he gawks at us. I try to cover my body with my hands. Suddenly I remember my backpack. Where is it? Was it only part of the lies that they told us to keep us calm? *Oh David, David*, my soul calls out to him. *Maybe you succeeded in saving the girls and making Vayibrach with Betje. Maybe your daughters will never have to be in this train. Maybe you will think of me sometime?* I am pushed along again because the other women are moving too. I no longer seem to have a will of my own. I understand and feel that I am in an enclosed space. It is dark here and I cannot breathe.

"I am 36 years old," I say out loud. "Just like Elina, I die without having known love." Where did I get that? *Ach*, that was written on her grave, she died a virgin. But my grave? Will anyone make a marker for me? I cannot breathe. It is dark but I can hear women falling on the concrete floor. I fall too, and then I do the only thing that is left, for even oxygen has been taken away from me. I lay myself into the hands of the G-d of Israel, for I was a good Jew all the days of my life. "*Shm'a Yisroel* (Hear Oh Israel)," I pray.

Then only the deadly silence. (Sobibor, July 9, 1943)

---

1. https://www.jewishvirtuallibrary.org/british-restrictions-on-jewish-immigration-to-palestine.

6

BELA PAGRACH: 1915-1943

In her best cursive script and with an elegant swirl, Bela Pagrach writes "Chapter I" and stops to admire her work. She is writing her first novel. Very carefully she blows on the damp ink, dips her pen into the inkpot, shakes off the extra ink so as not to stain the virginal page and starts writing feverishly, her tongue between her teeth, her head tilted to one side.

The sound of a bicycle bell sounded and the voice of a young girl called out, "Hey Viek, are you coming?" Viek van Hulen raised her eyes from her book. Her cousin Jo van Hulen was standing at the gate to the garden ready with her bike. She was wearing a white dress with a matching white beret, a tennis racket in her hand. Viek thought that she looked cute. She gestured a greeting and called back, "Be right out. Come and sit down inside, I'll be ready in a minute." So, Jo leaned her bike against the gate and stepped onto the patio. She dropped into a chair. "Hurry up already. The weather is perfect for tennis."

The sentences race through Bela's head and she can barely keep up with her thoughts. The pen races along as well and in a second, so it seems to her, the entire notebook is full of words. "If I stop writing now," she says out loud, "I will lose my momentum and inspiration." So, instead of getting up to look for a clean notebook, she continues on the inside of the cover. There is no time to waste. She certainly can't run to the store to buy a notebook now that the muse is sitting on her shoulder. She cannot stop. Bela's story is an innocent, optimistic tale of two cousins. She writes the end of chapter one on an old newspaper that was sitting on the table. Tomorrow, on her way to work, she will buy two notebooks and from now on she will write smaller.

Bela Pagrach's story is unfolding itself on top of an old newspaper article about the German occupation of Czechoslovakia and Hitler's threats to attack Poland. She ignores the headlines but switches to blue ink so that her words will stand out from the darker newspaper print. Tomorrow she will copy the end of the chapter into the new notebook.

By the time she is finished writing, her untitled novel takes up three thick hardcover notebooks and runs over 500 pages, all in her own handwriting. She worked without breathing. There are barely any crossed out words in her story. Here and there you can see that she tore a page from the notebook – especially towards the end of the book – but the text itself, aside from a few ink stains, is neat and easily legible, written by a young and enthusiastic woman in her best handwriting.

The characters in Bela Pagrach's book enjoy endless adventures, laugh themselves through life and have no worries. Elegantly dressed, they jump from armchair to bicycle or the dance floor. They run over green lawns surrounded by flower beds and swim in the river. Without hesitation, they reject the many young men who stare at them with lovesick eyes. They shake their hair and giggle together. Tomorrow a new, more suitable boy will come along. After all, they are pretty girls, dressed in the latest fashion, desirable and sought after.

The book is a shameless, romanticized idealization of life. On the very last page of the final notebook, one of the cousins finds a great love: *Just as you are now captured, my beloved, in my heart, I imprison you within my arms.* To emphasize this ending, Bela has underlined it twice. Two lines under those final words. This is it! Her heroine is imprisoned in love. The End.

The year was 1939, and time rushed swiftly and without pity through the river of life.

1941

The book of Bela Pagrach's own real and horrifying life begins when the end is already known – at least in Berlin. Over there, someone has drawn two thick lines under her final line: Sobibor, June 16, 1943. But Bela does not know this yet.

She has only just reached 1941 and is now keeping a diary. It is a diary for the time of the apocalypse, but even now she does not yet know the end of her biography, because her world has shrunk to claustrophobic dimensions, her life minimal and constrained. When Bela Pagrach puts pen to paper for her first entry in this new undertaking, it is October and there are endless indications of the hardships that a Jewish woman living under a regime which wants to destroy her must endure. She writes with hesitation, leaving many gaps in her narrative and using codes. Yet, Bela holds fast to the hope that in the end she may still be caught within the prison of her beloved's arms.

From the perspective of time, Bela's tragic reality stands in sharp contrast with the characters she controls because hers is controlled by the cruel thumb of rules and regulations that change almost daily. The result is that Bela's life unwinds in a frightful, chaotic world where logic holds no sway. Everything that happens to her now is the result of the new world order forced upon the Jews by the German occupier. Bela is caught, but not in the passionate embrace of her beloved Levi.

By the autumn of 1941, Dutch Jews are no longer allowed to move around freely, and also for the non-Jewish population in the Netherlands life has grown harsh: staples are scarce, and even if one has the money to purchase the necessities, they are hard to come by.

Money is no longer the only coin of the Nazi realm. Citizens have to pay cash and also hand over the appropriate number of their ration coupons in exchange for the goods. Everything is rationed by the size of the household. Each family receives what the occupation deems necessary for survival, and it does not take long before the ration booklets also become a weapon in the war against the Jews: when Jews no longer have the right to their existence, they can no longer demand the ration booklets, and as a result they cannot stay alive. Furthermore, without ration coupons, it is very difficult to help the Jews to go into hiding. This development happens slowly at a time when Bela is deadly ill with a physical ailment, but she, as a Jewish woman, suffers two equally deadly diseases. On the one hand she suffers because of her Jewish blood, which under German occupation has become a terminal, genetic illness, and on the other hand, Bela Pagrach – sister to Betje Samuel Pagrach – has also fallen victim to a disease she caught during her work as nurse in the Sanitorium at Hellendoorn: TB, tuberculosis! Our optimistic, first-time author, the girl who wrote her bubbly, heartfelt book after falling in love and becoming engaged to Levi Cohen, was about to get married. She should have been Levi's wife already but her newly diagnosed TB has put all their plans on hold. Her dream of happiness with a husband and children retreated with the invasion of Hitler's storm troopers, and not long after that, her entire future disappeared behind the dark cloud of the contagious disease.

The medical protocol requires that Bela keep strict bedrest for at least a whole year, but worse than that, the tuberculosis is a stroke of luck for the Jew hunters. Bela has become easy prey, confined to bed as she is. The battle for her life is now fought between two cruel contenders: if she recovers from the TB before she is sent to a camp, there is a chance that she might succeed in escaping death in Eastern Europe, and so she must remain one step ahead of the murderous bulldozers of the Germans.

In the final analysis, the bacteria in her blood are less fatal than her inherited Jewish blood.

7

BELA PAGRACH: 1941-1943

I caught a cold and cannot shake the cough. Just to be on the safe side, I wore a double mask when I took care of my patients, so that they wouldn't catch it. I drank one cup of tea after the other, and whenever we had a lemon, added a slice. Mama bought a little honey from one of the neighbors. Very slowly I felt better, coughed a little less, but still felt exhausted. Perhaps it was the pressure at work, who knows. Perhaps the preparations of my marriage to Levi were a little too much. No wonder I feel so weak. I really don't want to work fewer hours because the patients need many working hands. And then there are my finals at the nursing school. Of course, all of that is a lot of stress for one person. Mama scolds me that I am not strong enough to carry such a heavy load, telling me that I am much too thin, but Betje, my big sister, laughs at me and says that I simply want to be a beautiful and slender bride. The truth is that I simply have no appetite. I am always tired, and suddenly my cough is back as well.

Because I work in a sanitorium for contagious diseases, I have to undergo regular check-ups, including the subcutaneous Mantoux test for an early diagnosis of TB and I also have X-rays twice a year. Last time everything was fine, but now, all of a sudden, I saw blood in my handkerchief, and I just knew. When I noticed my temperature was also high, I ran to Dr. Pompen, the director of the sanitorium, and told him. A microscopic examination of my sputum made all my fears reality. I had the disease. I had TB! Especially now, when I need all my strength. What am I going to do?!

A few seconds later I found myself hospitalized in isolation, crying rivers. I could not stem the flow. The earth had moved and I had fallen off. The doctor came to let me know that he'd spoken to David, my brother-in-law, and had explained the situation. Shortly after, David had arrived at the sanitorium but was not allowed to see me. Dr. Pompen convinced him that I was in good hands, after which David cycled in the direction of Holten to give mama and papa the bad news. The next day they all came to Hellendoorn, but they were not allowed to come into my room. I was too ill and too contagious. For a second the doctor let them see me through the glass door. My darling Levi told me afterwards that no one was willing to leave the building, but how long could they just stand there? Eventually, Dr. Pompen had chairs brought into his office and in his own gentle manner, suggested that they write me a letter to cheer me up and give me courage for the battle ahead. "Then we will keep a close watch on the situation in the coming days and if she responds well to the treatment, we can talk again." The doctor came to read me the letters in person to prevent me from making any effort, but when I asked him for pen and paper, he forbade me to write even one word. "You must have absolute rest. That means that your eyes and hands have to rest as well." He sent me a nurse so I could dictate a few words for my family, but I was afraid to say anything personal, so at best, it became a polite little note. I did sign my name, but that was all.

I spent most of the day crying. I cried so much that Dr. Pompen feared the sanitorium might be flooded. "Of all the nurses you are the only one who took ill, Bela. In my opinion, you depleted all your energy and you simply did not have the reserves to fight the infection." For one moment the doctor looked me straight in the eye and then continued, "Even without your wedding plans, your study and exams, and even without this very demanding job, you had simply reached the limit of your capacity because of the situation."

He meant, of course, that it was because I was Jewish. That my body had simply given up. He was right. I was completely exhausted. What else could that Schreier take from me, then? Levi and I had already postponed our wedding because of the "situation" and now my body was disintegrating. So, what do I still have that can be taken? Of course, the doctor was right. I had so done my best to keep all the *tsures* (problems) at bay and to ignore them as much as possible. Everything was connected to our "situation". I had hoped that if only I worked really hard and left no time to think about the despair of our lives, I would get through this dark time. I left all the major decisions to the men of the family and listened to them. Not to my soft, inner voice. I could not handle it.

"You have been living under such unbearable tension," Dr. Pompen added softly. I had not even realized that he knew we were Jews. I had not spoken about it with anyone. The sanitorium's kosher kitchen was housed in a discreet corner of the complex and I thought I had managed to slip in and out unnoticed. No one had ever spoken to me about being Jewish. Suddenly, I thought that perhaps because of this, the doctor had chosen to bring me the letters from my family by himself and read them personally?! Perhaps he wanted to make sure there were no things that might be unpleasant if people knew them or things that might give away some of our secrets. What a wonderful thing to do for me, for it is true that we must be discreet and worry about all the *rishes* in every corner. If bad people knew things that they shouldn't know, they might use them against us. Oh, dear G-d, I think in despair, our life is much too complicated for a normal, healthy person, let alone for a person who is so sick. I no longer had any way of knowing who my friends were and worse, who my enemies might be.

It did not take long before we all knew that my TB was fairly light and my prognosis positive. The infection was curable and I could recover completely. As soon as I had this certainty, I did not leave Dr. Pompen alone. I begged him to allow me to be nursed at home. Mama could do it and everyone in the family would pitch in, but the doctor would not hear of this, saying "It is completely irresponsible to

73

release you from the sanitorium." He gave me a stern look and said, "You are still contagious, you know. What if you were to infect one of your relatives? Your mother for instance? Besides, you are much too weak and vulnerable. You must remain in isolation." I tried a different tactic and told him that I found it almost impossible to be a patient in an institution where I had been a nurse. This he was willing to deal with and after a while, a compromise was found. I would be transferred to Deventer, to the nuns. Dr. Pompen was the head of the TB ward there, so he could continue to look after me. Deventer was also much closer to Holten and there was a direct bus. Best of all, in Deventer no one knew me.

Shortly after my arrival, I received a package with a short note from Levi and a thick, hardcover notebook. For a moment I thought that he had sent me one of the notebooks I had used to write my book when I fell in love with him, but the notebook was empty. "This is a good time for you to start a diary," he wrote. As always, I listened to him, although I really did not feel like writing. Nevertheless, I wanted to believe that Levi was right. Perhaps it would be a good thing to write down all those thoughts bubbling up inside me. For later. For after everything. Still, I hesitated. I was afraid to truly write down what I was feeling. I was afraid to expose my emotions to the paper. I understood that I could write about things I did not want to forget, for when I would be allowed to stand under the *Huppe* canopy with my Levi, but not my secrets. Those I could not set free on paper. Also, the "situation" needed to be left out of my diary. A hospital is the wrong place to whisper secrets and too dangerous to write things down. So, my fears, my terrible trembling fears, would remain outside this project. I opened the notebook very carefully, for Levi, to make him a little bit happy. It was for Levi that I dipped the pen in the ink and turned that notebook into my diary:

First letter, October 1941

I must be crazy to choose these difficult times to start a new diary. Most likely there won't be too many good memories. But I thought that it might be interesting for later, if I could reminisce about my time in the sanitorium.

I feel as if in a dream, well, a nightmare, really. How can it be that I got this! This disease! And on top of that these difficult times too! When Dr. Pompen told me that I would need a year of bedrest, I did not even realize what was wrong with me... But I want to be strong! And with G-d's help I will recover. I can cooperate to make that happen. To make it happen faster... Levi just went home. I would have preferred him to stay later, but the new laws make that impossible. Well, nothing to be done about that. I will be writing little bits, each time when I think of something I must not forget, something that I can hold on to. Levi says that a diary is not really truthful because you never truly write down the way you think you experienced things. But I can make that choice and in my old diary, which I no longer have, I did sometimes write things down which were for my eyes only, and for Levi, of course. To tell the truth, I started this diary with the idea that when Levi also read it, he would know me even more profoundly, and also for later, when we can bring children into the world.

Levi got special permission to visit me once every day as long as he put on a sterile coat and wore a mask. I had to put on a mask as well. On one of those days, as he was sitting next to my bed, an oak leaf from the tall tree outside fluttered down into the room and landed on my bed. Levi picked it up carefully and handed the brown leaf to me with a comical bow. I even wrote about it in my diary:

26 October 1941, afternoon

This leaf dwindled down into my room a short while ago and Levi laid it inside this diary. He said, "One day we will reminisce about this. We will show it to our children and then laugh a little about the idea that we saved this dried up leaf so carefully. Perhaps then we will say to each other, remember when you lay there and everything seemed so sad." And yet, despite everything, when Levi is here it all seems a little better, not so hard. He really means everything to me. How strange that such things happen in your life. But also, wonderful.

November 1941

Actually, it is terrible to know in advance that you are going to be sick for such a long time. But I have to look at the sunny side. That with G-d's help

I will recover completely. My blood tests are improving, my pulse is slower and my temperature is down. As long as I do not develop pleurisy now. Dr. Pompen expects that I will. It is part of the disease. Levi also needs to be tested and has to have X-rays of his lungs. I wish our Betje came to visit. I cannot understand why she has not yet come. Perhaps it is not so simple because of the children (unbeschrieen - they should be well). Well, Levi and I love each other so much, but the wedding... we have to stop thinking about that. Even if the war ends in our favor, very soon with G-d's help, we still have to wait till I am fully recovered. Dr. Pompen told Levi about a year and a half, including the aftercare. Then I will already be more than 27 and Levi 31 years old. Nothing we can do about that. I always thought I was such a religious Jew and that this would give me something to hold on to, but sometimes that means nothing. Well, Levi brought me a tile with a phrase in our dialect – do not worry, it will all work out – and hung the tile on a nail above my bed. Everyone loved it. He gave me orders to look at the tile often, especially when I was feeling down. It will all work out. Think positive! I AM getting better! The doctor says so too. He also tells me that the nuns pray for me every day. It will all work out; it will all work out! I keep staring at the tile. That is my prayer. Well, and now I am running a fever again. Nothing to be done about that. But I have also gained two kilos and I am a fat woman, but that is part of the treatment, and the doctor is satisfied. Levi laughs at me and says that he has to get fat too so that "We will always be right for each other!"

That is how it was. Bela recovered well from her tuberculosis and the doctor was optimistic, but outside her sterile room surrounded with love, breathing for the Jews became more difficult day by day. While Bela was working on her health, the Nazi machine worked day and night and laid plans to destroy Yacob's seed down to the last Jew in Europe. Even this young woman who remained in isolation by the nuns was on the list of the condemned.

At the beginning of 1942, the order was given to make all the hospitals Judenrein. In other words, all the Jews must vacate the hospitals. For a short time, Dr. Pompen succeeded in preventing this. He used the ruse that Bela was still contagious and if she returned to the community now, this might result in an epidemic outbreak of TB, not only among the Jews, but among the Aryan civilians of Holten as well.

Bela was allowed to remain with the nuns until the family built an isolation chamber for her so as to protect the outside world from her. They decided that they would dismantle the sunporch of the house and use its glass windows to build a kind of hothouse isolation room. The windows could be opened, and there was room for a bed. When the structure was ready, Dr. Pompen inspected it, asked for some adjustments to be made, and allowed Bela to come home to Holten. He whispered that he would continue to look after her and monitor her recovery, even though he really is no longer allowed to do so. Jews may be treated by Jewish doctors only. The good doctor kept his promise and did much more than simply look after his patient.

Now that Bela is home, a stream of visitors comes to see her, but they must stay outside the glass windows. They write good wishes on pieces of paper which they hold up so Bela can read. They smile and wave to her. For the sake of her treatment, the first rule is that her disease must have lots of fresh air, and Bela, wrapped in many blankets, lies in her glass cage with the windows open, day and night. They are only closed to enable visitors to come or when it rains.

November 1941

Thank G-d, Levi's X-ray was negative. He brought me a beautiful bouquet of roses, and candy.

Every letter in the diary includes a long list of visitors, as if by naming them, Bela shows that those people are safe. Those who fail to come are also mentioned, and she often asks other visitors what the reason for a particular person's absence might be. She writes that she is moody and often depressed. It is all taking so long.

Even if you are healthy that happens, but this is something else. When I have the time to just lie here and my thoughts run wild, I know it is time to take pen and paper. They keep my worries at bay. Well, nothing to be done about that.

Levi refuses to keep his distance from the woman he loves. Every day he sits by her bed, agreeing only to don a sterile coat and mask, and then he tells Bela everything about life outside the glass walls of her isolation. He can see how weak she has grown; her difficulty in breathing has not escaped him. Sometimes Bela barely has the strength to lift her head off the pillow. She concentrates all her energy on getting oxygen into her lungs, and then expel it. As a result, talking remains minimal. Levi takes the lead in their conversations. He knows that there have been *razzias* (raids) on the Jewish communities in Twente, and that Jews have been dragged out of their homes on the other side of the river Ijssel too. They all live between hope and fear. Tomorrow the banging on the door could be at their home, with the Dutch police ready to take them away with undue force. Levi understands full well that should this happen, Bela does not stand a chance. She would not survive if forced to make a long journey to some unknown destination. He must do something! He must save her, and feverishly, he begins to weave his plans. He starts by taking a roundabout route through the forest to Nijverdal to talk to David, and then he walks in the other direction to discuss the situation with his brother Aharon. In Holten, he has Louis, his future brother-in-law, and Tante Klaar's son, Benjamin. He wants to know what all these young men plan to do to save their families and themselves. They all agree as far as the bleak future for the Jews in the Netherlands is concerned, and they certainly agree concerning the terrible situation for Bela and the older generation, but they have fierce arguments about how exactly they can save everyone from expulsion to an unknown fate, but which they believe is death. Louis and Benjamin lean toward accepting the occupation's solution: they are interested in finding out more about the notices in the only surviving Jewish newspaper: "Jewish men and women may come forward voluntarily to serve the Third Reich in work camps in Eastern Europe. In exchange, their families will receive special papers which will allow them to stay in their homes." Louis and Benjamin decide that this sounds like a solution, because at least the parents and Bela, and their married siblings with children would be safe. Since they saw nothing more promising than this option, the two cousins, without discussing anything further with Levi, walked into the police station to volunteer for a work camp in exchange for the appropriate stamp in their families' *Ausweis* (ID).

"You have to wait for a letter from Arnhem and follow the instruction you receive," they were told. The two young men, only in their twenties, wanted to be prepared, packed a backpack with warm clothes they scrounged together, a thick sweater knitted by their mothers, and almost new walking shoes. Then the waiting for the letter started. The parents opposed their sons' plans, and there were daily arguments about Louis' and Benjamin's stubbornness. "Don't believe anything those Krauts tell you. You must escape. We have some jewelry we can sell, or you can sell on the way. You have to make it to Spain." But Louis, Bela's older brother, dug in his heels. He was not going to change his mind, "Our Bela is much too ill! Only I can protect her! She would never survive such a difficult journey to the East. How could she even consider being in a work camp?! It is out of the question." Tante Klaar's Benjamin also faced his mother squarely. He had his parents to think about and his older brother was married and had a young son. He would keep them safe by volunteering.

When there were no more words left to say, Daniel and Marianne went to the photographer and came back with portraits of themselves. "You must keep these with you always. Put them in your pocket. That way we will keep watch over you. Look at the photos every night and know that we are praying for you. And make sure you eat well! After all, you are going to a camp to work." A week went by, and another week. Then two, three. Still no letters from the German headquarters in Arnhem. Perhaps there would be no letter. Had the Germans forgotten? Maybe Louis and Benjamin would remain with them in Holten. The clock ticked slowly, the pendulum swinging between hope and fear.

About two months passed, and then, on a Friday in the spring of 1942, a police car slammed to a halt in front of Daniel Pagrach's locked, empty butcher shop. It was evening and the family had already gone to bed. They were sleeping. Suddenly there was banging on the door followed by shouting in German. Louis was the first to get out of bed and opened the door while trying to wipe the sleep from his eyes. A German policeman in his green uniform pushed him aside roughly. "Come with us immediately. Five minutes to get ready." Louis barely had the time to embrace his parents. He did not want to wake Bela in her glass room, so asked his parents to tell her not to worry and to get better. He pushed the portraits of his father and mother into his coat pockets, and also the little bit of money his father had managed to scrape together for him. It was Shabbos, but this was an emergency, *pikuach nefesh*. He stepped outside. The policeman asked if there were other young people in the house, but Louis shook his head in denial. "No," he added for emphasis. It was his first act in protecting Bela. As they pushed him to the waiting car, he turned one last time to look at his parents at the window. He saw the shock on his mother's face, and his father holding his hands on his head in despair. He must keep a positive frame of mind, he admonishes himself. After all, he is rescuing his entire family. Meanwhile, he thinks of the warm sweater his mother had knitted for him and had pushed into the knapsack. And the food? He had forgotten it. His mother would be so upset about that, but with all the banging and screaming he had simply lost his ability to think. He, too, was in shock.

I am strong, and I am saving my family, aren't I? These are the words he repeats to himself as someone roughly pushes him into the car. Tante Klaar's Benjamin is already inside. He has a black eye and is not completely dressed. He too has been violently removed from his home. And all of that on Shabbos. He casts a final glance at his mother's silent scream behind the bedroom window.

Our home is now a house in mourning. Mama walks from room to room, choking on her tears. She does not want to keep on living. Stories of her little granddaughters in Nijverdal are of no help. Just the opposite, for she can no longer see them. The 10 kilometers between their villages is far too great for our Betje to walk; we are not allowed to take the bus, and we don't even have our bikes anymore. Betje surely cannot walk all the way through the forest with the two girls. She sent some photos, but studio portraits are expensive.

Levi comes daily, but he cannot stay long because of the curfew. I turn to my diary but am too afraid to put too much on paper. I cannot really tell the truth of our situation. I tell roundabout stories about the realities of our lives and choose my words with care. "*The present laws make evening visits impossible,*" I write with hesitation. I apologize whenever I discuss the daily tortures we have to accept under the occupation, but in my soul, I feel like a cold, hairy, dog which has been left out in the rain too long. I try to shake off the drops, but I never get dry. The gentiles also stand in the German rain, but the Jews are kept wet and shivering; in spite of that, the rain keeps pouring down. In my diary I write, "*Well, nothing to be done about that,*" after I finish writing all the half-hearted phrases. This is my code. Later those words will remind me how I truly felt. For now, the apologetic "well" has to suffice. The word shakes me back to reality, but I know that the one thing I can do is remain strong and courageous, recover my health, and live because my *Vayibrach* depends on that.

In the dark, all alone in my glass cage, I doze off a little. I daydream about Levi and myself. I had remained pure and had been saving myself for the wedding night. Now all is different, and I no longer know what the future holds. I have written about it in the diary openly and honestly. I wanted Levi to know how much I love him but in the light of our harsh reality, I regret my decision. "*My body hurts with a passion which has no outlet.*" I had written from the heart, saying exactly how I feel. I must hide this diary, for I would hate to have anyone read it.

When I confessed my feelings to Levi the next day, he started to laugh. "*Write down everything I am about to say,*" he said between laughs. "*Word for word. I dictate,*" and he unscrewed the top of the inkpot while handing me the pen. "*You did not spend enough time in*

Hellendoorn, so you did not get acquainted with what was going on. I regret that I could not send you to Switzerland for a cure." I wrote down everything. Word for word and I responded on paper, so that my diary became a kind of dialogue. *"Why do you think it would have been better for me over there?"* *"Not better, no,"* was his answer. *"But if you had been there longer, you would have seen that every day was a party and people were doing whatever came into their heads."* His answer shocked me deeply and for a moment I rested my pen, looked up at Levi and then continued writing, *"Why, on earth would people behave in such a manner?"* Now it was Levi's turn to look at me, *"Because they all think they are dying, and just imagine what was going through their heads! They say to themselves, 'Ach, why should I care any longer,' and then everything is allowed and there are no consequences. Yes, it is like a French whorehouse."*

I wrote it all down but could not believe that we were using such terrible words. Levi always treats me with the utmost respect and speaks to me as if I am almost a child. Suddenly, I felt old and tired, and I snapped the diary closed. I let my eyes bore into his, "Levi, do you want me, now...? Maybe the time has come?" He turned to face me squarely, eyes shining. For a second, I thought it was going to happen so that I could give free rein to my passion, but the man who had stolen my heart smiled sadly and said, "We have promised ourselves to each other. We know we belong together. Heart and soul. It will happen."

After Levi had left, I took up my pen again, *"The spot on my lung is no longer growing and the injections are working. In a few days I will start a new course of treatment. I have to sleep. I hope the war ends quickly."* Then I closed my diary and let the pillows embrace me. I knew with absolute certainty that I would give myself to Levi, body, heart, and soul. He need only ask.

I understand full well that the tuberculosis is not the only problem on our path to the future. It is the situation too: the Schreier. Levi and I did what Betje and David were unable to do and postponed our *Huppe.* That decision was made before I was ill. But the big difference between them and us is that they got married three years before the war, and all that time they believed that the Netherlands would remain neutral. Our wedding was planned for 1941 but the war destroyed all our hopes and dreams. We are, however, engaged. I wear Levi's ring, but we remain standing on the threshold of our life together, and now there is one more enemy which wants to take my body – the TB. Meanwhile, I am already nearly 26 and I do not see a clear future. I am so afraid that the years will pass and we will miss our chance of having a family. Because of Hitler who makes our lives unlivable with new regulations and also because of the illness.

Everything is so complicated but there is nothing to be done. Everything that happens outside my glass room is not supposed to touch me because worrying is bad for recovery. I try to put the worries aside and concentrate on good thoughts: Levi will come soon. I need him! With G-d's help I will recover. In my heart, however, I wonder whether postponing our *Huppe* was the best thing. Perhaps now that I am sick and bedridden, the fact that we are not married is not so bad. These are such complicated days for couples such as us. It is not so simple to decide to ignore the world, get married and live our lives in spite of everything. Already in the hospital in Deventer it wasn't any fun for me, and the family has a terrible time, and yet, in spite of it all, I want to get better. I do want to stand under the wedding canopy with Levi next to me. I want to live.

Levi told me to keep a diary and so I keep a diary. I am not really used to the idea of writing down my thoughts, but Levi encourages me and says that I will get used to it and that writing is good for me. Also, that it will make the time go faster... Every day I ask Dr. Pompen how much longer I have to remain in isolation, and only Levi is allowed to come in for short visits. I ask the nuns too. They smile and do not answer.

It was really stupid of me to ask. I should know they cannot answer. There IS no answer to this question. When I was a nurse, tuberculosis patients asked me that same question and I smiled and gave no answer. I turn Levi's ring around on my finger. Each time we see each other we make solemn vows to get married as soon as I am back on my feet. Meanwhile, Levi is buying furniture for our home and takes care of all the details. For us both. For us together. He brings me samples of upholstery for the dining room chairs and the living room set. It is all so beautiful. Red velvet, so royal. I caress the snippet of fabric and hold it against my cheek.

A letter without a date:

Mama came and told me that the Jews have to hand in their jewelry to the police, which means that my engagement ring must be handed over as well. It is but a simple, smooth ring and we intended to make this our wedding ring as well, simply by wearing it on my other hand. I had trouble taking it off my finger because I have gained weight as a result of the treatments. Mama brought me some green all-purpose soap and together, slowly, we managed to massage the ring off my finger. It left a mark. Mama opened her hand and I dropped the ring into her palm. She closed her fingers around it and left the room. We never said a word. I wonder who will wear my ring and whether she will be happy with it, even as she knows that another woman wore it before her. Well, nothing to be done about it.

And then, suddenly, another humiliation is dropped on our lives: All Jews now have to wear a yellow patch in the shape of the Star of David, with the word JOOD embroidered on it in pseudo-Hebrew letters. Everyone has to sew these yellow stars on their clothing at a certain height, and it is forbidden to cover them. The costs of this humiliating ordnance must be borne by the Jews themselves. It is a scandal, really, and one more way to rob us of our money. There is no limit to the occupier's cruelty! I, Bela Pagrach, TB sufferer, am the only exception to this new rule. At least for the moment because I am not allowed to leave my isolation chamber. As always, Levi can read my thoughts and feels what I feel. That is why he takes off the coat with that terrible yellow star before entering my little glass palace. Thus, he protects me from seeing him marked that way. In a way I feel as if I am living on a completely different planet. I am really just as the queen of the beehive. The wings of all the drones move up and down, make noise and wind and wave in the air. They fly in and out as they desire and come back loaded down with nectar. And their queen? She is busy with only one thing: making babies. The only difference is that I am busy getting healthy. Well, nothing to be done about that...

And then the worst disaster of all happens: Levi leaves. He disappears. In the diary Bela copies poems and bits and pieces of stories which describe how she feels. Now and then she opens up a little.

24 February 1942 "I miss Levi so." It is the last sentence of a short entry.

27 March 1942 "Betje will come from Nijverdal... I miss Levi so."

17 May 1942 "Last night I dreamt of Levi. It was so real. I sat on his lap and saw his face clearly. He was wearing his dark blue suit."

Bela's health is improving, and even Betje and David's children are allowed to visit.

7 June 1942

Today the family from Nijverdal is coming again. I am so happy about that. Little Marianne has changed so much. Louisie is sweet, and such a good little girl, unbeschrieen. And again, I dreamt of Levi and told them about it. I asked him "Where have you been? You were gone so long!" People can dream the strangest things.

Louisie said, "When you are all better, Tante Bela, then Ome Levi will come back too." I do not understand how a child gets those ideas. And afterwards she added, "Yes, when you are all better, all better. Otherwise, he won't come." I say, "Then Tante Bela will be so happy, darling." And Louisie says, "Can I come too, then?" "Then Tante Bela will be even happier still," I answer her. "Why are you so happy when I come too?" "Because I love you sooo much." It made her laugh. A clear sound.

It is getting too dark to write. Levi, Levi, Levi.

8

LEVI COHEN: HIS GREAT LOVE, 1942-1945

After that terrible day in 1942, when Louis and his cousin Benjamin disappeared toward an unknown destination, the family heard from them only once more. A postcard fell through the mail slot, one for each family. The cards looked identical, and the text was also the same word for word: "We have arrived safely. There is enough food and we are treated well. Do not worry. We are well." And their signature. For a short time, those cards succeeded in lowering the level of anxiety, but too soon the two Pagrach families heard that others had received those postcards too and that afterwards there was only the fearful silence. There were never any personal details on any of those postcards. Time passed, but no more mail arrived. It was as if the earth had swallowed Louis and Benjamin.

Marianne, my future mother-in-law, and her sister Klaar could barely keep themselves going. They were in deep mourning as if their beloved sons were already no longer among the living. Even Marianne did not really believe that everything was well; her conscience plagued her, and she was unable to forgive herself for having let Louis go, for having let him volunteer for that work camp to save her. The way in which he had disappeared broke her spirit. She sat there with her prayer book open in her lap, mumbling the ancient Hebrew words, and begging the Almighty to keep her child safe and to return him to her. Marianne had long lost her prosperous look and had grown very thin. Her skin hung loose on her once fat body, yet she fasted on Mondays and Thursdays, the days when the Torah is read, to rescue her Louis from a fate which he could not escape without a miracle from the G-d of Israel.

Now Bela's care fell on me. Her mother still provided food, drink, and clean sheets; she washed her, but she no longer sat with her daughter. Bela was recovering well and was allowed visitors in her glass house, which was now known as the glass palace of the princess. Betje hardly ever came. There really was no way to bridge the distance between the two villages, unless Van Egmond was able to drive her, somehow. Although they no longer had bikes, I did hear that David had not handed his over. Instead, he had gone to the police station to report that his bike had been stolen when he forgot it outside one night. His excuse was that he could not retrieve it because the curfew had already gone into effect when he remembered.

One time when he had walked to Holten through the forest, he told me that his bike had made a successful *Vayibrach* and had been taken apart by the owner of a bicycle repair shop. Now his bike hung there among the Aryan bicycle parts and was hidden in plain sight. It would be returned to the family when that became possible. "Nothing for those *reshomim* (evil people)! I will burn it all before I let them get their hands on it!" We discussed the urgency to organize our own *Vayibrach*.

David brought letters from Betje and a drawing from Louisie. Sending mail meant that the censor would open it and we had to watch our words. This was the reason why I had moved to Holten – to be near Bela and to avoid having to communicate via the censor. I could see my beloved every day now.

There are no pretty words to describe our lives: life has become so hard; it is almost impossible to keep going. Jews are allowed to shop for necessities only two hours a week. We are lucky that the Pagrachs have a vegetable garden and chickens. We still have eggs, potatoes, and lettuce. Daniel's brother, Bram, has an orchard behind his house and so we also have whatever fruit is in season, but bread? We cannot bake our own as we have neither wheat nor corn. And bread and flour are rationed. For one or two loaves we have to stand in line for most of those two hours allotted. There are only 50 Jews in Holten, and the occupier still succeeds in making our lives miserable and keeping a close watch on us. Of course, the non-Jews are also forced to wait in the lines outside the bakery, but they have more time to shop and are not watched as closely. And, of course, their lives are difficult too. No one has new clothes anymore. Coats remain in use until they are worn out and too small for the children who have to wear them. While the same is true for adults, children grow, their arms become too long for their sleeves, dresses, and pants too short. Outside Holten there is a marketplace where people barter for clothing, but we are not allowed to go there. There you can find shoes and secondhand clothes. Now and then, Mina, the neighbor, is willing to take some of Marianne's things and trade them for much needed items, but she is afraid to come into the house so that is not really a solution.

I saw the postcards the boys supposedly sent but I do not believe they are genuine. I believe they have been tricked into leaving. The occupation wants to use the absence of the young and strong to their advantage. That is what I believe. My greatest fear is for my darling Bela. She would never survive deportation. And our parents? Of course, they are not able to undertake such a journey. For Bela, however, everything is doubly difficult. Finding a place for her to hide is almost impossible. How would any family agree to hide someone who is still recovering from tuberculosis? Hiding a Jew is risky enough, but a Jew with TB? How can I possibly find her a safe place? It seems to me that we need to consider other options. We have to try to end the war as soon as possible and consider joining the fight, which is the topic I discuss with my brother Aharon each time we meet. Slowly but surely we make our plans. At this point we know what to do, but I have not told Bela. How, in G-d's name can I? In the end I know that I have no choice and the best way is to explain without making pretty conversation. That is the reason for my visit to her glass palace today. It is cold, but I still take off my coat. Because of that yellow stain of humiliation. The cursed yellow star with the word JOOD. We are forced to walk around like lepers in the Middle Ages. We have been stigmatized and expelled from the community. People point at us in the street. I am a proud Jew but little room for pride remains. Before I enter Bela's territory, I always take that coat off.

"Bela," I start, and try to take her hand, "Are you writing in your diary? Do you know what is going on outside? Do you know what the Jewish newspaper is publishing lately?" Bela does not like the tone of my words. She cuts me off mid-sentence. "Levi, what is making your heart so heavy?" She pulls herself up on top of her mountain of pillows and I take her other hand in mine too.

I take a deep breath. Oh, how beautiful she is, my girl. So beautiful in spite of the TB or perhaps because of it. She appears fragile and pale but her cheeks are very red, an indication that the illness is still in her. I would pick her up in my arms and fly away with her, but I know that we have missed that chance. All of us. All the Jews who have been caught in the trap of their own false hope. And it is exactly for that reason that I am about to do the one and only thing still possible: I am going to fight. I am going to find out exactly what happens to the Jews and then I will make my knowledge known so that there can no longer be any doubt. "Bela, I love you so much. I want you to be my wife. I want to live with you and grow old with you and I want to fill our house with our children. Many children." I have finally succeeded in raising a smile on her lips. It gives me the courage to go on. "I must do something positive to help bring this war to an end. I must join the fight against the Nazis. I am convinced that fight will come, including here in Western Europe and my task will be to liberate you from the persecution. I have made detailed plans together with my brother Aharon." My courage ebbs away and I cannot look her in the eye. I cannot watch her rising panic. It will make me too weak to do what I must. So, I race ahead with my speech to spill all those words I had prepared. They must be spoken. They roll off my tongue with difficulty and yet, stumbling over the words, I have my say. Bela must not think that I am abandoning her. "Aharon and I want to get to Spain. We can do it! We have the physical stamina to do so. We have planned a route across the mountains. It is no longer so cold and in most places the snow has melted. We will make it. I am certain of it. We will get there. And after Spain, we will sail across the ocean to America. Once there, we will enlist in whatever army will have us and the minute the Americans invade Europe, we will be there too. We will help them liberate Europe. The Netherlands too. And you, too. Then we will get married. All you need to do is hang in there. Get better. Be strong."

The way Bela now looks at me is like a knife pointed straight at my soul. I try to embrace her and to hold her to me. For a second, she allows this, but then she pushes me away with all her strength, faces me squarely and does not speak. Oh, my poor girl. But I must do this! "Bela, you will know where I am. I will take care of that the entire time we are away. I swear this to you. I will find a way to let you know my whereabouts. I will send postcards to Dr. Pompen and he will pass the mail on to you. And the second we leave for America I will write a letter to tell you that I am crossing the street to visit Eva. And then you will know I am on my way and that I am safe." I stop talking once again and wait for her reaction. She breathes in and out, and then she lets go of my hands.

"Bela, promise me that you will keep on writing the diary. Then later – when we are reunited – I will know everything that happened here. From now on you are writing it for me. Like letters you could not send me. Something like that. But you wait for me. You must wait for me! And you must do your best to recover. Before the most terrible thing can happen, we will find a place for you to hide. You know that we are working on that. And by then you will be all better already. You will do it for me. The spot on your lung is shrinking all the time. You know that very well. You are almost done with the illness. Within a few months you will be well enough to leave your little glass palace; you won't be contagious anymore, and you will go into hiding. Perhaps with a family that also had TB and recovered."

I sense that my despair is giving me away, so I stop talking. Now is my one chance to give her the strength to survive this nightmare. "Bela, the diary! We will read it after the war. We will tell our children about it. We will show them that leaf, you know. Do you still have it?" She nods and then asks me, "Levi, when are you leaving?" I face her directly, looking straight into her blue eyes. I must imprint her face onto my heart. This is what I will fight for. For this woman. I look at my beloved's face. No pretty stories. "Tomorrow," I manage to say to her. And then, in a rush, for the curfew is near, I escape from Bela's glass palace.

We have worked it all out. Aharon and I present ourselves at the police station in Holten. Very early in the morning we walk in and announce that we would like to volunteer for a workcamp in order to exempt our parents from being deported. Yes, we want to be sent to a workcamp. Voluntarily. In the East. We have good reasons to act this way: we must find out how that deportation system works, so we want to get as far as Westerbork and take a look around. We know that all the Jews pass through Westerbork. We believe that if we can get there it will give us a good idea of how the system works, and then we can pass on this information to our families. We will work as their spies. We will know what the Germans are planning to do with all those Jews who are forced to leave their homes. Aharon and I have been working out and we are strong, muscular, and young. Furthermore, Aharon is the wrestling champion of the Netherlands. We are certain that he can overcome any opponent and that we can escape any place no matter where we are. Our will is strong. Our bodies are in the best possible condition and our despair gives us an edge.

We sat in the police station for an entire day before they finally gave us an answer. We were told to report that very next day. We were given a list of the things we were allowed to bring with us and then we went home. As soon as we were allowed outside at six in the morning, we returned to the police station and were loaded into a lorry which brought us to the train station at Deventer. A few more Jews were there waiting in a pitiful group at the end of the platform.

Among them were some old people, a few pregnant women, and small children in their parents' arms. Were these selected to be the German work force? Were they the ones to support the German war effort? Impossible! The Germans had other, more sinister plans with those poor Jews. I signaled Aharon to keep his head down. We must not draw attention to ourselves. We needed more information before we could make our *Vayibrach*. We had to get a look at Westerbork. We had to make sure that they would not beat us up, because we needed our strength. I put my head down between my shoulders and waited.

Finally, a train came into the station, blowing smoke. It was nearly evening. We had been standing there for an entire day. We were not allowed to use the toilet and we were given no water. The people were pushed into the train and cramped into a compartment that was too small. Not everyone found a place to sit. The swaying of the train made people stumble and fall. There was cursing and screaming. The children were crying of hunger and thirst. It was horrible to witness all that and to realize that no one would lift a finger to help. We finally reached our destination and the train slid to a halt. The shouting of the guards indicated that we had to descend. It was dark outside, and we continued the journey on foot. We stumbled on. Perhaps we walked for an hour. Even Aharon and I were exhausted. We had been in German hands for only one day and already we had grown weaker. "Keep your chin up!" Aharon whispered to me, and so we kept going. Everything I saw I committed to memory. We were spying for our family.

From the corner of my eye, I noticed a sign with the name Westerbork. So, we were on the right path. That felt good. Suddenly, the camp loomed before us, surrounded by watch towers, search lights, and barbed wire. "Our first step of the way," I whispered to my brother. "Don't forget this," he whispered back. After a moment he added, "Wasn't Westerbork a refugee camp for German Jews who had fled to the Netherlands?" I shrugged my shoulders. I did not remember that.

We needed no more than two minutes to understand that Westerbork was a horror. We arrived on a Monday. The next day we saw a cattle train pull into the station and watched how many people were loaded onto it. Again, I saw the elderly, children, and young women with infants. It was insane. How could this be happening? And why a cattle train? But I kept my head down and stole a look at all that I saw. Aharon and I were put to work outside. We were ordered to clear the areas between the barracks and clear away all the heavy objects such as tree stumps and large rocks. In one of the barracks, I saw women and young children seated at long tables. There was a sharp scent in the air. I saw that they were holding batteries which they opened with a small hammer and then removed the carbon inside. This material they scraped into a central vessel. I later understood that the Germans reused it to make new batteries. The people inside coughed incessantly because of the tar-like substance laced with acid from the batteries, and the tight air. It seemed that the children had been especially selected to do this work because of their small fingers.

I was happy to be outside. At least the air was fresh; it was the beginning of summer and thus no longer cold. Outside was much better than the poorly ventilated barracks. We received reasonably sufficient food and water, but everything was dirty and tasted bad. I worried that a long stay in the camp would weaken us. We had to finish our spying tasks quickly and then continue on our journey to Spain. Searching out the camp was my brother Aharon's task, and he soon found a perfect spot for our escape: the barbed wire ended a little above ground, and if we tried hard, we would be able to get under it in order to get out. Even better, this part of the fence was in a spot where the searchlights did not reach, and the place was not so heavily guarded. The German soldier or Dutch policeman on duty might even wander off to smoke a cigarette while he waited for his watch to be over.

We figured that the best time to get out of Westerbork and start the second phase of our *Vayibrach* plan would be around two in the morning just before the changing of the guards. The guard on duty would be tired and would only want to go to sleep.

That is how we arrived at that spot near the camp fence. We were without our knapsacks or any other luggage. We had long spent our last cent, so our pockets were empty too. I approached the soldier in such a way that he spotted me easily and I held up my hand to show him that I was holding something that looked like the butt of a cigarette. I gestured that I needed a match to light it. Aharon came from behind, and the guard never had the chance to ask what a damn Jew was doing outside the barracks, nor did he get the chance to shoulder his gun and aim it. By the time he realized that I was not alone, it was already too late. In one second Aharon had him in a chokehold and knocked him out, and then, with a superhuman effort of flexible muscles and strong legs, we got our bodies under the barbed wire. Just to make sure, we remained on our bellies and crawled on for a few hundred meters, until we were certain that we would not be caught in the search lights. We then stood up and ran for our lives. Somewhere in the back garden of a small house there was some laundry on the line. We pulled down some clothing and a thin blanket. Then we sprinted onward until we found a bicycle in a yard. That is how we made our escape from Westerbork. Now our fear and despair drove us onward. I simply had to warn Bela, David, and the whole family: make your *Vayibrach* now! In the German camps there was no hope. The end would be terrible. After all, Aharon and I had seen it with our own eyes!

We fled south towards our final destination: Spain. On the way we stole everything we needed and fought with anyone who tried to stop us. Sometimes we slept under a hedge and sometimes we ate chicken feed. Sometimes someone offered us a place to sleep in the stable, the haystack, in the attic, and sometimes we were given a warm meal. We had to get across the border. In small villages where the police were less vigilant, we found picture postcards with the name of the village, and these I sent to Bela via Dr. Pompen so she would know where we were. I wrote my name in a hidden mirror script: Ivel Nehoc, no longer Levi Cohen. And so, I was Ivel Nehoc as far as Barcelona.

As unbelievable as it sounds, my brother Aharon and I succeeded in reaching Spain. We smuggled ourselves across a few frontiers. Sometimes we had help from the locals and sometimes we had a little money to grease the border guards' palms. At times, Aharon had to use his muscular abilities. Every step of the way I saw Bela's beautiful face before my eyes in her white bed in Holten. She would never survive Westerbork and the subsequent cattle wagons. If the Jews received such terrible treatment while still in the Netherlands, it would only get worse when they reached the camps in the East. Perhaps the intention was to murder those young women and their pitiful babies. The scenes I had witnessed while we were in the hands of the Germans and their helpers gave me the strength to justify any crime we committed on the way. In the end we succeeded in overcoming all the obstacles. Our plan was simple and our task clear as day: we had to warn everyone not to postpone their *Vayibrach* any longer because by the time they received their deportation letters, it would be too late. After we succeeded in that task, we would cross the ocean to the American army.

In Spain we found an organization that helped Jewish refugees. We received clothes, food, and a place to rest for a while. It had taken us four months to bridge the distance between the Netherlands and Spain. When we had somewhat recovered, the organization gave us a tip on how to find a ship that would take us to America. It was actually a very simple idea: you accepted any job offered to get onboard, and once in New York, you had to make sure you succeeded in exiting the harbor and then you would have to look for a recruitment office and enlist.

Aharon and I got it all done. We arrived in New York, got out of the harbor, found the recruitment office, and presented ourselves there. What happened then was too insane for words: the clerks did not believe us. They claimed that we were probably deserters from the Dutch army, escorted us back to a ship to Europe and left us there...

And so, we found ourselves at sea again. We needed a new plan and had to find a country and an army willing to take us in. Once more we jumped ship without ceremony. This time in England. Aharon simply showed the guards what he could do with his strong muscles and wrestling training. In England, they accepted our story that we were Jews who had managed to escape the German-occupied Netherlands. We were allowed to enlist. Aharon joined the air force and I the marines, but it still took another long two years before I returned to the Netherlands to liberate Bela. Finding her alive was the hope that made me brave.

I told myself that Bela would be writing her diary for me and that I would learn everything that had happened in Holten, but first I wanted to imprison her in my arms. In the prison of my embrace. Just as she had written in her novel about Jo and Viek.

Yes, Aharon and I survived the battles. Every bullet that reached its destination gave me satisfaction. Aharon's Royal Air Force bombed Germany and every whistling bomb was revenge for our dear and near ones who had been caught in the occupation's trap. Aharon screaming their names above the screaming bombs.

After a Canadian division liberated Holten and its surrounding cities and villages, I was able to reach the village. Daniel and Marianne's house stood empty. I knocked on the door, rang the bell, banged on the windows for a few moments or perhaps an eternity. The neighbor came outside and walked over to where I was standing. She recognized me immediately and without a word, took my hand and led me into her kitchen. I was still in my Royal Marine uniform. Mina gave me a chair and made me tea. I actually didn't want any tea! But Mina gestured for me to have patience and added, "One moment. I have something for you," in her Holten dialect. I had to drink the tea. Ah, I raised my eyes to the ceiling, and I knew! No one left. The house is empty, stupid man! It was over. Bela was gone. I wanted to get up and slink away like a wounded animal, to hide somewhere to lick my wounds, my pain, but Mina returned and placed two metal tins in front of me on the checkered cloth of her kitchen table. One round tin, one oblong. "Marianne gave me these tins only a few days before they left. They had received letters from the police, and they had to go somewhere for their travel papers. I do not remember exactly where. They also had to clean their house and bring the key with them. Marianne asked me to hide these boxes very well, and to give them to the first person to come to the house. 'Keep an eye on our house,' she begged me, 'Someone must come.' And that is what I did. Here!" and she pushed the tins across the table, closer to my hands. "I never opened them," Mina added.

I pushed the tins away, afraid to open them but Mina bent over me and spoke softly, "Come, we can do it together." The round cookie tin contained the notebooks with the novel about two lively cousins, and the other, the diary. I also found the picture postcards I had sent during that desperate flight to Spain, the cards sent by Ivel Nehoc. And some family photos. One of Bela from 1943. She smiled at me, softly. I turned it over and read, "for my love, Levi." The oak leaf still lay in the diary and had barely aged. And then there were many letters addressed to Bela that were sent by her friends and relatives when she was ill. At the bottom of the tin lay Bela's childhood memory book, called a poetry book, which she had received one *Sinterklaas* eve, a Dutch gift-giving celebration. All the pages were covered with little poems written for her. The Pagrach family was such a big one then. And Bela had so many school friends then.

I picked up the diary, but it could not revive her and bring her back to me. I brought her portrait to my lips. Oh, my lovely girl. My beloved Bela! Again and again I read the letter I had sent the family through Dr. Pompen when Aharon and I had finally reached the safety of Barcelona and were about to set sail. It was the letter I had promised to write! The envelope had been opened by the German censor, resealed, stamped with the Nazi eagle and sent on to its destination. It had been the right decision to send mail via Dr. Pompen. That was one thought that flashed through my head. Right? Right! What was right about that! They had not fled and had not tried to hide. They had remained in their trap. Here in my hands was the postcard with a picture of a hotel in Barcelona. "My beloved Bela. A final greeting from Europe. Keep your chin up. Regards to all. Your loving Ivel."

And there was my letter too! "I am crossing the street to visit Eva and Sol. I have seen many landscapes and places. You have to make your *Vayibrach*. As soon as possible. I embrace you and send greetings to all. Ivel Nehoc."

In the end I handed the tins and everything in it to Betje, and we stayed in touch. Miraculously, they had found Louisie and Marianne, and in 1946 Betje gave birth to another child. They called her Bela. I bought a gift for the little girl, but I could not say her name. I even got married, but children did not come. My brother Aharon remained in England. He had been grievously wounded. Physically, he recovered fairly well. Mentally, he never was able to overcome all the things we had been forced to do during that cursed war.

In 2014, my daughter Hani and I came to Holten and walked down the Oranjestraat where many Jewish families had once lived. We stopped in front of Opa Daniel and Oma Marianne's home. The Dutch autumn had already started a little and the sidewalk was littered with wet, rotting leaves. They hid the Stumble Stones that had been laid there. Four small, metal squares, each only 10 square centimeters. We pushed the leaves aside with our feet, kicking them away and searched for the memorial tiles. They had been copper colored, but now, nature had darkened them and made them hard to find. Hani and I tried to stack the leaves on one side, and slowly we uncovered the surface of the sidewalk. We did not stop until we found what we had come for. The tiles had been placed side by side in a straight line, parallel with the eastern wall of the house. All the Stumble Stones in Holten had been placed that way and if we had started our walk at the tourist center in the village, they would have explained that to us. Four memorial tiles for four people I had never known, but for whom I had been homesick all the days of my life.

Everything had changed here. Even the house standing at this address was no longer my grandfather's butcher shop. It was a modern, white, nice-looking bungalow, its windowsills full of begonias. I saw some people standing at the window but ignored them. They had never even known my family! It was more important to finish what we had come for. I wanted to make a speech. I needed to say something. Perhaps something about my aunt, my mother's murdered sister, whose name I bore. I closed my eyes and searched inside my soul until I found the words. To my aunt whom I never met. To my Tante Bela who left me her name. To the aunt whose meager surviving possessions slowly came to me when my mother gave them to me as gifts. Things you, my aunt, had touched, but I wasn't allowed to. Somehow, I was never deserving enough to touch your things. My mother put your makeup table in my room. It stood there, painted in a kind of shiny cream color with a black stripe along the border. The pain was chipped and peeling but mama never allowed anyone to renew the paint. The makeup table had a beautiful, oval mirror. When standing, I could see my entire body but not my head. To see my face, I had to sit down, but there was no chair. On the makeup table I had your toiletry set consisting of a brush, comb, and hand-held mirror, as well as an empty perfume bottle with a silk fringe. The brush was so soft that it did not do a thing for my untidy, thick hair. Oh, yes, it all belonged to me and it was all there in my room – your makeup table, your hair care set – but every night mama came into my room and touched her hair with your comb and brush. She also looked into the oval mirror but did not find you there. She did not see me standing behind her.

Later, I also received your *magen david*, the Jewish star of David. Mama put it around my throat. The pendant was decorated with marcasite, three of them missing. Mama closed the necklace and then she hid the star inside my blouse. I was expected to wear it all the time but always hide the pendant from curious eyes. The silver necklace and pendant were cold on my skin.

Downstairs in our living room stood a silver frame with a portrait of you. You were so pretty. You wore a beautiful blouse, and your hair was all wavy and perfectly done. I did not see your arms, and when I was little, I thought that perhaps you had none, and that because of that, you looked so sad. It was a disturbing thought, and I did not like to look at that photo. I also avoided the family portrait, you between your brother and sister – my mother – not long before the war. You all stare directly into the camera but no one is smiling. You are all so serious.

I often had to hear how beautiful you were, how good-hearted and how sick you had been, and how brave. I was none of those things. It would still take time before I could be your worthy niece. *Ach*, when I got married, I left the makeup table behind in Nijverdal and felt no regret. It could not come to America with me, or later, to Israel. I have no idea where it might be now. I lost your *magen david* with the missing stones at some point, but I bought a new one once without realizing the significance. This time, without any stones. Simple gold chain. I always wear it, taking great care to keep the pendant outside my clothes so that everyone can see it. I also left behind the brush and comb with that mirror together with the perfume dispenser. They did not fit in my new life. And I had long ago understood that my mother could not truly relinquish these items, so I made the gesture to give them to her without a word. Just left them, neatly placed at straight angles on the lace doily on the makeup table. But there is one thing that has become my inheritance and it was freely given to me. Mama gave it to me many years after I got married, long after my children were born. We had been in Israel for years already.

I was in Nijverdal visiting my mother, a yearly tradition. Mama brought me a small package from her linen closet and placed it in my hands. "For you. Take it over for me, Bela," she said, somewhat strangely, sighed and withdrew her hands from the wrapping paper. "Should I open it now?" Mama nodded. I pulled the string, pulled back the paper, and looked inside. It was a white tablecloth with an open-work border, embroidered in colorful flowers so that a garden grew all around the tablecloth. I could see that it was very old. "What is this, mama?" My mother took a deep breath as if the air pained her.

"My mother, your grandmother, made this Shabbos cloth for your Tante Bela, for her trousseau." Suddenly, the tablecloth became as heavy as lead. But it was a gift to me! My mother had given it to me because of my name, because I already had your name, Tante Bela! I had become worthy of having this part of your life. The precious tablecloth embroidered lovingly with my grandmother's living hands for her living daughter, the bride, and left in the hands of my mother who had never once used it on her table because it hurt too much. Now I had it to honor and own. A tablecloth that returned to the living, to the land of the Jews, to my festive Shabbat table. I use it for very special occasions, but no one is allowed to eat off it, and no one may put anything down on it. It is holy. My heritage. My inheritance. I wanted to pass it on to Yad Vashem, the Shoah Museum in Jerusalem, but I couldn't let go of it. I will leave that task to my children. The tablecloth is here in your honor, in your mother's honor, my grandmother. I return to the present and turn to my daughter.

"Hani, let's go. We can look at the house where my mother was born." We turned around and walked away. The people inside the house waved a friendly village goodbye. We returned their greeting with a slight nod. Then we let the autumn leaves flutter in the wind to cover up the tiles once again.

1942

Because of the blackout and the fact that Bela Pagrach lies in a room surrounded by glass walls that remain open day and night, her glass palace had no electricity. When evening falls, she has to close her diary and with a mumbled word of apology to the empty pages, she puts the notebook in its place. She remains lying down feeling out of sorts, with too much time to worry and think. She tries to turn off her brain, but in vain! She is bedridden and barely allowed the writing. TB patients are on absolute bedrest and all they are supposed to do is try to get well, take in the cold, fresh air, absorb some sun rays, and eat a lot. Nothing else. "Well, nothing to be done about that," Bela says to herself and writes those words down at the end of her diary entry for that day.

Her life has shrunk so much and is even more constrained and more impossible than that of the other Jews in Holten. She is like that dwindling leaf which landed on her bed. That leaf also had no control over anything! And the cold, cruel wind blowing in from Germany pushes her away from her tree of life and she is incapable of changing that. Bela is so completely dependent upon others that she has fewer choices even than the other members of her family. When she was in the hospital, the nuns nursed her with love and compassion, and every day she was read a few verses from the Bible intended to raise her spirit. Levi gives her proverbs, some of his own making. He wants to give Bela the willpower to carry on. She must go on, fight the disease in her body, become healthy again, and then return to life. But that is a life that is not really livable. Levi keeps saying, "When we come to that bridge, we will cross it." Notwithstanding those pretty words, Levi knows just as well as David, that the Jews no longer have a bridge. The time to cross one into concrete action has long gone. Now they have to build bridges where none exist. Build one, steal one, learn to swim, do whatever they need to cross to a safe bank. The Jews have to climb over the threat of the German occupation and search for safety. If life for the Dutch Jewry has become a stormy river, they cannot be afraid to find a way to get across it. If not over the water, then under it, around it, past it, perhaps find the source of the river and jump over it while it is narrow, but they must get away. On the other side there might be life. Theirs is a desperate battle.

When Bela, my aunt, was healthy enough to be allowed visitors, Betje was still afraid to bring the little girls. Instead, she took them to the photographer and sent her sister portraits of Louisie and Marianne. They were like two living dolls: Louisie, tall for her age, standing with a protective arm around her baby sister who had been placed on a high stool. They wore their best dresses, sewn by Betje. She had trimmed them with lace from her wedding gown, and there were pretty bows in the children's hair. How serious they looked! Not even a hint of a smile.

In her diary, Bela wrote:

Dr. Pompen tries to give me courage by saying that I will recover 100 percent, and he also told me that his own wife had been sick with TB in the same way as I am. I remind him that in the sanitorium he had thought that the situation (of the Yidden) had made it so hard for me, and that I was sad all the time. That is, he said then, why I was too weak to defend myself against contagion. "It is all because of these difficult times. You take everything too hard." When I remind the doctor of that conversation, he nods, "That is what weakened your body." "Well," I added. That was for myself, to remind me what I really thought, for later, when these times would be over.

I read this letter once more. My aunt had written those words more than 70 years ago. *Enough! Enough writing for today. I am now closing my diary.* I follow suit, close her diary too and use the old oak leaf that had been put inside it by my aunt and Levi as a bookmark. For 74 years this dried out leaf had remained whole, but it lies there so naked, and it is beginning to disintegrate. I find some absorbent paper in the form of a nice green napkin, place the leaf inside it and lay it to rest. Our hands have touched this piece of life, my aunt and I. Gently, I return the oak leaf to the right entry and do not understand how it survived all those years while my beautiful, innocent aunt, who was so filled with hope and love, and those like her, all those others, did not. How simple it was to rob them off their lives. I cannot get my head around it.

Under the diary there is another document I inherited from my aunt, the poetry book she received for *Sinterklaas*. All her friends and relatives had written little poems for her and pasted cute little illustrations of pastoral scenes covered in tinsel. Those who had no store-bought pictures drew something. It was all sweet, sentimental and traditional. Part of being a child in the Netherlands. Her poetry book is filled from cover to cover. It is a mirror to my aunt's youth – a world filled with aunts and uncles, cousins and friends; a world overflowing with life. And like this world, that is gone forever, her poetry book's color is fading and retreating slowly into the not-being. The brown leather cover is cracked, and the rose on it almost gone. Also inside this poetry book were a number of picture postcards sent by Ivel Nehoc, her beloved Levi.

9

DAVID SIMON SAMUEL: THE DESPERATE RACE FOR A RICKETY BRIDGE, 1943

No matter how hard I tried, I did not succeed in softening any of the new laws against us. I did not give up easily and tried time and time again, but with every new regulation, the small Jewish community of Nijverdal became more vulnerable. I continued working but my body rebelled, and I was plagued by cramps and pains I had never known before. From Enschede I received the terrible news of an extensive roundup. A hundred Jews had been picked off the streets or taken from their homes and sent to a camp. Shortly after, their families were notified that their fathers, husbands, or sons had died somewhere in Austria. Through Irma, my cousin David Samson's girlfriend, and a refugee from Germany, we heard horrifying stories of what was happening there. I was certain that the beginning of the end had already started for us, this tiny group of Jews in Nijverdal-Hellendoorn. It had started the moment the young members of our families had voluntarily presented themselves to the Germans to work in the East somewhere to help the German war industry. They had all disappeared in the mist surrounding those so-called work camps. And notwithstanding the German promise that the elderly and the very young would not be molested because family members had gone East voluntarily, this turned out to be yet another lie.

Neither the aged nor the young were spared. Quite the opposite: Hitler and his henchmen worked day and night to isolate us even more, to impoverish us even further, and to weaken us relentlessly. We were to be easy prey to all those German plans. The young men and women had disappeared, sacrificed themselves to save their families, and almost at that very moment a proclamation was published in the Jewish newspaper to notify us that the phone lines of all the Jews in Overijssel would be cut off shortly. I tried to fight this decision with words. I am a man of brain, not brawn. I have always been a man of words and so I wrote a polite letter full of logic why at least one telephone had to remain, but my heart was breaking when I thought about the moment when we would be cut off from the outside world and remain in the dark about our fate until it was sealed.

My request was denied but the authorities did not even bother to notify me. No reaction to my letter arrived, nothing, neither in writing nor orally. Nothing! No response fell through the mail slot of our home. The mayor had simply forwarded my letter to Arnhem, the German command post for the area. Meanwhile, instructions to cut off our telephone landed on the desk of his superiors and from there, stamped with their approval, were sent to the PTT, the government mail, telephone, and telegraph service. On the day, perfectly on time, according to German punctuality, a technician arrived at my parents' house to disconnect the phone line and repossess the instrument. My father ran across the street to get me and I ran back with him to try and stop the PTT official. "One moment, please," I gasped. "Sir, I have submitted a request to retain this phone connection here and have not received a response as yet." I waved a copy of my letter to the mayor in his face. He, still without a single word, showed me what he had in his hand: the same letter. "Read what it says here," he said, with a shamefaced smile. He pointed to a few words, written in barely legible pencil, "and here," pointing to the Arnhem command post stamp. He shrugged his shoulders. He obviously felt bad. He was not one of those who enjoyed watching us cringe. The words he pointed to were smudged and hard to read. They had not even bothered to sharpen the pencil. Next to the first word of my letter, "we," it said, "Who are those 'we'?" with a comment about the Jewish community being so small that "a phone is not a necessity." So, no more phones. Do everything on foot, passing on messages, following orders. I would have to do it all walking! And then, one more comment that my words about "adhering to regulations" was superfluous. Of course, we would do what we were told, this comment implied. A real insult to me, the author of that letter. The technician cut the line, picked up the phone, and left. It was all over!

For me, this meant that I no longer have a direct connection to Mr. Menko. I try to convince myself now that I have sufficiently internalized the idea of *Vayibrach* and can act on my own. I am absolutely certain that I must keep everything secret, that I cannot share any of my plans with anyone. I also know who I can trust and who has a loose tongue. The former are so few. What I still do not know is how to convince the Jews that I am trustworthy. That is the hardest nut to crack. And time is running out. As for me, I have no doubt that taking away our telephones is a clear provocation. The occupier has removed his gloves. And now his iron fist is out in the open for all to see. If we truly wish to stay alive, then we must go into hiding, to "dive" into the hidden spaces of society. No wonder the Dutch use the word *onderduiken*.[1] We must disappear from the surface of life. However, it is also very important to remain out in the open for as long as possible. This is especially true for myself and my wife and daughters. People need to see me walking around for as long as possible, for should I go into hiding before the rest of our community, the Germans might take their revenge on the remaining Jews. And that must not happen! We have to keep pretending that we are easy prey. We must look like a goldfish in a bowl swimming in circles, easily accessible at any moment. That is the illusion I want to create. We are engaged in a battle of nerves and our lives hang in the balance.

Slowly, so slowly, a network has been created with the help of the underground and I have set up a clear plan of action. I know that I can trust the pastor and his organization, even though I have no idea who they are. The truth is that I do not need to know. None of the Jews who have expressed a willingness to go into hiding know where they will be taken, except for the first stage, and even that they will know only at the very last moment. That is the cautious way to act. As far as the mayor is concerned, I am not sure how trustworthy he is, but he is nevertheless an important link in our *Vayibrach* plan. I hope that when he does know something, he will pass on some of that to me. In the final analysis, our mayor is also but a goldfish in the bowl of his German overseers in Arnhem, and he too pretends to be a dumb fish swimming in circles.

The plan to help the Jews in the village to find suitable hiding addresses is nerve-wracking and slow. Every move takes time, even though time has essentially run out. Abraham Hijmans is trying to get us false identity papers to protect the people that are willing to hide us. For Betje and me, he wants to find papers that show that we are strangers to each other. In this way he hopes to protect our children, for should we be discovered, there will be no talk of offspring because we are not married! With every visit to my aunts and uncles and the other Jewish inhabitants of the area, I keep on saying that we can save ourselves. That rescuers are waiting in the wings. That they can survive this horror. That all they need to do is to disappear and there are people willing to reach out to them. "Just say the word, and we will find you a place!" This is my line each time I speak with someone face to face. "You have to be willing to take this step and the rest will be taken care of by the resistance. As soon as you make up your mind, wheels will start turning and that is all you need to know for now." The time has come to take a desperate leap of faith. They must say yes or no. It is as simple as that. They say the word, the underground will open up for a second and they can disappear, escape the net that is pulling tighter and tighter around us. The other option is to listen to the German instructions and allow ourselves to be evicted from our homes and deported. I need the Jews here to realize that this option is virtually a death sentence, but the elderly among us are incapable of seeing this and cannot believe that hiding is an acceptable alternative. They cannot understand that they have to become illegal residents, that very soon a Jew living in his own home will be a criminal. How can they! Our innate Dutch obedience to the law is a real impediment in my work to convince the older generation. They are blind to the writings on the wall. They ask me, "What does it mean that we are outlaws?"[2] We are law-abiding people. Never had any trouble with the police. Why should that change all of a sudden? Every time I sit in their kitchen, sweating in the heat of our discussions, this is the word they stumble over. I scream at them, "When we have no legal standing, we cannot allow ourselves to be law-abiding!" I am close to despair, especially when I try to convince Ome Sander-Shmuel and Tante Schoontje. "Get it through your heads! We no longer have the right to our lives!" The few men and women of my generation who have not gone off to workcamps in the hope of saving their parents remain silent. Betsie, my sister, who continues to live with our parents across the street from Betje and myself, and also the sons of Ome Abraham and Tante Lewia, stare at me and shrug their shoulders in helplessness. I cannot give up. "Think of all those who have gone to a work camp until now. Where are they? They have all disappeared without a trace. And why?" I feal tears of anger and tension welling up but I must say the words clearly. "Everything is a lie! All lies! Accept the help those good Dutchmen are offering you. Save yourselves!"

All those desperate and difficult conversations are having a little bit of impact and success, for Ome Abraham and Tante Lewia have decided to entrust their youngest daughter to the *Vayibrach* program. Truusje is only 12. She is a child, really, and the family has had some experience with the German cruelty, which started with a bicycle. Yes, a bicycle! When we all had to hand them over to the police, Ome Abraham did so, but someone told the authorities that he actually had a new bike, and yet, he had handed over an old one. He was arrested and beaten to a pulp while he tried to explain that he had sold that new bike because of financial distress, and the old one he handed over was the only one in his possession. He was not released until his story checked out and Arnhem gave permission to let him go. At that point he was beaten some more and then dumped in front of his home like a sack of potatoes. All because of a bicycle. And from that moment on, Ome Abraham refused to hear any more talk of workcamps for his young daughter. "Wild animals are not as horrible as those beasts! No one is going to touch our little girl." And so, Truusje will go into hiding with the help of the resistance.

We are in the countdown to zero hour. Everything must be in place when that moment comes. In the following months, Hijmans visited through the backdoor and picked up small packages of clothing for our little girls. Everything sewn by Betje and Betsie. Dresses and knitted sweaters for a time when the children cannot be under our roof. Everything made with extra material in the seams so the clothes can be let out when the girls grow. After they make their safe *Vayibrach* it will be our turn and hopefully, there will be enough time for that. We follow the same protocol with Truus. Everything we prepare disappears into the secret world of the underground. To where we do not know, do not have to know, must not know. Everything through the pastor.

With the clock close to zero hour, our plans can be put in operation as soon as we receive official letters ordering us to present ourselves at the starting point for our journey to a camp in the Netherlands. Shortly before that date we will activate the *Vayibrach* plan, Nijverdal-style. First, the children will disappear into the safe shelter offered by courageous and noble Christians. In Holten, all is in the capable hands of Louis, the son of Ome Bram and Tante Klaar.

Every day we wake up filled with fear, and every night we go to bed and have bad dreams. I have nothing to take my mind off the situation. The business is dead. Everything has been closed down. Dutchmen are not allowed to buy from Jews and there are not enough Jews to support our store. Besides, I am no longer allowed to work. Once in a while, someone knocks on the kitchen door, asks to buy some yard goods, thread or perhaps a coverall. Mostly I do not accept money and prefer barter. We still have a little bit of cash stashed away from the funds Eva managed to get back to us before our accounts were stolen from us. The only way we can survive is by "eating up" our house. We sell things, repurpose furniture for firewood and try to keep warm.

The 1942-43 winter was severe. And when there is no money for food, coal becomes a luxury. We have taken to sleeping in the big bed together with the girls. In this way, Betje and I keep their small bodies warm. During the day, we heat only the kitchen. The rest of the house has been ceded to ghosts and spirits, dust, and neglect. Some of our furniture is now kept in the Salvation Army's second-hand store, and some of our possessions are in storage by Teesselink. Some of it I have broken up for kindling.

In February 1943, Pastor Hijmans whispers that through the resistance grapevine there are rumors that the deportation of all the Jews in Overijssel is imminent. "The Krauts call it a voluntary departure," he grimaces. Voluntary. Right. Another ruse to keep criticism at bay. Another lie to fool the world around us. There are no limits to the web of fabrication. All that matters is that the population be kept under control. Lies and more lies until it is too late. We must continue to believe that the Germans will send us somewhere and that they mean us to survive.

A few days later, I received a letter with the municipality's official stamp. The letter was a demand for clarification concerning the status of the local Jews. I was ordered to present myself at the town hall in Hellendoorn, the seat of our local government. I had to walk. Once outside, the cold bit into me. There was a hole in the sole of my left shoe. I had put on two pairs of socks, added a little newspaper and hoped for the best, but the shoe was tight, and I could probably get some blisters. Even worse, in spite of my efforts, the water still seeped through the hole and my foot was getting wet. I trudged along, my head kept low, walking against the wind. I was ashamed of my appearance and tried not to think of that, but I looked more like a beggar than who I actually was. My coat was worn out and Betje had already turned the collar and cuffs. I should have had a new coat long ago. I was tired and thin. I was also hungry all the time because we never had enough money or food coupons to pay for what we needed. And the girls came first. Their growing bodies needed nourishment. I was no longer carefully shaven and I did not smell so good. Soap was a luxury. We saved the tiny bars for the girls, and Betje and I made do with green all-purpose household cleanser. My wife did boil up some flower petals to improve the odor, but it only made the soap more liquid while the smell remained the same. And in this state, I was expected to present myself to the mayor! I was the head of the Jewish community here, yet the way I looked won't make him respect me in any way...

As always, Jewish affairs were of little concern. A Jew can wait. I was told to sit down outside the mayor's office. People came and went. They avoided my eyes and I theirs. Time slowed to a halt. I felt pressure on my bladder but did not know what to do. I was afraid to walk into the restrooms, but I also did not dare do my business outside near a tree. Who knows, that will give someone an excuse to arrest me for daring to release Jewish urine against an Aryan tree.

My chair was across the receptionist's counter. To my surprise, the girl stood up suddenly and approached me with a hot drink. "The ombudsman is not here today," she whispered. Yes, that ombudsman, that rabid Nazi, that monster! So, he isn't there today? That may explain my presence here, I thought to myself. I raised my eyes to hers with a question and she turned around and came back with a large key. "This is for the ladies' room," she said as she handed it over, softly adding, "Please be quick, and remember to put down the seat. I do not want any problems." I gave her a closer look. I know this girl. She is Teesselink's daughter. I smile my gratitude and hurry off with the key. When I returned, the cup with the hot drink was still there. I took a sip. It was real coffee and boiling hot. Not Ersatz! I enjoyed the drink slowly. I wanted to thank her once again but she had already buried her face in her work.

The day was endless and when my turn finally came it was already getting dark. I had been sitting there like a fool since nine in the morning. That was the time written in the summons, but only now did the mayor deign to call me into his sanctuary. Of course, he too played his own games. It was expected of him. I was mostly concerned with the problem of getting home after the curfew goes into effect. And isn't that the whole point? He had to torture me a little. It was part of the game to keep me in my place. I am, after all, nothing but a dirty Jew pig. The mayor was seated in his leather chair. I remained standing at his desk. He did not invite me to sit down. And then he began a rambling speech about obeying instructions and keeping to the rules and being careful not to oppose the proclamations regarding the Jews. He yelled at me. He got a little red in the face. He banged his fist on the desk; he even said, "Heil Hitler," and raised his arm in salute, but in between all of that, he also pushed a sliver of paper toward me after which he dismissed me. It was completely dark outside. But I knew that would happen. The curfew had gone into effect. I had no choice but make my way home through the meadows.

I returned soaked to the core, blue with cold and exhausted. But I was safe. Only now did I dare to take the paper out of my pocket to see what the mayor's message said. There was only a date, "April 9" and one word, "everyone." I understood. I threw that sliver of paper with our verdict into the glowing embers of the kitchen stove. And then, despite the dire consequences of being found outside, I slipped around the back into Brinker's swept yard and gave him a message for pastor Hijmans, "What time is the prayer meeting?", and another for the Salvation Army to inquire after a table for us.

The next few days were nerve-wracking but eventually, there was a knock on our kitchen door and my friend Jacques van Egmond, my true friend was standing there, smiling gently. This man had done so much for us already. He had smuggled us to Holten so that Betje could see her family. He brings the mail back and forth, so that the censure won't open our letters, allowing us to write a little more openly. Van Egmond quickly stepped inside and closed the door behind him. He laid a hand on my shoulder just for a second. "Tomorrow someone will come to pick up Louisie." Before his words could penetrate, he had already gone past Brinker's backyard.

Tomorrow is the deciding moment for our first-born. We knew this day would come and now it has. Betje and I have already learned to keep our emotions in check. During the few weeks, we had tried to prepare our four-year-old daughter for the fact that she was going to live in the house of strangers. We told her about this very kind aunt and even kinder uncle where she was going to spend some time. Oh, they were wonderful people who were so happy to know she was coming. They had prepared a room for her. They will take such good care of her. And on and on. We told her about an exciting trip she was going to take. Perhaps she will go by train. Or bus. We told her that she was a big girl and that she was expected not to cry. To behave like a big girl. To listen. That she was going to have a wonderful time with that wonderful aunt and uncle. Not with us. With them. We told her that over there she will be allowed to play outside, use the playgrounds and perhaps be taken to the swimming pool. Perhaps to the cinema! "You are going to have fun there! Isn't that wonderful?" We repeated the words like a mantra, hoping that in saying it, it will be so. And she nodded in agreement, without meaning it.

I take a deep breath. This is the last night with our little girl under our roof. And who knows for how long? But I suppress those thoughts. I must be practical. Stay in the now only. I have to give my child strength. Give her courage. Give her something to hold on to. "Story?" I ask her in my normal "father voice" and I wink, because she loves when I do that. I try to appear relaxed. Louisie answers quickly, "Papa, tell me already." And she leans against me in absolute trust. Her intensely blue eyes bore into mine. She has my eyes and also smiles the way I do, a little crooked like that. Louisie is a slender child and tall for her age. She is a sweet little girl, a little sickly at times, and I worry that she will have enough to eat and drink where she is going, but I push those thoughts far away. Again, I look at my daughter. She is wearing the pajamas Betje sewed for her from an old flannel nightgown. One for Louisie and one for Marianne. I swallow my fears for now and lean over this little girl. Perhaps for the very last time, I begin to tell her a story so old that my father told it to me, and which he heard from his father. And so on, and so forth. It is a story half in Dutch and half in Yiddish. I gave her this story as an anchor, to make her a link in our chain of generations.

There was once a child whose name was Alte Bobelte. And that Alte was a good boy who listened to his mother but was not very smart. Sometimes he completely misunderstood what he was told. Or perhaps he did not hear all that well... and here Louisie takes over, "But he was the oldest and he was the biggest. And he had to help his mama with his brothers and sisters." I pull her closer to me and sitting on my lap, she leans against me, full of sleep, full of trust. Close to my heart.

And then, one day, Alte Bobelte's mother had to go to market, and she just could not take all those children along, so she told Alte, "Alte, Alte, I am going to market, and I cannot take all the children. You have to..." And Louisie knows and finishes the sentence for me, "Watch over the house" and she burst into laughter because she knows the rest of the story already too. "Yes, absolutely right, my cuddly bear," I take up the thread of the story again. But when Alte's mama came home from the market, loaded down with vegetables and fruit and sweet candies, she found that her house was in shambles. The children were jumping on the chairs and sofas, and there were broken dishes everywhere. Pots and pans were being used as drums. Alte was nowhere to be found. I look down on Louisie's hair and stroke her head gently. "Papa, don't stop now!" She kicks her legs impatiently. This is the best part. Finally, the mother found Alte outside, on the roof. "Alte, what happened to you? Why did you not watch over the house?" she yelled, furious at her big son, but Alte did not understand. "Mama, I did exactly what you told me to do. Didn't you tell me 'Alte you have to... pee on the house!?'" Louisie giggles as she says the words together with me. This was the part she had been waiting for, and Alte, she knows, was up there standing in a huge puddle he had made because he had misunderstood his mother. (In Dutch, watching the house is 'op het huis passen' and Alte peed on the roof because he understood 'op het huis plassen' [to pee].) And now the story is finished, almost. Louisie gets the punch line, "What a schlemiel (dummy)." She says with a satisfied sigh.

"Louisie," I speak to her softly now, "tonight, I will tuck you into bed, ok? Sleep well my darling and tomorrow you get up bright and early to get ready for your wonderful adventure. By train. Good, no? Have you ever traveled by train?" She shakes her head. "No, so that will happen tomorrow. You are my big girl, my little darling cuddly bear, and you remember everything your mama and papa have taught you. You are such a good child. And you are a sweet child too. And so big already. Listen to the nice uncle and aunt. And enjoy your stay with them."

The next morning, we said goodbye as if she was going on a short sleep-away. Jacques van Egmond picked her up in person. He lifted her up in his arms and put her behind him on his bike. Then they rode off toward the train station. Everything worked according to plan. Jacques had arranged some food as well as Louisie's little suitcase, which was filled with the things we had smuggled away through the church. Once on the train, he put the innocent-looking bag down between his feet. Louisie bit into the sandwich Jacques handed her and drank some of the lukewarm tea he offered from his thermos flask. She enjoyed the food. He even had a lollypop for her and with that in her hand, the child fell asleep.

They arrived in Nijmegen, an important hub in the center of the country, and crowded with people mingling or waiting on the platform. Jacques descended the train with Louisie in his arms. Her head on his shoulder. Four-and-a-half years old. A refugee. A child without identity. She had crossed over to the Aryan side. Jacques quickly made his way toward a tall man in the uniform of the Dutch Railway. That was Mr. Bemelaar, David's good friend. They had served on the Tourist Bond together, and before that he had been in the army with him. Bemelaar, who had promised his help before the war had even started. And there, on the busy platform, he made good on that promise.

Bemelaar was the station master and had no problems with the documents. The German Green Police saw him every day and he was waved through without having to produce his papers. Jacques nodded once, handed over the sleepy child to Bemelaar, turned around and returned to Nijverdal. Louisie was barely awake, and everything happened so fast that she did not even cry. Bemelaar held her close to him, and quickly left the station. The two men never exchanged even one word.

The next day Jacques van Egmond let me know that Louisie had arrived safely, and that everything had gone according to plan. He could honestly say that she had not even cried. He did not tell me about the sleeping powder he had added to her tea. And from that moment on we heard no more about our first-born.

Tomorrow, Betje will carry out her inhuman task: she is going to bring our little two-year-old Marianne to Dr. Bakker, the starting point of her *Vayibrach*. Marianne looks much younger than her age, but none of that matters. She will escape through Dr. Bakker's clinic. And then? Then it will be our turn. Everything for our escape must be in place before April 9th, for that is the designated date for the deportation of all the Jews here. We cannot make any mistakes. We cannot betray any of our secrets. We have to see it through and stick to our plan so that we survive the war. We are not allowed to die or be caught, and we must not be killed. Our daughters are waiting for us. And that knowledge must sustain us.

"Papa," I call out in despair across the barriers which keep my world of the living away from his realm of the dead. "Papa, all those people around us, all the people who were your friends and colleagues, they were your saviors during those terrible times. I met them. I knew them!" And suddenly I remember something important, meaningful, a sharp shock. And to my father's spirit I say, "I am going to pass this on to Hani, your granddaughter." I can almost touch him. "She was the one who initiated this quest. She asked me to find your path and follow in your footsteps to discover the source of the stories I tell her and to understand them better. She was the child, my Hani, who pushed me in the direction of the bridges of your life and together with her I was able to cross them."

Now I turn to her, Hani. At 30 Rijssensestraat, even before the house was built, my father planned a garage for our car, but he never parked there even once. It was soon given a totally different purpose and slowly turned into the parking area for goods my father sold in the store. In the end, it was only one more section of the store, although we kept calling it the garage. And the car? Well, the car was only one more way in which my father expressed his gratitude to the people who had helped him during the war. The rescuers of our family were important, and he never forgot what those people had risked to save him and his family.

In any case, the car never slept in front of the house. Every evening, my father put it to bed in Jacques van Egmond's garage. Jacques ran a gas station, a car agency, and a repair shop. At first, he sold Vauxhalls and so we drove a British car, but when Jacques switched to Opels, papa had a dilemma: the Opel was German and if it were up to my father, he would not own anything with a German trademark. However, he reasoned that Van Egmond's hands were pure and good, and that even the German origin of the Opel could not sully them. So, now an Opel was no longer a problem and Van Egmond must have our business. To my father, the Opel was reduced to its pure origin, no longer a German car to be avoided, but a Van Egmond car and in such a car my father was proud to drive. His loyalty to his daughter's savior weighed more heavily than his hatred of anything German. He also paid for overnight parking in Van Egmond's establishment. Every morning, he jumped on his bike to pick up the car before he opened the store. "It is easier for me that way," he said, "The car keeps its value better if it is not left outside." And that is how it was. No long speeches. It was simply so. Papa was not a man of many words.

From that moment on, papa parked mattresses in our garage. They stood there in neat rows leaning on each other. I was not allowed to go in there for fear that a mattress might fall on me, and that was bad for the mattress, but also for me. What if a whole stack fell on me and I were caught underneath and could not breathe? I was told to stay away from the garage. Well, not being allowed to do something only made it more attractive, and my urge to play among the mattresses only grew stronger. For me, a little girl living in Nijverdal, blessed with a good imagination, the space was kind of a Disney World. This was my private playground. Even better, it was Mattress World built for me by my father and was adjacent to that other wonderland, my mother's laundry room. Yes, that was an equally magical place. I had my water-world in one section of the back part of the house and next door, the mattress mountain. When it rained and I had to play indoors, I was never bored. To my regret I experienced the dangers of a mattress avalanche which taught me to keep myself far away from papa's warehouse garage. The avalanche happened when I tried to move the mattresses around and make them stand straight up rather than leaning against each other. I also wanted some of them facing up and others sideways. Like soldiers marching. I got stuck once too often and struggled to free myself. That was not fun, and neither was my punishment after I was caught. In the end I set my compass for mama's laundry room, my water-world.

My mother owned an ancient Miele washing machine. It was made of wood and looked a lot like a water barrel, including the iron hoops. This Miele was open on top, and my mother filled it with a hose connected to the faucet of the laundry room. Before she put the dirty laundry inside, she boiled up the white tablecloths and bedding on a kerosene heater that stood on the floor, and then with a brass laundry stamper, which looked like some kind of pogo stick with a retractable bell-shaped contraption, she pushed the laundry up and down until the stains came out. Only then did she remove the now steaming whites from the bubbling water with the aid of huge wooden tongues and moved everything into the Miele. She plugged it in and let its agitator go to work. This went on until the water was properly dirty and the laundry clean. She drained the washing machine into the grid on the floor and refilled it with clean water. Again, she turned it on, repeating the rinse process until the water was clean enough to drink. Water in, water out, over and over again. The Miele had no spin cycle, so the laundry had to be wrung manually. My mother did this with the help of a kind of torture instrument called a mangle. It was screwed onto the Miele, and the sheets and tablecloths were fed into it slowly while she or her maid turned a handle and moved the laundry along. This was laundry day, for doing the family laundry took an entire day. In our village, this was Mondays. By the end of the day, everything was hanging on the line, sparkling clean. I observed, amazed at their prowess. Like the mattress garage, the laundry area was off limits for me unless an adult was present, and of course, here too things did not really go the way the adults expected because they had me to reckon with.

I brought my little friends into the laundry room and together we worked out games to keep us happy. One included the wringer contraption: one of us inserted her hand and someone else turned the handle until a hand was sucked inside the mangle and the girl cried out in pain. Whoever had a red welt the closest to the wrist was the winner.

In time, my father bought a centrifuge for my mother to ease her hard work. That first one was a very narrow, tall machine with a transparent cover. It did not hold much laundry and needed to be carefully balanced or it would pull on its cord and dance away like a calf in spring, until it unplugged itself and came to rest.

I quickly discovered that when I threw a wooden building block into the centrifuge and turned it on, it spun around and filled the entire machine with color, and if I threw in different colored blocks, the colors mixed and made new ones. I was not good at balancing the centrifuge but solved that problem by simply sitting on it. It was all fine as long as I was not discovered. When either of my parents walked in on me while I was mixing colors in the expensive new centrifuge, I was punished but that did not stop me for long. What choice did I have, after all? There was a limit to the amount of time I could sit in my room and read a book. In the end I climbed out of my window, walked across the flat roof and, hanging on by my fingertips, jumped down onto the coal storage bin behind my mother's laundry room. And I was back in my water-land!

I lost my playground to technological advances. The Miele company published an advertisement that stated they were in search of ancient Miele, like our wooden one. If such a machine existed, was indeed as old as the company hoped and the owners were willing to give it up, Miele might replace it with a shiny new machine. Our washing machine was prewar. It was in good condition and well maintained. Our machine won, and in the blink of an eye a brand-new front-loader washing machine showed up in mama's laundry room and killed my magic playland. It was the end of the centrifuge, the mangle, the dancing laundry stamper, and the bubbling and steaming vat of water cooking our whites. The new machine was capable of doing it all. Yes, as Miele advertised, a child could do the laundry, but I wasn't allowed to come within touching distance. I mourned the loss of my wonderful fantasy world with its unusual entertainment and was angry with my mother for being so delighted with her machine. I hated that omnipotent new, shiny Miele, but it had no feelings for me.

All that was left was papa's mattress world.

One day, I found a box of matches. I was playing hide-and-seek with myself and climbed under my mattress hill and wiggled until I felt that I had made a cave. It was cold on the concrete floor, and to warm myself a little I lit match after match, each time dropping it on the floor before I burnt my fingers. It was a bad idea – one of the mattresses caught a spark and began to smolder. It scared me and I fled my cave, ran through the garden, and then onto the dirt path behind our house. Fortunate for me, my father smelled the smoke and ran into the storage area to check. With the orphaned hose from mama's wooden washing machine, he managed to prevent a full-blown fire. Yes, one of the mattresses was scorched, and yes, I got a well-deserved beating. I was also sent to the prison of my room. And yet, the worst punishment was the way in which my father reacted to my disobedience: he was insulted and sad at the same time to think that I had done this to him, and for a while I was not allowed to help in the store. The latter punishment taught me an important lesson! I had broken my father's trust and it took some time to regain it.

1. The literal meaning of *onderduiken* is to dive beneath the surface. At times I have even used the word 'diving' to illustrate the perplexing meaning of this word to a post-war child.
2. The Dutch term is *vogelvrij*, literally free as a bird, and as a term, it is indeed confusing. One would expect free as a bird to be a good thing. However, *vogelvrij* means that birds may be hunted and shot down, snared, killed.

10

BETJE SAMUEL PAGRACH: THE BRIDGE OVER THE IJSSEL, 1943-1945

For two years we were allowed to keep Marianne with us and watch her grow. David does not like to talk about his feelings, certainly not during these difficult times, but whenever he sees our little girl, his features soften and I can tell that he is breathing easier. She radiates some kind of inner serenity as she studies the world through her clear blue-green eyes. This is the child who came into the world in spite of everything, and I find a little solace in this knowledge. She brings light into our lives and is surrounded by an aura of quiet happiness.

For two years we have fought a desperate battle to create a normal home environment for our Marianne. For Louisie too, but today I cannot think about her. She has already disappeared into the underground and I cannot dwell on this now, for today I have an impossible task. Maybe if I let go of Louisie for a second, I will have the strength to deliver Marianne to her destination. And then I only have to just stay alive until we are all allowed to live in our house once again. Until we can all return from some hopeless exile, back to the family.

I look at my poor little girl, how her curls fall down over her face playfully and how absorbed she is in her games. Sometimes she sits back on her knees and follows my every move, and now and then fondles her blankie that lies next to her. Marianne is a Wunderkind who sings better than she talks. Once she hears a tune, she never forgets it. When she is tired and a bit restless, perhaps any time the mood strikes her, she sings to herself and soothes her little soul. I have never seen anything like this in such a young child.

The bond between the two sisters is also extraordinary: Louisie, the older one, leads and Marianne follows without question. She still has that baby wiggle. She is so adorable! I cannot stand to think about what is hanging over our heads because then I will start screaming and will never be able to stop. I am filled with a young mother's rage, fury at what we never really were allowed to have. We did not get to enjoy normal days with our children. From the moment of their birth, their lives were lived in the shadow of the persecution. All those evil intentions aimed at their small bodies. In my anger, I am ready to destroy everything; I want to tear down the world and blow it up. I want to scratch the walls with my naked nails until they crumble. I am capable of scratching out the Germans' eyes and also those of the Dutch police who are too cowardly to resist the occupation. I want to set the silent world on fire, all those people who have turned their eyes away, and all those countries that have closed their borders and do nothing to aid the Jews trying to flee the German talons. Oh, I hate this world filled with people unwilling to see that good and loving parents are forced to smuggle their children to safety, to relinquish them in the hope of saving them. When Louisie was taken away by the underground no one spoke up in protest, and no one heard the screaming deep in my soul. How can this be allowed; to tear a child from her parents' arms while they have done nothing wrong. And I am also very angry with myself because I did not force David to emigrate to Baltimore when we had the chance.

The war has robbed the Jews of all their legal protection: we are stateless; I am not allowed to complain to the police about the way we are treated, for everything they do to us is legal. These are the new laws promulgated by the occupation. We are practically penniless and we stand naked in this terrifying storm. We are only Jews. That is all that is left of our lives and to be a Jew is a crime against the world. Jews must disappear. We are in the way. The fate of my two-year-old toddler emphasizes how inhumane and cruel our lives are now. That Schreier from Germany has only one objective, or so it seems to me, and that is to wipe out all the Jews on earth. "Heh!" I say out loud, and my sharp voice shocks me. "Enough! Stop it!" and then, speaking a little softer and in a different tone, I still continue to talk to myself. "You have work to do, get started." I must find the courage to let my little girl go. Today I will bring her to Dr. Bakker and from his house she will disappear with the aid of the resistance and be taken to a safe place. I must see this through, so she may live, but before I can do this, I must imprint everything about her in my memory. I must carve her image onto the tablets of my soul and carry her within when David and I go into hiding. *Onderduiken!* I must accept that we will live with strangers and be hidden away inside their lives. I must accept that we must depend on others to survive. Yes, that is what we must do, what I must do, because the tiny hands are waiting for me. I must live toward that moment. Wait and live. That is why I am able to hand my children over. David and I are doing this together and every day he says to me, "We are giving them over to life. To life, Betje!" Not to suffering and death. To life. The moment we succeed in hiding their Jewish origins, a whole new world will open up for them: parks and playgrounds and perhaps a swimming pool or the cinema. They will be allowed to play with other children. If we succeed in peeling away their Jewishness, they have a chance.

We are at the crossroads of our family life. We will continue as two childless, unmarried people, strangers to each other, but right now my little one is still with me. She is so tiny but she is already toilet trained, doesn't need diapers even at night, and is quite independent. There is only one thing that she insists on holding on to and that is her blankie. I am not allowed to wash it – I tried once, and her crying brought the neighbors running to ask if someone was being murdered. That blankie is but a leftover piece of an old blanket and it has been part of her for as long as I can remember. She takes her blankie to bed with her, and holds a corner in her little fist as she falls asleep. Her blankie lies on the ground by her side, or she sits on it as she plays. Louisie, who can have anything that Marianne owns, does not touch the blankie. She sat down on it once but Marianne turned to her with a deep frown, planted her feet, and closed her fists around Louisie's arms until she moved.

I have no idea how it is possible to prepare a child of barely two for what is about to happen and so I really did not say anything, not even when we allowed Louisie to depart. She did ask after her in her high voice, "Wiezie?" but we had no answer. By evening Marianne was tearful and cranky, so when I put her to bed I lay down next to her until she fell asleep. The next day, she said "Wiezie?" again, and pointed to the empty swing in the garden. She turned her hands and palms up, and raised her shoulders in question. Wiezie wasn't there. And that was all. We had no answer and she stopped asking about her big sister. And today, this tiny, miniature little girl is also going away.

I am not going to cry. There is no time for that. I am not going to scream. I am not going to bang my head against the wall and shatter my skull. I am only going to carry out the task I have taken upon myself and know that for the past two years I have lived in constant fear that this day might come. And now that it has it will pass without theater. If I should die now, I would still succeed in handing Marianne over to Dr. Bakker. I would not fall on the floor, dead or alive, but would put one foot in front of the other. A walking corpse, but carrying out my task till the end, if I must. And then, when this first part of our *Vayibrach* is behind us and the girls have life, then the rest of the family will have life too. We will live. All of us. Yes, that is the scenario. Bela will find her *onderduik* address with people who have recovered from TB, just like her. Last year, they were already talking about that. Last year, when we were still allowed to visit Holten. I heard David talk to Tante Klaar's Louis, didn't I? Even then Bela had almost completely recovered. My *moesje* and papa are in good hands with Tante Klaar's Louis and he will find everyone a safe address. He is so like my David, unafraid and resourceful. The entire family will succeed in making their *Vayibrach* and Levi is going to war for us and he will liberate us. He will shoot Hitler to death and then my brother and all the cousins can return from their work camps. And then we will once again have control over our lives. That is how it will be. That is how it will be.

Marianne looks at me and says something, but I am only half listening. In a way she is no longer even mine. I have already given her up. I have closed off my heart and my emotions. There is no other way. I have this one task to see through: step out into the Rijssensestraat and walk down the street to the end. Cross the Grotestraat, cross the train tracks and reach Dr. Bakker's clinic. His house, really. Leave early, they told me. As early as I am allowed to go outside. "Finish your breakfast my darling," I say to my little girl. I made her porridge, half water and half milk. We have no sugar so I added a little home-made applesauce, from the tree in our garden. Marianne eats. She is used to the taste. I drink hot water with some ersatz coffee and chew on a piece of sour bread. "Say bye-bye to papa because we are going for a walk and then we can sing together on the way. Yes?"

The morning is chilly with the cold wind of early April. Marianne is wearing a woolen dress and underneath I have put a pair of long pants. Above the dress, a vest and a jacket. Over all of that I have given her one of Louisie's old coats. She is drowning in it. The boots, also her sister's, are huge on her tiny feet. I wrap a blanket around her and inside the stroller I hide a few things: her favorite little wooden truck on a pull string and a nightgown I just finished sewing. I have also added a letter addressed to the people who will take in my little girl. I have tried to explain who Marianne is, the things she likes to do and food she likes. Even songs she knows how to sing. And I have written that I am grateful to the woman who will rescue my baby. I wrote, "For saving my little darling."

I quickly spy up and down the street. Thank heaven, our neighbor the Nazi has already left, so he is not here to see us. That is good, for he is certainly not allowed to see where I am going. He would betray all of us to the police, including Dr. Bakker. I have no doubt. The street is actually completely empty because it is early and the stores are still closed. Women are busy at home.

David insisted that I memorize the route I must take in all its details so that I do not take a wrong turn. First, I enter the street through Brinker's yard and then I cross our street at an angle to take the narrow path through the meadow. There are no cows in the field, the grass is almost dry, but still it is not easy to walk where many feet have worn down the grass, especially because I am pushing Marianne in her stroller. Nevertheless, I prefer to tax my muscles rather than taking the chance of meeting a Nazi policeman who will demand to see my papers, although he knows perfectly well who I am. All just to torture me a little. Marianne is enjoying our walk. We have not been in the street much this past year. I cannot bear wearing my coat with the shameful yellow star. That star of David, which was once our pride, has been turned into our humiliation and fear by the screamer in Germany. I mostly stay indoors with the girls or take them into our garden where they can play safely. "Hey, focus!" I mumble under my breath. Marianne is singing softly to herself. "Clap your hands and smile," and as she sings, she makes the gestures with small, perfect little hands. What a darling she is! Still almost a baby. Barely two. And so small. And so innocent. I remind myself once again why we are trudging through the damp soil: Hitler wants to kill her. He wants her, and the only way I can protect her to prevent that murder, is by giving her up. I will not be the one to raise her. That I must leave to strangers. But even that thought is almost too much for me. I can only live in the space of putting one foot in front of the other, and to control the expression on my face. In no way must I look sad or shed tears. On the outside I must look as always. *Ach*, I keep my eyes on my feet so that I will be able to avoid the eyes of anyone I might run into. What if they can read my mind! What if they understand that this is the last time I will take my baby for a walk! I am so glad that the street is mostly devoid of pedestrians. I am already back on the main road and walk in the gutter, as I have to, by law. With difficulty I push the stroller through the muddy puddles where the rainwater drains into the sewers. There are rotting leaves and other debris left over from the last downpour which makes walking more difficult. Yes, that Schreier knew all the tricks to torture us. I was a loyal Dutch citizen and an equally loyal Jew but now I live in a society which has dreamt up laws that are there to make my life impossible. There no longer is any logic in my world.

"Oh mama," I say out loud, wanting to bridge the gap between our generations. Here I am, sitting in my luxurious 21st century, calling out through a wrinkle in time which allows me to be part of my mother's 20th century. I see her as if she is more than a figment of my feverish imagination, and I see her breathing hard as she pushes the stroller with that little girl toward her uncertain future. "Mama, you were afraid of your yellow star, the 'Jew star,' and you became a prisoner in your home because you could not bear to have to wear it. Why then, why in the name of all that is sacred in the world, did you save those coats?"

I have a confession to make to Hani who is sitting next to me in the here and now. She must hear this story. Yes, it is connected to something I did to my mother many years ago, when I was a little girl myself and we lived in the same house, under one roof, in the previous century. "You were my mother, and I was your naughty daughter. But mama, I had no idea that you would faint and fall down on the cold stone tiles of the kitchen when you saw what I had done. I could not know that."

Hani, this is the story: Yes, it was a rainy day, and when it rained my mother hung the laundry in the attic on the side close to the stairs. We were already living in the big house at 30 Rijssensestraat and because of the rain, I too could not go outside. And so, I was playing in the attic together with a friend. We played tag and hide and seek among the wet sheets and towels. I thought we were as quiet as mice, but mama heard us. She had warned us not to touch the wet laundry. "What is going on up there?" she called from the hallway below. We stopped dead in our tracks. "Nothing mama, nothing, honest. We were cold and were stamping our feet to get warm."

After all, the attic was unheated and the concrete floor very cold. I hoped my mother would leave us alone, but my friend got scared, and worried that my mother would yell at her, so she went home. I did not feel like coming downstairs yet so I wandered around the big, shadowy space, looking for adventure. Because it was large, I expected to find lots of interesting things up there, but it was really cold, and the wet laundry did not help. I wanted to climb into the huge double bed with its heavy oak frame and jump up and down on the sagging mattress. That would warm me up quite nicely, but my mother would hear the noise and order me to come downstairs. I did climb into the bed and on top of the several spare mattresses piled up there and pulled one of the heavy woolen blankets around me. When I was no longer shivering, I climbed onto the pile of pillows and blankets, and standing on my toes, I managed to get close enough to the skylight to open it a little. I was able to see outside. The forest spread out before me, and the village leaned into the trees. Everything was mysteriously shrouded in the mist; the rain splashed on my face, and I imagined that I was somewhere in the depth of the forest. Oh, I would search for a hollow in the ground, a small cave, dug by the resistance, and used to hide weapons or people, during the war. I imagined that if I were forced to flee when the war came back, I could easily get on my bike, pedal to the forest, and hide there.

Standing on tiptoe was tiring. I pulled the string to light the bare bulb above the bed and lay down on my stomach. The light was a circle around me, and the rest of the attic remained hidden in the spreading dusk. I loved that half-dark period of the day and was at my most creative then. Soon, however, the cold reasserted itself and I was also getting hungry. One final adventure, I thought. I looked around, knowing that I had to start moving. My eyes fell on a green painted wardrobe that was almost hidden under the eaves. I did not remember that closet at all. And even if I did, I had certainly never opened it. Now was my chance to open its doors and search for treasure.

I climbed down and carefully wiggled the handle. The closet was not locked. Good, the door opened easily and silently on well-oiled hinges. The attic hummed around my hands and eyes, and whispered stories about mysterious, lost treasures just beyond my reach.

As soon as I had opened both doors, I knew that I had landed right in the middle of a new adventure. This gave me a wonderful feeling of accomplishment. I bent down toward the low shelves and let my fingers search inside, for the light was fading fast and the bulb's halo did not reach there. All the way on the bottom I felt something rolled up. Papa had taught me to finger fabric and to know what I was touching. I caressed the material. No, I was not touching a blanket, but the material did feel like wool. My fingers were sure. I closed my hands around the fabric and pulled. It came out of the closet reluctantly. Once out, the mysterious find unrolled a little and I could now see that I had found a winter coat. Two actually. They were of a dark gray, or perhaps black, and felt a bit old and dusty. I picked up the first one and laid it on the bed. "Well done," I mumbled, for I had found a solution for my shivering self. Lit by the bulb above the bed, I saw that someone had sewn a yellow star on the breast of the coat with the word 'Jood' embroidered on it. That was strange. Why would anyone want to wear a coat like that? Especially here, in the village. Mama always pressed upon me to keep my David Star pendant safely hidden inside my dress, for although I was expected to wear it, I was not supposed to flaunt it. It was nobody's business what I wore around my neck. Why then was this star on the coat? I did not get it and decided to go ask my mother. Actually, I kind of liked that yellow star with its unusual letters.

I put my arms into the sleeves. That coat was huge on me. I looked a little like the little Prince with that long train of coat dragging behind me. It was also very heavy, but I refused to take it off. That yellow star made it worth the difficulty of moving around with that coat, and perhaps mama would give it to me and sew it onto my winter jacket.

With careful, dainty steps, I walked down one flight and stopped off in my room to admire myself in my Tante Bela's oval mirror. Yes, it looked great. Now I was ready to take the stairs down to the kitchen. One foot after the other, tread after tread, walking like a princess and carefully holding on to the banister, I reached the corridor and walked into the kitchen to show my mother what I had found in the attic.

And then, all of a sudden, it seems to me, Marianne and I have arrived at the doctors. I quickly look around to make certain that no one has followed me there and with a single movement, I push Marianne's stroller into the space near the front door. The walls form a kind of alcove and the roof juts out to shelter people waiting outside from the frequent Dutch rain. Today this small niche shelters us from curious eyes and protects a Jewish woman and her small daughter. I knock timidly, and the door opens immediately. I see the doctor with his hand on the doorknob, as if he had been waiting for me there. He motions me to enter. For a second, he puts his arms around me, and I have to swallow hard to contain my emotions. This is not the time to burst into hysterical tears. He whispers, "Everything is ready. We are all clear on moving out from here. Do not worry, Betje. G-d will protect us." And he stretches out his arms toward Marianne. She willingly gives him her little hand and walks away with him. He is a familiar face, the trusted healer.

The moment the door closes behind my little girl, I do not waste another minute. I turn around, grab the stroller where the doctor has placed some potatoes and a loaf of bread as a ruse to explain why I had taken the stroller with me. I must not raise any suspicion.

Slowly, dragging my heavy feet, I make my way home. My body feels hollow, and my hands touch only the emptiness. My feet sink into the abyss. The entire world is a bubbling morass, treacherous quicksand everywhere.

I catch a glimpse of my face in one of the shop windows. A crazy person stares back at me. Her teeth and lips are an insane grimace. Quickly, I force my face into a normal mask, for now I too am a soldier in the war for my family. This is the moment when our battle truly begins. It is 1943, April, Nijverdal. Our weapons are the *Vayibrach* plans and we go to war without informing Germany. There will be no declaration of war on our part. This is the most secretive, silent struggle. We will fight till our last drop of blood and last breath of air. For a moment I close my eyes tightly and my hands into hard fists and do not utter a single word. This will be my stance. This is how I will keep myself standing so that I can keep on living. This will be how it will remain until once again small arms and hair as soft as silk can embrace my legs and lean into my body.

Back home, I find David in the kitchen. He is warming his hands around a mug of hot water, but he does not drink. The house is silent. Oh G-d, so silent. This is a house of the dead. We could not even console each other by saying that we were doing the right thing. There are no words. From now on and until Levi stands before me with Hitler's head, I will remain silent, for all the words in the world are done.

I walk to the sink for a minute to rinse out Marianne's breakfast bowl. I wipe down the counter without thinking and immediately regret what I have done, for now I have erased all traces of our two children.

In the afternoon someone knocked on the backdoor. The knocking was insistent and loud. The doctor's wife was outside. I let her in quickly. My heart was beating so loudly that I thought the neighbors could hear it. "The child won't stop crying, and she is saying something, but we do not know what it means. She says mebelankie, I think. What is that?" And then I burst into tears. I had thought of everything. Everything was so carefully planned, but Marianne's blankie, her hugsy blanket, that I had forgotten. "She is saying 'my blankie,' I managed to whisper, and she means "my little blanket." She always has it with her. I am so sorry I forgot!" and I ran upstairs and picked up that piece of old blanket and handed it to Mrs. Doctor who immediately stuffed it inside her coat, and before she slipped away she asked if there were other words they should know. "I have done my best to explain all of that in my letter to the woman who will take in my little girl. Marianne speaks quite well and mostly she also knows to point to things so that it is not difficult to understand her." What more could I say? For a moment the doctor's wife embraces me with all her strength. I cling to her, but then, quickly, push her away. As I hear her footsteps receding on the stones outside, I realize that I had not even thanked her for everything she and her noble husband were doing for us. I knew that their help to us brought great danger for their entire family and yet they were doing it. For our little girl.

I held on to my routine. Cleaned the kitchen once more and my husband David walked into the closed store to clean up the empty shelves and display cases. On that day we felt like we had reached the absolute rock bottom of despair, but it was only the beginning.

11

DAVID SIMON SAMUEL: THE JEWISH COUNCIL OF NIJVERDAL-HELLENDOORN

For David Simon Samuel, the fact that he was the local representative of the *Judenrat*[1] (The Jewish Council) was a double-edged sword, even if he had not volunteered for this position. On the one hand, it gave him access to information that would otherwise have been hidden from him, and it is almost certain that as the representative of the Jewish Council in Nijverdal-Hellendoorn, he was in a position to help people marked for deportation. It certainly helped him to find a way to bring his family to safety.[2]

Most likely, it was David Simon's contribution to the village's growth and prosperity that had made him stand out. As everywhere in occupied Europe, such Jews became the German occupation's choice to carry out the thankless task of being their liaison with the local Jews. However, his prewar endeavors in public life had also brought him into partnership with people who did not forget his tireless work for the village. Now, in his time of need, they came forward and offered their help.

Even before the Germans forced him to be their local go-between, David had already started his secret guerilla war against the occupation. It did not take long before David knew exactly what his long and torturous official title entailed. He was the Jewish Council for Amsterdam, district Nijverdal-Hellendoorn, local head representative of the Jewish Council. However, this official, dubious honor, as he described it after the war, also made him privy to the secret guidelines of the Enschede District Jewish Council headed by Mr. Menko, whose policies were in total opposition to those of the Amsterdam Council.

The Netherlands knew *razzias,* the public rounding up of Jews. Non-Jews sometimes witnessed Jewish men, women and children being dragged out of their homes, or picked up on the streets. Such roundups mostly took place in the large cities where the concentration of Jews was much higher than in the eastern provinces, the small towns and villages far away from Amsterdam. The Germans apparently believed that in the outlying areas, it would be enough to show their iron fist only once with one very public, extremely violent razzia. This would put the fear of reprisals into the population, Jew and non-Jew alike, so that most Dutchmen from then on would be too afraid to resist the new regulations. The non-Jewish population would fear that helping the Jews would put their own families in danger, and in general, make people accept that if Jews followed German orders, everyone might be better off.

The Amsterdam Council echoed the German demands for obedience, fearful of reprisals, but in Enschede, things were handled in a different manner. It is quite possible that the Germans had chosen Enschede as their venue for that *razzia* over, for instance, Leeuwarden, because Enschede had a larger Jewish community, or perhaps its closeness to the German border had something to do with it. Whatever the motivation behind picking Enschede for the German's 1941 action, they closed off entire streets with army trucks and a major roundup took place: Jews (mostly men) were picked up off the streets, dragged out of their homes and stores and sent to a camp. A short time afterwards, their families received notice that their husband or son had "passed away".

There is another important fact that needs to be mentioned: the Jews of Amsterdam lived largely in their own neighborhoods, but in

Enschede the Jews and Gentiles lived side by side and the two communities were well integrated and on good terms with each other, making the roundup visible to the non-Jewish population.

Two things happened: The *razzia* made the Jews of Enschede understand that the Nazi occupation was not interested in simply making their lives difficult but were planning to deport and perhaps murder them. If they wanted to live, they had to disappear from view. The non-Jews, whose papers had been checked and waived on after a stern warning to go indoors, had witnessed the roundup from behind closed curtains, and the cruelty with which their fellow residents had been dragged away did not leave them unaffected. They understood that they could not possibly stand by and do nothing. They could not hide their heads in the sand in the hope that the war would simply pass. They had to "join in", as the term was coined. People would talk about the *razzia* and ask each other, "Are you in or out?" In a way, the result of the roundup was the opposite of what the Germans had intended, and the backlash was that a movement to rescue the Jews of Enschede and surroundings started toward the end of 1941. Thanks to David's friendship with Mr. Menko, he too got the somber picture of what might very well happen to the Dutch Jews, and he joined those who did not believe the German occupation did not merely intend to separate them from the general population. He also believed that what awaited the Jews could only be much worse than they might even imagine.

The Germans, however, apparently thought that their Enschede action had had its desired effect, and Jews and non-Jews alike now feared the regime enough that there would be no opposition to any new measures against the former. This solved the need for further roundups in the east of the Netherlands, and at some point, in the large cities in the west as well. From now on, Jews would receive letters advising them that they were no longer allowed to remain in their homes after a given date. Any Jew receiving such a letter was told when and where he was to present himself; what to bring with him; what to do with the key to his home, etc. The murder machine was a well-oiled, bureaucratic one, and the polite and obedient Jews of the Netherlands mostly responded by cleaning their homes, handing over the keys to their possessions and disappearing into the void of the gas chambers. The deportations were euphemistically called relocation, but in the German doublespeak, it was simply legalized looting and mass murder. The fiery ovens of the death camps burned day and night while most Jews continued to believe that what was happening to them could not be happening to them. Only a very few had the foresight to act in opposition to the German regulations.

For the province of Overijssel, the Jews' final stay on Dutch soil was supposed to be in the temporary holding camp of Westerbork, but in 1943, the stream of Jewish walking dead into this camp became so enormous that the Germans did not have enough trains to Sobibor and Auschwitz to control the intake into Westerbork and the deportation east. An additional temporary holding camp had to be found. The choice fell on the fearful punishment prison of Vught which was enlarged to absorb the influx of still warm bodies, and so Jews were detoured to languish there (under terrible conditions) until more death trains had left Westerbork, freeing up space there. Every Tuesday, a train pulled up at the platform there and the weekly quota of soon-to-be dead Jews was shipped out. Vught could then schedule a transport to Westerbork until, eventually, trains from Vught still passed through Westerbork but the Jews on the train were not interned there. Instead, they continued on to their destruction. Those sent to Sobibor would be murdered on the day they arrived. And so, Vught, unlike being a permanent work camp as the Germans had proclaimed, was simply the Dutch Jews' first step into the abyss.

The well-oiled death machine worked like a major industry: Jews received letters from the German occupation, cleaned their homes and presented themselves at the collection site. They came. Have you ever seen how a slaughterhouse works? Pigs walk in on their feet and come out neatly wrapped in cellophane, plastic, stamped and ready for cooking. I know this is a horrible comparison, but the way the Jews were murdered was too similar to deny. The greater the distance between the Gentiles and the Jewish deportees, the worse the way the latter were treated. Yes, far from the public eye all pretense of German humanity ended.

For the 70,000 Jews living in Amsterdam, the same system was put into operation. The Jews came to their collection point in the city, fearful of the consequences if they did not. Their holding pen was a small theatre in the middle of the city, known as the Jewish auditorium (De Joodse Schouwburg).[3] But before the Jews allowed themselves to be locked up and deported, they tried to obtain a legal postponement of the inevitable. Only the Jewish Council could issue papers stating that they were essential workers, or perhaps that they were too ill to be moved for the time being. Every day, long lines of despairing Jews would wait outside the council's offices and beg for those magical papers. Unfortunately, the council policy was simple: follow the instructions in the letter and present yourself at the Jewish Theatre with your suitcase. Therefore, going into hiding was mostly an individual decision for the Jews of Amsterdam and certainly not supported by the *Judenrat*. Furthermore, because many of the poorer Jews of the capital had little or no contact with the non-Jewish population, they did not really have anyone they could possibly turn to for help. As a result, the non-Jews also saw little of the deportations, and only when most Jews had disappeared from the big cities in the west and the terrible overcrowding and inhumane conditions in the Jewish Theatre became visible, did a resistance group go into action to help Jews, focusing mostly on the children. It was too little, too late.

In the district of Enschede, the Jewish Council followed a different policy: the *Judenrat* there operated on two levels. By day, they followed the official guidelines as had been decided in Amsterdam: do what the German occupation tells you, pack no more than what you are allowed to bring according to the instructions and present yourself at the designated place on the date given. After all, the council wished to maintain a semblance of obedience to the German orders, but after dark, after the onset of the curfew, a member of the Enschede *Judenrat* visited the homes of the Jews who had received their fateful letters of deportation. It was all in deep secret. All in whispers. Mr. Menko put this dual program in motion but kept himself outside these night-time visits. In this manner, he would be able to maintain that he had known nothing. He set the policy, but other members, especially Mr. Sanders, and probably also Mr. Van Dam, made these house calls to enlighten the Jews to the alternative to their "voluntary relocation" to a venue of German choosing. Supported by the heroic actions of Pastor Overduin and his group, hiding places and ration booklets were supplied with funding supplied by Menko's fellow industrialists.

In Nijverdal, David had no council members to take over part of the *Vayibrach* work. He had only himself, and so, he defied the danger of being arrested if he were discovered during one of his trips to Enschede by train without Aryan papers. He maintained the contact with Menko for as long as possible. The Overduin group of Nijverdal operated through the Dutch Reform Church, led by Pastor Hijmans, David's good friend since 1928. The *Vayibrach* plans fell into David's capable hands, and it was up to him to convince the local Jews that if they wanted to survive the war, they had to go into hiding. To achieve this, he put everything on the line, including his personal safety and freedom. Although his bicycle had already "gone into hiding," he risked using it from time to time. Eventually, he received false identity papers someone from the city of Hengelo had "lost" and to which a local resistance forger had affixed his photograph. He used them when he needed the train. In the village he visited family after family, tried to organize hiding places, and to supply more information to those who were still too afraid to say yes to his escape plan. He walked, talked, yelled, and begged, just so that some might be safe. In the kitchens of his aunts and uncles, he talked till he was blue in the face, and of course did the same at his parents' and sister's.

It is a historical fact that David Simon, his wife Betje, and their two young daughters survived the war. They came through with their bodies intact, but after 1945, in the years that David Simon was my tortured father, I saw his suffering and I saw how he swallowed sleeping powders (the time before pills in our village) to keep the nightmares at bay. "It wasn't my fault, was it?" was his leitmotif. My older sisters heard him say these words when the sterile letters sent by the Red Cross fell onto our door mat, with the notice that his sister, his parents, Betje's parents and her brother and sister, just as all the uncles, aunts, cousins had "passed away". It was a tidal wave of death letters in which he drowned. It was the sheer volume that overwhelmed him. The Jews found their own euphemistic denotation for this massive loss – the people had not returned. This was the term for the murder of their large, extended family, men, women, and children. Toddlers, babies. Old people and young people. They did not return. Papa blamed himself – he had not done enough to save them. Mama threw oil on the flames of his self-castigation. He **was** to blame. We, his children, witnessed this, time and again. She cried those words out of her own pain and loss, but still without compassion for his. "It was all your fault! Why did you let them go? G-d shall punish you for this," and other difficult phrases which washed over all of us as a daily ritual. Like a statue papa listened and let the poisonous words wound him. He never defended himself against them. He never said a word about the German murder machine or the sinister way in which the Jews had been caught in the Nazi trap. Mama's words fell like salt on open wounds, but he remained silent. To us, his children, this seemed like a kind of confession, for otherwise he would have refuted her words. If he finally did open his mouth and words did come out, it was mostly about the help he had given our mother's family before the war, the house he had built for them and the improved quality of life they had enjoyed thanks to his generosity. Instead of helping, those words made everything even more complicated, for as soon as papa had yelled out his words, he turned around and walked away into the store, where he stayed out of her sight until the evening. But that did not end the quarrel; it followed him. Mama sent one of us after him to repeat a few more wounding words, verbatim speeches mama put in our mouth. This usually happened after the midday meal, and at some point, this encore to the fight between my parents fell to me. Louisie and Marianne were in high school and did not come home for lunch, so only my little sister Danielle and I still ate at home. When my mother told me to go after papa, I obeyed immediately and followed him. I was just a child. Perhaps six years old. I was afraid of my father, who seemed a hard man in my eyes and exactly the way my mother characterized him. I wanted her protection and hugs, which were given, but at a price. Mama carefully choreographed what I was to do: open the door between our living quarters and the store like this, stand like that, say what she told me to say, and when I was done, to slam the door and run back to her to tell her exactly what had transpired during those few moments I stood behind my father and yelled at him. She wanted to know how he had reacted. And then I was allowed to return to school for the afternoon session. It was a daily ritual and continued until that day when the balance of power in our home shifted and the battle ground of our family existence changed into different shades of right and wrong.

As far as my father was concerned, he was motivated by his overwhelming feelings of responsibility and guilt. He could not leave the Shoah alone, even though he never, ever, ever said a word about it. What had been a secret battle in those terrible years remained hidden to us now, but the war continued to gnaw at him. Perhaps he needed to relive it, the way an unreachable itch continues to nudge, but there is no relief... For papa, the end of the war was merely the beginning of a new battle. As soon as the guns and canons fell silent, in 1945, David Simon Samuel, my father, began a new conflict at a new front, once again, sitting behind his Royal typewriter. But this time he fought a stubborn battle with the bureaucracy to redress the injustices that were not resolved for the handful of survivors. He believed that if family members had not "returned", the very least the world owed the survivors was to return their possessions and, of course, their own. They were the rightful owners and were entitled to their inheritance. "Nothing to the Krauts" was his motto. "I'd rather burn everything down," he usually added to that tightlipped phrase.

———————

"I have to mail a letter," my father said. "Who wants to come along?" Such an innocent phrase, but in our family, it was a loaded one.

Mailing a letter usually came as a dessert to the evening meal. When Louisie still lived at home, she usually joined him, but after she got married, I took over. We walked to the red mailbox outside the drugstore. Arm in arm. A short walk. Papa let the letter fall through the mail slot, and we walked back. There wasn't much conversation. Papa walked like a dancer, arms swinging in a rhythm that did not change, moving back and forth on the balls of his feet as we walked. We stopped at the post office. He called out a hello and went in through the service entrance. "Any mail for me?" he called out, although in those days the post was delivered twice a day. But papa did not have the patience to wait till the next day, and the postal workers were used to his evening visits. A small pile of letters was ready for him, tied in a rubber band. He picked it up suddenly in a hurry. Flipped through the mail. Business correspondence. Not what he was waiting for! Suddenly, in tense silence, we returned to number 30. For years I had no idea why we had made those daily pilgrimages to the mailbox and the post office.

Over time, the Shoah had grown into a genetic syndrome inside me, and now and then I needed some treatment for it. When that happens, I take a digital IV by connecting to the Jewish Historical Museum in Amsterdam and the digital monument on site with 104,000 names of deported and murdered Dutch Jews. Time and time again I stumbled over the names of our family, read once more name after name, as if doing so would make them less dead. I never succeeded in bringing them back to life. Meanwhile, I already knew all the names by heart. The letters and phrases remain sterile and unchanged: Daniel Pagrach, head of the household, born, plus date, lived at, plus street name, murdered, and a place and date. My grandfather was a name between the brackets of his minimal data. On the bottom of the Daniel Pagrach family page was some more information: "A JOKOS dossier exists for this family."[4] Well, perhaps that might help me learn more, I wondered. I looked up what the acronym stood for. Ah, this JOKOS file held the remnants of the family Daniel and Marianne Pagrach from Holten and was on file at Jewish Social Work. As a direct descendant of this family, I was entitled to open it. It felt like a Pandora's Box to me. What could possibly be inside? I continued surfing and found out how to request the file. I read that this was essentially a collection of papers from after the war, concerning efforts to reinstate the Jewish survivors' rights to their dead relatives' possessions. It was a bureaucratic collection of dusty papers. Why would I even want to see it. What could it possibly add?

Since I learned of the existence of this JOKOS dossier and how I could see it, I started a kind of dance with myself. Two steps toward the file and one panic-stricken step back. The academic inside me wanted to look but the child in me fled. One step forward, two steps back. Ten years went by since I first found out about the JOKOS file. And yet, someone had collected papers and documents, someone had fought for the survivors. My dance went on with its own rhythm until 2015, when I flew to the Netherlands accompanied by my two big sons in order to participate in the solemn placing of memorial tiles, Stumble Stones, in the village where I was born. In front of the house where I had grown up, number 30 Rijssensestraat, now a pedestrian mall called Keizerserf, someone handed me a microphone and I was expected to tell the story of that house. Flanked by Moshe and David, I related how I had learned about the original occupants of the house, my father's aunt and uncle, Schoontje and Shmuel-Sandor Samuel, his cousin Sientje and her husband Mauritz. Only I could pass on their story, for none of them had returned from the killing fields of Sobibor and Auschwitz. My son David and Danielle's son Dave laid the tiles with the names in front of the house, and at that moment I knew without a shadow of a doubt that it was not enough to simply say their names and tell a few anecdotes about the people. I had to know beyond, something that only a member of the family was allowed to see. The JOKOS file! I had to learn the meaning of the term redressing justice. The sterile dates of murder and birth after a name were not enough. I screwed up my courage only after my feet had safely touched the embracing earth of Israel. I called the Jewish Historic Museum of Amsterdam.

"Ah," said the lady on the other side of the line, across the sea. "It is nothing really, only a request for compensation and other financial affairs. This particular file was put together by a David Simon Samuel Prins."

Of course. It was papa. He had gathered the documents. He had built the case for justice. Even the word redress brought some deep echoes from my childhood. Redress of justice. He had been preoccupied with it. But how exactly? I had no idea.

I was told to download some request form. The museum had three dossiers listed, one for the grandparents of both sides of my family and one more for Tante Schoontje and Ome Shmuel-Sandor of number 30. A separate form for each. I filled in my personal details three times and sent them off to the Netherlands. And then I returned to the routine of my daily life. JOKOS was parked on a little cloud somewhere in the back of my head.

Two months later I discovered a large, torn, gray envelope in my mailbox. I took it upstairs, made coffee, sat down in my comfortable computer chair, and with a feeling of excitement, carefully opened it.

My coffee grew cold, the avalanche of papers fell from my hands and landed on my desk and the floor. I cried without understanding why but that cloud in the back of my head did. I was sucked back into a film in monochrome which overwhelmed my organized workroom in Israel. I was back in Nijverdal, in my father's office. Papa was there sitting at his oversized oak desk with the typewriter at the ready and was in the middle of his trek to reinstate the family's rights to everything the German occupation had robbed the Samuels of. He did it for all those who had "not returned." From the moment when Jews were allowed to make their claims for the lost property in 1952, a whole new battle began. Yes, it had taken until 1952 before the Dutch government finally established a commission to handle the reinstatement of rights for the Jews because, as papa wrote in one of the letters I have in my possession, the Jews had to wait until the [real] victims of the war had received their compensation. So, the Jews had not been victims of the war? Why was that? Because they had been safely hiding? Because they traveled to camps, a vacation in

Poland or Germany? No, they were not victims in the eyes of the Dutch government. For six years, the Germans, assisted by many Dutchmen who had willingly collaborated, had grown wealthy from stolen Jewish possessions. The Jews had no redress, no way to claim their inheritance and restore their own homes and bank accounts. The government was less than enthusiastic to overturn the way they had been robbed.

This was the reality in our home: whispers, muted arguments and discussions, and endless reams of paper. The lists my father made filled innocent folio sheets. Papa paid the stamp tax, which was part of every claim, for the Dutch government wanted to make a little profit from the Jewish disaster. Papa handed over every request in triplicate and his lists traveled back and forth between the commission in charge of restoration of ownership and his desk for more than 10 years. Ten long years, but he did not give up. Give in. Desist. Neither did Germany. They wanted ever more forms and calculations. They wanted further proof that his claims were based on goods that were stolen by the Germans. Only then could a balance be made up. So, papa owned a beautiful bookcase filled with expensive books, didn't he? Perhaps all those books were in Dutch, weren't they? Germany will not compensate him for that. Germans don't read Dutch. So where did those books go? They were on the shelves when he was forced out of his home. Well, that was not Germany's problem.

I read through my tears and remembered one of my father's adages: "When you are right, you never step aside, not even for the queen!" And he dug in his heels before those colorless clerks with their endless paper ammunition. There he was not stepping aside. For no one. He also had ammunition: he took a lawyer, hired a typist, wrote more letters and did not desist, retreat, stop. Restitution! Rights! It was all about his family's inheritance and no one else was entitled to their possessions. He surrounded himself with an army of legal assistance. And the clerks in their gray jackets in their colorless offices read my father's lists. And they wondered: Perhaps he can trace the goods? Perhaps he can demand them from those who now own them? Let him continue searching a bit by himself. Oh, he knew about his mother's samovar, the counter that had stood in his father's store. Go and find where it could be now by yourself and then prove that you are entitled to it. Lists, more lists, endless words, and typewriter ribbons.

Finally, I picked up the last paper in the file. A stamp which had run a bit. A date, 1961. And a row of numbers and a sum of florins. And then a large, dark line under it all. This insulting sum of money my father divided among all the heirs of the Samuel family fortune, each one receiving a miserable pile of coins. A coin thrown at a beggar. Ten years of his life! He had dedicated 10 years of his life to ensure that the enemy would have nothing, absolutely nothing of what had once belonged to the Samuel and Pagrach families.

When the end of the battle for restitution was in sight, I was already 15 years old and, for years I had accompanied my father to the mailbox. Arm in arm. To mail a letter. To check at the post office to see if there was any news. How had I been able to ignore the tension and how had I failed to understand that my father was still busy with his efforts to rescue something, even years after he already knew that the family was gone? It had all passed me by. I had never felt any compassion. I had never truly looked him squarely in the eye to see all that pain and grief.

And yet, there is a memory that sticks in me like a knife: a rainy day, a cloudy sky. It is Sunday. My father is busy at work at his desk. He is typing a letter. I bring him a cup of coffee. There is a stack of papers near him. "What are you doing, papa?" He raises his eyes to me for a moment, but his gaze seems blurred and out of focus. As if he is seeing me for the first time. He smiles with difficulty. I come closer and try to read over his shoulders, to see what he is working on. Papa spreads his hands protectively over his work and sends me away. I must not be infected by the fallout of the restitution battle. Only he has the courage to do so. He alone makes the desperate attempts to gather in his arms the ashes spreading in the wind, to gather them and make life whole again.

All the family's possessions, from the dirty mop that was left behind on the bathroom floor and which was looted from his parents' home, up to the homes themselves. The occupation and the murder made the Third Reich rich, but now my father demanded it all back, down to the last item. The careful inventories German lackeys had taken after April 9th, became the basis of his claim for the pilfered goods. This process reached its conclusion only in 1961. One dossier for each murdered family, and the echo of my father's despairing cry, "But what could I do about it?"

The emotional connection to this terrible phrase reverberates through my adult life. I grew up and became a woman saddled with an often exaggerated sense of responsibility. I saw it as my task to fix every problem. I carried solutions up my wide sleeves. And when I failed, that was not the end. It only meant I would try a different approach. The stories from number 30 and perhaps number 82 Rijssensestraat have already stuck to my soul in nagging flakes and shards. The stories are puzzles with missing pieces. The picture remains unclear. The colors are never reliable and the lines are partly erased. Even those I had in my possession did not fit well. There were always gaps and black holes in my information. "Papa," I whisper into the cold winter wind crying toward my house, up from the Mediterranean, "Papa, I read only one file. I lacked the courage to even open the others. I am so sorry."

Our mother said, "*Moesje* died on the train. At least she evaded the gas chamber." Dying on the train was a consolation. It was also a victory, for my grandmother Marianne, mama's *moesje*, had chosen the time of her own death and cheated her executioners. Sometimes my mama sits for a moment in a corner, hands in her lap, her thoughts so far away that she is almost comatose. In her monotonous voice, she talks about piles of human cadavers that were thrown away without ceremony. One on top of the other. People beloved by her. Thrown away without prayer, without Kaddish, without honor.

Mama had four eyes: two for the living and two for the dead. Sometimes I thought that she could see her dead family more clearly than she saw us, for she remained focused on them and loyally tried to honor their memory. She took it upon herself to light the memorial lamp for each of them once a year, for the entire Pagrach family, for there was no one else who could do this. But mama did not know when exactly her parents, brother, sister, aunts, and uncles, and all her cousins had found their death. That should have been the time to light a *yizkor* light for them, but lacking the information, she would light our special memorial lamp with the light bulb in the shape of the Jewish star on their birthdays. It was but a small light, that *yizkor* lamp, a bulb screwed onto a Delft blue base, but no one else had such a lamp, and so, I would look on in fascination every time mama placed it on our sideboard in the dining room. After plugging it in, she would sit down and burst into bitter tears. When I asked her once why she was crying so, she shook her head and pushed me away. There was no place for children in the presence of so much sorrow. Now and then she softly said the name of the person in whose memory she had lit the lamp. *Ach*, it burned for so many days, that in the final analysis I went to play outside, to run with the children of the neighborhood, or to sit on the stoop in front of the neighbor's and to observe village life happening without disturbance, without *yizkor* lights and mama's tears.

My mother died years ago and there is no one who might still light a candle in memory of her family, but the Delft blue lamp with the purplish *yizkor* star still lives. It stands in Danielle's home, and I mail her to remind her to light the lamp on the Hebrew date of our parents' death and now that of Louisie, our big sister too. She sometimes sends me a photo to show me. "The lamp is lit," she writes, and we honor our mother's tradition together.

I was always a curious child, bursting with questions. I wanted to know everything and understand everything. But there were so many taboo questions. Without explanation, a child knows. It was the hourglass of time which slowly made my hesitation fade, and the day came when I had enough courage of my own and was ready to ferret out the facts, like papa.

During a short vacation in Jerusalem, while my husband went in search of books in the Jewish Quarter of the Old City, I took the bus to Yad Vashem, and sat down with Dutch Jewry's *Books of the Dead*. It was all so organized. All in alphabetical order. Black books, severe and silent, row after row, on one shelf among other books with other names from other European Jewish communities, all swallowed up in Hitler's murder industry.

The names of the Samuel and Pagrach families stood neatly in a row one after the other, parents and their children, so for the first time, I saw my parents' cousins, uncles and aunts, and their parents' siblings, nieces and nephews. The whole extended family, forever together in those black books. The municipality of Nijverdal-Hellendoorn was there, as was Holten. All standing on this narrow shelf. Black on white: Oma Marianne did not die on the train to Sobibor. She arrived still alive, sent from Vught, passed Westerbork without getting off the train, then on through Europe all the way to Poland, standing in a cattle car. A woman in her sixties. Days and nights. In Sobibor, she was beaten out of the train and forced to walk to her death. Not a single word about heaps of bodies in those books. I assumed that the crematoria of Sobibor and Auschwitz were in good working order and that all the victims were quickly reduced to ashes. My grandparents, uncles and aunts I should have known. They were exterminated like vermin, exactly like all other Jews who wound up in the death camps. There was no compassion for them from anywhere. Not for mama's *moesje* and not for her beloved father. And there was nothing I could have done, was there? I made two copies of the lists in the books. About six folio pages. Now I held them in my hands, rolled the paper up carefully and put it inside my bag. Then I had no idea what to do next. I took the bus to the Old City and descended near Yaffa Gate. I walked through the Arab souk till I reached the steps leading down to the Wailing Wall and walked toward the Wall of Lamentation, a remnant, like me. It towered over me. The time was still before the afternoon prayer, and I found a place close to the wall so that I could caress the ancient stones with my hands. A book of psalms lay on a chair next to mine, and I found psalm 91, my family's *onderduik* psalm, and said it twice. And then I did not know what else to do, so I just sat there. I raised my eyes to those stones which had witnessed so much destruction and suffering, saw the thousands of notes people had pushed into the crevices of those enormous stones, and then I knew what to do! I took the scroll of names from Yad Vashem from my bag. All the names of my tortured family still on them. Carefully, very carefully, I tore the paper into strips until each name stood by itself on its sliver of paper. I stood up as a sign of respect, and with infinite patience pushed them one by one between the stones of the Wailing Wall. First mama's family and then papa's. All united among the moss-covered stones. And then I said the 91st once again. And sat down in silent contemplation. When I stood up to leave, I first said Kaddish, the prayer for the dead, then added some more traditional words and said a eulogy, speaking directly to them.

"Today I have given you a place of honor in the bosom of the Jewish People, in our Holy City, Jerusalem, in the Wall. This is now your gravestone. It must be the most famous and certainly the largest gravestone in the world, and this is where you are! You will never be alone again. You will be here to listen to the Jews who say Lamentations on the 9th of Av and you will hear songs of joy and celebration. Children will come with their families to mark their coming of age, and to dance here with the Torah scroll. The Jewish army comes here to have its ceremonies. You will never be alone again!"

I left my place at the stones of the Wall, walking backwards in the way one leaves the presence of a king. I found a place to sit opposite the Wall on a low fence, still admiring the beautiful gravestone I had found all by myself. Perhaps I couldn't have done much, but I had done all that I could, all that I knew how, what I understood. I had done my best. "Mama," I whispered softly, letting the words be lifted in the soft wind of Jerusalem like a caress. "They have a stone, mama! And they are together. There are no more piles of bodies. They have found a place of eternal rest, and their names are bound up in the Sacred Wall of our people."

Many years have passed since I laid my grandparents and all their loved ones to rest in the Wailing Wall, and now I am back in the Netherlands for a special trek to find our roots deep inside the earth of Overijssel. My daughter Hani is with me and thanks to her I have succeeded in touching the safe bank over the bridge of our family's life. Following our journey, the avalanche of documentation found me which clarified the truth: David, my father, had gone into battle against the Nazi Goliath empty-handed, except for pen and paper. He lacked even the most primitive of catapults, had only his intelligence, his voice, his way with words, and his feet. That is how he fought the enemy. For hours he walked from one Jewish family to the next, talked himself blue in the face to convince them that *onderduiken* and *Vayibrach* were the only solution to escape the murderous clutches in which Dutch Jewry had been caught. Most of the relatives did not listen to him because they could not believe that the Germans were cold-blooded murderers, and they could not grasp that in order to save their children they had to separate from them, for it was easier to find hiding places for children who were on their own. Taking in an entire family was much more complicated. People spoke in phrases that no longer meant anything in their devilish world, but how could they make that switch! They still believed there was logic in their universe and it was that very insanity that the Germans counted on. And so, the Jews would say things like, "What are you talking about! The Germans only want us to work for them. They need us to work for them. There is no way they are planning to kill us!" The same reactions had come from the younger generations who had already offered up their lives in 1942 in the belief that this would save the elderly, the little nieces and nephews. They had been swallowed up by planet Auschwitz. What else could David then have done? He had tried everything, all his talents of persuasion, and he had no more ideas. He had tried so hard, and his most overwhelming emotion now was the despair at his failure!

In 1943, the elder generation had already passed 60, and they said, "No, we have no need to make *Vayibrach*, we have no need to go into hiding. After all, our children have voluntarily moved to the work camps so that the Germans would leave us in peace. They promised!" And then, when the deportation letters came with the order to clean their home, leave the key at the police station, and present themselves at the train, they said, "Well, you know, that is simply the new law. There is nothing to be done. Jews are no longer allowed to live in Overijssel. That is just the way it is. But we did remind the police that our children, sons and daughters had gone to the work camps voluntarily so that we would not be molested. And the answer was that we would get stone houses to live in. They promised! Our children did not leave for those camps in vain!" The day before they left their homes behind and walked slowly, a sad parade of the condemned, David tried one last time. They raised their eyes to him in surprise. "We are in G-d's hands now," they said. "We have given our fate over to Him. If He wishes, we shall live, and if He does not, so be it. In G-d's hands we are." People had never even given a thought to the possibility of mass murder. Perhaps they thought that life might become more difficult, such as not having warm clothing or enough food, and who knows, perhaps they were too old to survive such hardships. Only when they reached Vught or Westerbork, their final destination on the Dutch soil, perhaps only then, as they were being pushed and shoved into cattle cars as mere dumb beasts, did the truth become clear. There, on the platform of the holding camps, under the cynically lying signs, Westerbork-Auschwitz, and on the other side of the platform the opposite, even though no train ever came from Auschwitz, only then did they perhaps know that David had been right, but the gates to *Vayibrach* and life after *onderduiken* had closed. The younger generation that had put their lives on the line to save their parents and young relatives were long dead. The plan to pick off the younger men and women had left the elderly and the young families with babies without protection just as planned, and had succeeded at almost 100 percent. In *The Drowned and the Saved,* Primo Levi wrote that the survivors cannot relate the entire story, but neither can the dead, for they have lost their voice. And yet, there is one fact that cannot be disputed: Those of the Nijverdal-Hellendoorn Jews who had listened to David, made their *Vayibrach* and went into hiding, survived the war, but David found no consolation in this fact.

The way in which David and Betje succeeded in reaching their hiding place in the Dutch Reform church sounds a little like a fairy tale, the kind of story parents tell their little ones; a bit of an adventure, a bit of humor just before the child falls asleep, but I have the letter my father wrote to the mayor and the head of the police of Nijverdal. He wrote it in 1945, shortly after the liberation. Now he could openly say how Pastor Hijmans and the Overduin group helped his family, and he describes his escape route very clearly. And so, the following is not me telling stories. It is history.

The bald fact is that on April 9, 1943, my parents reached the church. It was a Friday night and the sun had already set. The huge structure loomed before them under its impressive bell tower, and the verger, Mr. Smit, was waiting for the Jewish couple just outside the church doors. He beckoned them to enter. It was Shabbat already, but my mother had no candles to light and my father no wine to welcome and bless the day of rest. Nothing of that tradition had remained. They had run, bent low, fleeing from tree to tree, hiding in the hollows of the forest, and near the railroad tracks they threw themselves against the pebbles near the sleepers. And again, they ran, always bent low, hiding in shadows. Until they got to the church. And there, once inside, were people who smiled at them and offered them some food and a bowl of warm water to freshen up a little. And then they were helped upstairs into the huge church attic, and to their enormous surprise, found other Jews from all over the country. Pastor Hijmans took David aside for a moment and told him that his resistance cell was hard at work to find them safe addresses and that they just had to be patient for a while. But he assured them that they were safe. For now, he thought to himself, but that he did not share with David.

Chronologically speaking, David and Betje arrived at the church after dark, but if we turn back the clock to Friday morning, at least 10 hours earlier, we can see someone standing at the front door of 82 Rijssensestraat. This man closed his hand around the copper knob of the bell and pulled it. The stick connected to the knob activated a chain which pulled the clapper against the bell and made it chime. This mechanism proves beyond a doubt that Nijverdal's Jewry was traditional and followed the laws of their religion to the letter. The mechanism of this bell is called a Shabbos bell because one is allowed to ring it also on the day of rest. On that day, Jews do not play any music instruments, and pushing the doorbell is considered making music. However, the mechanism on the door of number 82 activates the bell indirectly, a movement called *"gramma"*, which is allowed. The copper bell was still there after the war and we called it our Shabbos bell. The man who rang the bell that fateful morning, however, knew nothing of the subtleties of Jewish law. He simply pulled the knob out to make the bell ring twice. Two short bursts, one after the other. Then he waited a little, counted to five and pulled it once more. As that was the signal they had been waiting for, Betje hurried to open the door. Mr. Teesselink from the furniture store was standing outside. "Are you ready?" he asked quickly. "I have the truck outside. The boys are coming in a minute." He saw the fear in her face. She was doing her best, but her mouth was tight with tension. Teesselink looked at her high, almost Slavic, cheekbones for a second and those unique, large, blue-green eyes under her dark hair. In spite of everything, what a beautiful woman, he thought to himself. She looked neatly dressed, and her hair was mostly hidden under a scarf she had knotted under her chin just like the other women in the village. Teesselink gestured the two young men leaning against the moving van to come inside, and in a short while, the entire content of the house had been moved into the truck. There wasn't that much left in the house, after a large part of the family's worldly goods had disappeared via David's *Vayibrach* program, and after other pieces had been sacrificed to keep the stove burning. The young men quickly smoked a cigarette and waited while Teesselink signaled that he would have a smoke inside and check that they had not forgotten anything. "Ready?" he asked the couple. They nodded and together they waited for the sharp knock on the front window, to let them know that the coast was clear. David and Betje hurried outside and climbed into the back of the moving van. The first stage of their flight had begun.

David, unlike the rest of the Jews of Nijverdal, had received a letter ordering him to take his worldly goods and his family to Amsterdam and to present himself to the authorities at the Jewish Theatre. After all, he was the local representative of the Jewish Council, and the time had come for him to join other members already waiting for deportation.

Teesselink locked the front door of number 82, handed the key to David, or perhaps put it in his pocket for safekeeping, climbed behind the wheel and drove away. He drove out of the village in the direction of Zwolle. The truck was old and the hill in whose shadow Nijverdal had been built and whose valley had given the village its name was steep. The motor groaned and sputtered, but he crested the hill and when the truck descended, it passed the entrance to the tourist road which David had helped become a reality. Then, at the bottom of the hill, the truck slowed to a halt on the shoulder of the road. Teesselink slid out, quickly opened the hood and reached inside, covertly pulled out a part with some cables and pushed it deep into his pocket. Then, no matter how hard he tried, the motor refused to turn over. The second stage of the *Vayibrach* plan had begun. He walked to the back of the truck, pulled back a corner of the tarpaulin, and explained that everything was under control and going according to the plan. He pointed to a basket where he had packed some sandwiches and a flask of lukewarm tea. There were a few wrinkled apples from his garden. He winked, "Keep up your courage, we are doing just fine."

Teesselink made effort after effort to get the truck to start again, but it was in vain. Few people passed the stranded van and if they offered their help, Teesselink politely refused their assistance. Even a German jeep which stopped, glanced at his papers, and understood what it was all about, drove on without much ceremony. For the rest of the day, Teesselink mostly just guarded his precious cargo which was camouflaged by their chairs, table and beds.

Under cover of the dark, two forbidden Jews returned to the village. A man and a woman. They had turned their coats inside out to hide the yellow Jew star. They hurried up the hill, passed the turn into the tourist road, and then turned right through the garden of a beautiful villa opposite the Catholic cemetery. The back gate was off the latch and opened easily. Now they were in the forest, walking as far as the edge of the ravine, and then stumbled awkwardly down the sandy slope until they reached the railroad tracks. They followed the sleepers until they were close to the church, and then ran, keeping their bodies lower than the top of the hedge, and prayed that no one would see them. They reached the safety of the church portal, stumbled inside, and disappeared for more than two years. No one had seen them, neither their silhouettes against the dark night, nor their fear and shivering anxiety. No one? Almost no one. The postman looked up at the very moment that David and Betje Samuel were swallowed up by the shadows of the church portal but kept this knowledge to himself. "I didn't even breathe a word to my wife about it," he said to David with pride when he met him again in 1945.

And Teesselink, that courageous upholsterer of furniture and smuggler of Jews? He walked home and only the next day did he return to the moving van. To his chagrin he discovered that it was empty. Everything in it had been stolen. And where did the items go?

This was the third stage of the *Vayibrach* plan: David and Betje in a safe place, the furniture too. In the dead of night, a few members of the resistance had moved everything to the furniture store's storage and to the secondhand store of the Salvation Army in the village. There, properly aryanized, the living room set and the dining room table found a home in a dusty corner, far from curious eyes, and patiently waited for the return of their owners. That had been David's request: nothing for the enemy. And the *Vayibrach* plan worked perfectly in all its stages. For a while...

During the years I lived in the house of my father David Simon Samuel, another truck covered in tarpaulin pulled up in front of the house. The driver also slid from behind the wheel and rang the bell of our living quarters. It was Monday afternoon, and the store was closed. We were living at number 30, the big new house near the center of the village. The doorbell was electric for there were no longer any Jews who might come calling on the Sabbath, our day of rest. I heard the truck stop in front of the store and because I was curious by nature, I went to take a look. We lived in a sleepy village and a truck might be interesting. Perhaps papa had bought something exciting for his business. Something that would live up to the slogan on our wrapping paper: always something special by Samuel Prins.

"Delivery," said the chauffeur with the cigarette dangling from the corner of his mouth. "Open the store, please, so we can bring the goods inside." I followed my father, and I was the one to slide back the bolt on the entrance to our store while papa turned on the lights. "Take it upstairs, please," he said. "To the wholesale department." Two young men carried in box after box. They were enormous. I counted at least 20 huge cartons but waited till everything had been taken upstairs, my father had pushed a generous tip into the hands of each of the delivery boys, plus something for the chauffeur whose hand he shook in parting, and then locked the store again. The truck had already driven off.

"Papa, what did you buy?" For a second my father gave me a thoughtful look as if he searched for the right answer, but then he gestured with his thumb and we walked back to the wholesale department on the second floor. Almost the entire space was taken up by those cartons. Papa brought out his boxcutter and cut the adhesive tape. I saw multicolored blankets, but a strange smell wafted up from them. "Papa, those blankets smell like Van Egmond's gas pump!" He smiled and answered, like always, in a few words, "Touch them, feel them with your fingers" because he had taught me to assert the quality of goods by fingering them. The blankets were rough and greasy. They were not pleasant to the touch. It definitely was not wool, but I did not know what material had made them. My father looked at my face and smiled in satisfaction. I had been a good student. "Those are synthetic, cheaply pressed blankets made of leftover materials. I bought them from a factory that was going bankrupt. I bought a thousand pieces. Twenty-four per carton, figure it out. They cost practically nothing, and I can sell them for a nice profit, but they are only for the wholesale trade. Certainly not for the people in the village."

Those blankets were but one of the ways in which my father found revenge against the Germans and all they had done to our family. He placed an advertisement in the newspaper, invited house-to-house salesmen and marketeers who worked across the border to come and look at the goods, and promised them colorful, large, synthetic blankets. The sales took place once a week on Monday afternoons by appointment only, when the store was closed to retail shopping, and papa always made certain that the person who came to buy up a carton or two really worked only in Germany. He refused to have them sold in the Netherlands. The blankets were very cheap but still too expensive at any price. They reeked of gas, but by the time the housewife realized that she had made a bad bargain, the peddler had disappeared. The blankets were not warm and once washed shrunk so badly that they were useless. In the end, they simply disintegrated after a short time.

Every time a carboard box left the store, papa rubbed his hands together in pleasure, especially when word of mouth also brought German peddlers to buy up blankets. Thus worked my father's revenge: slowly, unexpected, but with an aroma that lingered.

For five weeks David and Betje remained in the fortress of the church where they held fast to the hope that here, like in a Biblical city of refuge, they would be safe. During this time, men and women alike did their best to keep their hands busy in order to make the heavy hours of the day pass a little faster. They peeled potatoes which had been left by anonymous farmers at the entrance to the pastor's residence, no questions asked, but the work was done much too soon. They asked *Dominee* Hijmans if he perhaps needed some help with the maintenance of the church, and in secret, the women were given copper ornaments to polish, while the men fixed some of the sagging pews. Betje asked for wool so as to knit warm caps and scarves for the resistance. This became a hit and assisted by other knitters, a stream of mittens and caps reached the men who helped to keep the Jews of the DRC (Dutch Reformed Church) far from the clutches of the German occupation. Those who did not know how to knit well labored at unravelling old sweaters and socks and to recycle the wool thus received.

While the Jews worked at their tasks, they whispered among themselves, carefully withholding information that might be dangerous. Perhaps they even gave each other false names. Perhaps they said they had come from other cities than the ones they mentioned. No one spoke of relatives, children, or parents, and no one asked about the families of their attic-mates. They were an artificial island, afloat on a raft constructed by naive resistance fighters. Keeping silent about their lost children was better. It was better for morale, for the silence that had to be maintained and the despair to be kept at bay. No one spoke of the past because it was too dangerous, and no one knew what might happen tomorrow. They were truly adrift.

Over time, the hapless group of fleeing Jews shrunk and expanded slowly, as new refugees joined, while others disappeared further into the nooks and crannies of the resistance. David and Betje were also waiting for their so-called permanent address, but nothing opened up for them. The pastor whispered to David that he might be able to keep him and his wife in the church over the long haul. The year was 1943 already, and how long could the war still last! Via the clandestine radio, David listened to the BBC and faithfully translated talk of a turnabout in the war: Hitler's troops had not succeeded in breaking through the Russian lines. There were rumors about an imminent counter offensive to push back the Wehrmacht. Could it be that Hitler was losing the upper hand? The little group of Jews together with their protectors, *Dominee* Hijmans and Verger Smit, drank a glass of home-made liquor from the verger's still. They accepted cigarettes he had rolled with heaven knows what home-made tobacco. They all lit up and downed their drinks, eyes tearing from both the liquor and those horrible cigarettes, but no one refused the treat. They laughed through their tears. It was a moment of celebration, just a moment, a tiny hiatus in the horror. And that night, when a tiny spark of light had entered the lives of the Jews in the attic of the church, there was a careful, yet insistent knock on the door of the rectory. David and Betje were trying to adjust to their strange existence in the secret hollows of the sanctuary and life without their children, but the reality of their precarious existence was brought home with that knock on the door, even though they did not hear it. When Hijmans opened the door, he saw a young man whom he knew as a member of the Overduin group. He had a burlap sack slung over his shoulder. He slipped inside, gently put the sack on the kitchen table and opened it a bit so that the pastor could see what was inside. Those were not potatoes. Not illegal weapons either. It was a little girl deep in a narcotic sleep. She had been drugged for her safety, and that of the boys and girls who had smuggled her from courier to courier, to take her back to Nijverdal as a matter of life and death. The little girl was Louisie, Betje and David's firstborn child. Something very terrible must have happened to compel the underground to brave the curfew and get her as far away as possible from the Bemelaar family.

For six weeks Louisie had been with the family, camouflaged as a little niece. They had a perfect cover story: the child's father had been killed in the 1940 bombardment of Rotterdam, and now her mother had fallen ill with tuberculosis and was incapable of looking after her daughter. "We had no choice", they told anyone who enquired. "There was no one else." And Mrs. Bemelaar shrugged her shoulders as a sign that she felt a little saddled with the child. "What is your name?" people asked and reached out to touch the child's silken hair, but Louisie remained silent and pulled away. Time passed, and she learned to say her new name: "Wiesje". Yes, Wiesje was her name now. Louisie had disappeared on the way to Nijmegen, and in her place there was a new girl with a more Aryan sounding name. She also learned very quickly that her best defense was to say as little as possible. Her introversion was interpreted as homesickness or shyness and people went out of their way to be kind to her. "Oh, that poor girl, no?" they said to each other, and came with clothing or toys and perhaps a piece of candy. "Yes, first her father," the neighbors said clucking their tongues, "and now her mother, and who knows…" they said behind their hands and looked at Wiesje in that meaningful silence. Some stroked her hair with compassion.

One neighbor was especially taken with the Bemelaar family's new house guest. He was a widower and father to a five-year-old girl. He encouraged the children to play together and invited Wiesje to come to be with his Anneke. With Wiesje's Aryan bloodline firmly established, the Bemelaars thought encouraging the connection might be a good idea and help the poor child to adjust to her new circumstances. Visits began back and forth. Everyone was delighted to see that Wiesje began to relax a little, to smile a little. The two girls preferred to play at Anneke's house because of her many toys, and because she had the run of the house. The girls dressed up in

Anneke's dead mother's dresses and looked inside her jewelry box. They walked hand in hand when Francien Bemelaar took them to the swings, or whenever they played in the shared garden behind their homes.

Slowly and painfully, Wiesje emerges a little from her traumatized silence and begins to talk. Anneke's toys and games are wonderful and she loves joining in the make-believe balls and dress-ups. She loves Anneke's mama's necklaces and other pieces of custom jewelry. Life is normalizing somewhat, and Wiesje instinctively knows that if she behaves, the Bemelaars will let her stay. She is adjusting.

Just about six weeks pass. Life becomes routine. There is no weeping mother here, or a mother who hides her tears, and there is no father who paces back and forth and mumbles to himself. There is no tension of all those things that are not allowed. Nijverdal was a prison, but here, in Nijmegen, with the Bemelaars, she is free. Wiesje feels the difference in everything that happens in her new home. Her father's stories recede, and it seems that she is beginning to forget.

Till the sixth week. Six weeks after that sleepy child came to her hiding address, started befriending Anneke, and watched as she opened her dead mother's jewelry box once again. Anneke fished out a long necklace for Wiesje and searched at the bottom of the box. She found what she was looking for: a large brooch which she pinned to her dress. "Look, so nice," she said to Wiesje with pride. "So nice with those yellow stones, and so fancy. You can wear it to church. You can pin it to your coat and then you will be the most beautiful of all the girls." Wiesje is not quite sure what a church is, but the bejeweled brooch is lovely in her eyes, and she admires it out loud. Then she holds out her hand to ask for her turn. "Can I have it now?" Anneke pulls back and covers the pin with a protective hand. "No! That is my mother's favorite pin. But isn't it the most beautiful pin in the whole world?" And she waits for Wiesje's agreement. For a moment, Louisie Samuel, till now safely hidden inside Wiesje Bemelaar, stares at the brooch on Anneke's dress. Then she shrugs her shoulders and dismisses what her friend has said about it. "No, not at all! My mama has the most beautiful brooch in all the world. And she keeps it on her coat. And she wears it every day, not only on Sunday for church. And it is a star. A yellow star. That is the most beautiful in the whole world," and she turns her back on Anneke. Both girls burst into tears and the woman who looks after the policeman's daughter runs into the room to see what is wrong and sends Wiesje home to her aunt and uncle next-door.

That evening the policeman, Anneke's father, bangs on Bemelaar's front door. He is furious. "I am not a child killer," he yells, "But that dirty Jewess pig must be gone by morning, or I report you to the Gestapo. Tomorrow!" he repeats for emphasis, turns on his heels and storms out. Mr. Bemelaar, shocked beyond words, remains seated in his living room. The child must go. That is clear. But how and where can he find another address for her on such short notice? Night is falling and curfew near, but he pulls on his coat, slaps a hat on his head, and leaves through the garden. He needs to talk to someone in his resistance group. He knows that David and Betje have already disappeared into the underground warren of hidden Jews, so he cannot bring Wiesje back to them. In the end it is decided that she must be returned to the central point of the Overduin group – to Nijverdal. The pastor and his people will find her a hiding place, but until then, the church can shelter her.

And now she is there, deep in a narcotic sleep, on the pastor's kitchen table. *Dominee* Hijmans knows that no matter what else may happen, he must prevent David and Betje from finding out that their daughter is under the same roof as they are. And vice versa. At any price! They cannot know about the danger their daughter is in right now. Suddenly, finding a hiding place does not guarantee safety. He must prevent them from thinking that. The underground is inexperienced and still learning from their mistakes. They may have been naive enough to believe that the Jews are safe the moment someone agrees to take them in, however, Hijmans now realizes that this is an illusion. They are caught in a macabre marathon with fate and the prize is the life of the people over whom he wants to spread his protective wings. He must win that race! Once again, he looks at the little girl who is slumbering in innocence on his table and he is lost. Where can he possibly find a place for her on such short notice!?

The pastor does the only thing that may give him insight: he folds his hands, bends his head low and slowly, with desperate intensity, prays for a solution to save the lives of the members of the Samuel family. And suddenly he knows: the baker across the street, 18 Kerkstraat. The Scheffers are not members of his congregation, nor are they part of the Overduin group, but he has heard rumors about their resistance work. That they rescue British pilots and smuggle them back to the coast where small boats ferry them back to England, so they can fight another day. He has also heard it whispered that the Scheffers are in charge of getting weapons and communication equipment dropped from British planes. As far as Hijmans knows, the Scheffers are members of the *N.V.* or *Naamloze Vennootschap* (Limited Company), a group which has already done much to hamper the Germans, but he does not know for sure. With one last glance at Betje and David's sleeping child, he puts everything on the line. He will let her stay in the rectory for one night. One night does not seem too risky and he will make every effort to smuggle her parents away from the church. He sees their anxiety as they wait for a hiding place and Betje was pale and jittery. The only thing that sustains them is the belief that their two little girls are safe.

As long as they held on to that belief, they would have the courage to wait, remain out of sight, and adjust to their impossible circumstances. However, should they find out that Louisie was in danger, who knows what they might do. This would not be the first time that a desperate Jew committed suicide.

Hijmans had been told that he must keep all information inside the Overduin group and never trust an outsider, but he did not see how he could do this now. Betje and David had to disappear from inside the church, and there could be no mishap. Curfew had already gone into effect, but he had no choice. Like Bemelaar, the pastor also pushed his arms into his coat, pulled a farmer's cap low over his forehead, and left the safety of his home. After a quick look, he ran diagonally across the street and hurried into the shadows of the Scheffer's home.

The aroma of freshly baked bread wafted toward him before he even entered. Bakers work at night and in the morning offer their clients freshly baked loaves. Scheffer did not have a shop; he delivered his bread from door to door. Because of the occupation, bread required ration stamps in addition to cash, and he carefully collected them. Used ration stamps had to be returned to the distribution office in exchange for a new allotment of flour. The rationing made for a lot of extra work, but that was just the way things were now!

The entire family was busy with the production of bread. The wife, Hendrika, called Henk, kneaded the dough and her husband Cornelius, Cees, formed the loaves with quick, economical movements. Every loaf was weighed, but from each Cees pinched off a bit of dough so that he accumulated a few extra loaves for the illegal inhabitants of his home, among whom was his firstborn son, Cees Jr. The latter was in hiding to avoid being sent to Germany for forced labor. During the day he stayed out of sight, but now, late at night, he was at the hot oven and slid the loaves inside for their baking. His bolt hole was a secret compartment under the bed in the front room. This was also the place where the family hid the N.V.'s radio, ammunition, and a few guns. The Scheffer daughters, Ina and Jo delivered the bread before they went to work. It was also their task to glue the collected ration stamps onto cards. Even the two younger ones, Tony and Henny, helped with the deliveries before school, but now they were asleep.

As soon as the pastor enters, Cees understands that something is up. This is hardly a time for calling on neighbors and like Hijmans, Cees too has heard whisperings about the *dominee*. He nods once in greeting, invites the pastor in and offers him his hand. Hijmans gestures with his head that he wants to talk to Scheffer in private. That understood, Jo steps in to take over the shaping of loaves and Scheffer gestures the pastor to follow him into the "good room." This room is the pride of most village homes and was never used except for weddings or funerals. He opens the door with its blue and red stained glass insert and the two men go inside.

Hijmans does not mince words, "I have an emergency," he begins and in as few words as possible paints Scheffer the picture of what is happening at his residence. "For one night." He is almost begging. "One night! A man and a woman. They even have false identification papers. Their names are Piet and Geertje. Two lost human beings."

Of course, Scheffer understands perfectly what the *dominee* is saying to him and he also knows the questionable usefulness of forged documents. He knows that the underground does not always have the best equipment or skill. They are still too new at it all.

"I need to discuss this with my wife," the baker says in the end and adds that in any case, he already had quite a few so-called guests in his home. He shrugs his shoulders. "Even my oldest son has been forced into hiding and he is not the only one here." Scheffer walks back into the bakery and returns to the pastor a few minutes later. "One night! One night, you solve your problems on your side and then Piet and Geertje can return to the church. Will that help you out?" The two men shake hands again and Hijmans slips out into the dark night and hurries back to the rectory.

One more hour passes, and once again, a knock on the back entrance of the bakery. Cees opens immediately and sees Verger Smit standing outside with two people who look familiar. "Come in, quickly." He hurries them inside. "Welcome," he adds, and watches when Betje, white as a sheet, stumbles over the threshold and falls down in a dead faint on the stone floor of the bakery. He helps David to pick her up, and together they carry her into the front room to a large bed. "Sit with her until she regains consciousness, and make sure she does not scream," he whispers in David's ear.

The next day *Dominee* Hijmans drops in to say that he has not yet found a solution to his problem and asks for a few more days.

Scheffer's home is not very big. He has six children and several secret guests who all need a place to sleep. The discussion is painful. Furthermore, there is always the terrible fear that the Germans will suddenly show up in their street for a house-to-house search. Scheffer is afraid for the safety of his own children. Henk also worries about the consequences of sheltering Jews. Cees tries to calm his wife but has no clear answer to her question what would happen to their children should they be caught and sent to a camp. "Especially the little ones," she adds. David feels the tension and takes the baker aside. "Sir," he says carefully, "you barely know us. You do not owe us anything. We have papers and perhaps you can simply help us reach the coast where there might be a boat to take us to England? Like those pilots you told me about." Scheffer does not answer right away but rubs his hand over his chin, carefully thinking about what words to choose. "Give me a day to consider this," he says finally, and the next day he comes to talk to David once again. Scheffer is very tall and towers over David. "A few things," and he places his hand on his shoulder. "You two cannot possibly go outside in Nijverdal. Too many people would recognize you, so that is much too risky, and for sure, false papers will not protect you then. But Piet (he always called them Piet and Geertje, for safety) you are of G-d's People, and deep in my heart I have come to the realization that our situation is the opposite of what you think. I do not protect you, but you and your wife protect us, so that we can be safe to do our resistance work and finish the war by defeating the Krauts. And besides," he continues in a serious voice, "What kind of example would I be giving my children if I taught them that our lives are more important than that of others, yours, for example?" Now he smiles for a second. "You know, Piet, I have never thought about this so much, but every word I have said to you goes to the heart of the matter. I do not want to live in a world that does not have room for everyone and besides, none of us are safe at the moment. This is war and we do not know who will live and who will die. We simply try to improve our chances, and for me, keeping you and your wife safe is a good beginning. With G-d's help we will succeed by working together. And now, enough talk. Come, help me move those sacks of flour. They are heavy!"

Slowly, a routine grew at 18 Kerkstraat. At times, the young children were sent into the street carrying baskets of bread, so that people could buy from them. However, once the younger ones were out of the house, David and Betje could come out of the closed front room for a little human interaction with the adults. The children were told they were outside to look out for German patrols on the street. The reason for this, their parents said, was to protect their big brother Cees Jr., but Louisie and Marianne's parents also needed time to pry open the floorboards that hid the entrance to their hiding hole under the big bed.

One time while Henny and Tony were in school, a large army truck with GP, the German Green Police stopped under the trees in front of the Scheffer family home. Neither Cees nor Henk had seen the truck because of the trees and there was no time for David and Betje to go into their hiding place. Cees Jr. was also outside, but he dove under the table where a tablecloth that reached the floor covered him, and the Samuels ran into the front room. David threw himself behind the bed, but Betje only managed to close the door and press her body close to the wall. They could hear German inside the house. One of the uniforms opened the door with the stained-glass panels. A young face looked in, checked behind the door and saw the woman standing there, silent but shaking with fear. For a second their eyes met. Then the German policeman in his green uniform closed the door and told his superior that the room was empty. The rest of the house turned up no illegal residents or contraband. It was all legal. Still pale as death, the Scheffers and Samuels came into the central kitchen, and everybody hugged for a long time. They read the 91st Psalm together and the next day Scheffer cut down all the branches, leaving only the bare trunks. "I need firewood for the bread," he told the villagers who wondered why. Until now, he had left the trees grow thick thinking they protected the front room from view, but they had turned out to be a threat to their safety. Cees had to be able to see the street!

For those two years, the 91st psalm was their close companion, and it has remained with the family ever since. The psalm is even inscribed on my parents' headstone. In our home, when bad things happened, we would simply say "Psalm 91" without actually reading it. We said the number, and G-d did the rest. We knew that by saying those magic words "Psalm 91", we had done all we could to keep the family safe, just as then in 1943, when the German policeman saw my mother and did not betray her.

Years later, when I traveled to Canada to take part in the Yad Vashem ceremony in honor of the Scheffers who rescued my parents when hope was nearly gone, Henny, the youngest of the Scheffer children, gave me a handmade wall hanging with the psalm. It was decorated with crowns and flowers, each crown topped by a small cross. Perhaps she saw the way I looked at the embroidery, and perhaps I was a little taken aback by those crosses. In any case, she apologized profusely. "I wasn't thinking, but if you do not want it, I will understand. You can leave it here." Still focused on the crosses, I searched for something to say, but suddenly I had the feeling that we were not alone, and that my father was whispering something in my ear. I listened intently and embraced her with all my strength. "A cross embroidered by you with so much love is an honor, and this beautiful sampler deserves a place of honor: I will frame it and hang it in my room." It is still there, and I meant every word my father spoke through me.

———

Tante Henk Scheffer, called mama by my father and aunt by us, was a nervous, tense woman who often struggled to survive even one more day with her house so full of contraband and illegals: radio, resistance weapons, Jews and other people fleeing from the Germans, but she never said one single word to give my parents the feeling that she wanted them to leave. And she never tried to convince her husband, Cees Jr. or daughters Ina and Jo to stop working for the resistance; in fact, she encouraged and orchestrated it. She chose to sanctify life. The life of every human being, including Piet and Geertje's. Including the British pilots and a German deserter who could not bear the way Jews were mistreated. Perhaps this is where her true courage lay, a pure and holy courage which emanated from a woman who had not had much school learning, never had much money and had never traveled, perhaps not even outside Nijverdal. Tante Henk was a unique soul who clearly knew the difference between right and wrong. And so, notwithstanding the fear that kept her awake at night, she stood by her man, supported him in all that he needed to create a world where Piet and Geertje would not be condemned to live their days in a darkened room, hidden behind curtains, floorboards, and false names. She did not even complain when Ome Cees was unable to leave his protegees during the intense bombardments that destroyed much of Nijverdal during the final year of the war, and instead chose to stay with the Jewish couple rather than run to the shelter of the church cellar. Tante Henk accepted his dedication and found excuses to explain why her husband was not there with her and the children.

There were times when the Germans came too close to 18 Kerkstraat and *Dominee* Hijmans had to step in. The Samuels returned to the church from time to time, but there was never any question where Piet and Geertje belonged.

Who can better tell the story of the Scheffers' purity of soul than my father? After all, he was there. He saw it. He saw everything and in his own manner he was even part of the family's resistance activities. Years later he wrote about this in the local newspaper, *De Twentse Krant*:

"Cees Jr. always went out dressed in two suits in case he found a British pilot hiding in the Nijverdal forest, after parachuting out of his burning plane. Such a person had to strip off his uniform before anything else. It was much too dangerous to come out in the open wearing it. And so, Cees Jr.

went out searching every time an allied plane was hit. He had to find that pilot before the Germans did. One day, he returned with a young man, a child, almost. The boy was wounded and panic-stricken. Once, safely inside the Scheffer home, he was handed over to me, because I knew English. My wife and I took care of his scrapes and bruises, cleaned the wound, and made sure that he ate and drank something. He slowly recovered a little. "We want to smuggle you back to the coast, where a small boat will get you across, back to England." Within a few days the boy was well, and the mission could start. "Do you know how to ride a bike?" He said he did. "Just remember that here in the Netherlands we ride on the right side of the street." Yes, he knew that as well. Very early in the morning, the pilot, together with Cees Jr., left. On bikes. I followed the pilot's progress from behind the curtains. He lurched back and forth like a drunken sailor. "To the right! To the right!" I said out loud and gestured with my hands even though that boy could neither see nor hear me. I hoped to reach him through telepathy, perhaps, but he kept on veering back to the left side. That day G-d was with us a little, for there were no German soldiers or policemen in sight, and it ended well."

From my own research on this story, with the help of the name my father used in the newspaper, I learned that this pilot had safely returned to England, rejoined his squadron, and survived the war. He lived to a ripe old age, surrounded by children and grandchildren.

For two years, my parents lived in the Scheffer home. For two years, they only whispered, were not allowed to argue, yell or cry. For two years, their life was like a feather in the wind, protected by people whose lives became fragile and temporary as a result of that protection. No one could prophesize whether their lives would still be safe the next day. Two years like that. Twice 365 days, times 24 hours, times 60 minutes. Two years with a clock that did not move. And every day anew, David and Betje had to convince themselves that their little girls were safe. That they were alive, that the war would end, and they would all be able to go home. And then they would be a family once more and would put these years behind them. They would forget. That had to be possible. But even when the German soldiers were already in retreat and even when the Canadian division came to liberate the village, David and Betje did not venture out. They were too afraid. The liberation festivities passed them by. For them, the time for celebration had not come. It took a month before they dared to venture outside. First, they made it as far as the swept yard with its scrawny chickens. Then past the vegetable garden, and only then did they make a trip of perhaps 100 meters to *Dominee* Hijmans' rectory, to his church. The understanding that they were free came slowly, but once they felt safe enough, they set out in search of their children. Louisie was found first and quite some time later, Marianne too. During those days they also went to visit their home at number 82 Rijssensestraat to see how it had survived the war. The store had been hit in one of the bombardments that had destroyed many homes along the street. The back part – the living quarters – was livable, but the house was not empty. A Dutch Nazi had moved in after quasi buying it from the Germans who had confiscated all Jewish property after April 9, 1943. This family refused to vacate the house, but soon enough, a few muscular young men of the resistance came along and without ceremony, furniture and the members of the K. family were thrown out into the street. As soon as that had been taken care of, neighbors showed up with buckets and soap, cleaned the house from top to bottom, and Teesselink and the Salvation Army returned the Samuel furniture. The next day, many of the villagers who had heard that David and his wife had survived the war and had been hidden at the Scheffers' showed up at the bakery, and a parade of honor brought the Jewish couple back to their house. The living room table bore Betje's candle sticks, where she had lit her Shabbat candles, the menorah where David lit the Hanukkah candles for eight days, adding one candle for each consecutive day, and the silver cup used to bless the Shabbat. It was all there. The family which had hidden their Judaica, heard about the Samuels' survival and rushed to bring back everything, but first they polished the silver and copper and then placed the items in a place of honor inside the home.

Jewish Canadian soldiers found a warm welcome at the family home as well, and very quickly, soldiers were quartered with them. The couple had only one room left for themselves but were happy to sleep on the floor of the returned children's room. Aside from the chocolate the soldiers brought, they also carried a small edition of a newspaper that was printed in Brabant, in the south, a region that was liberated late in 1944. The paper, called *Le'Ezrath ha'Am* (In Aid of the [Jewish] People), was designed to help restore a semblance of Jewish life to the survivors, but also to help them find relatives. In his first public act after he came out of hiding, David gave his address to the editor, and to ensure that post would reach him, he gave the Scheffer address, 18 Kerkstraat. That is how his name appears in subsequent editions of the paper. He was the liaison for Jews looking for other survivors in the region.[5] None of his relatives, however, made contact.

Their first Passover after the liberation was celebrated with the Canadian soldiers and the following year, just before Purim, the Feast of Lots, Dr. Bakker came to number 82, for a new baby was coming into the world. It was March 10, 1946, exactly one week before that carnival-like celebration of Jewish survival long, long ago. That was the day I came into the world. The third Samuel daughter. Yelling and screaming (I was told), red in the face and blessed with a head of black hair, I arrived, full of life. So full of life that no one was able to control me.

And Louisie? Wiesje? Just like her parents, she did not stay in the sanctuary of the church long. It was much too dangerous for her there and like her parents, she too reached a place where good, courageous people took her in. Also there, the intention had been to keep her for just a short while until a more permanent address could be found, but she ended up staying for two years. The venue was Hengelo, an industrial town not far from Enschede, part of the area where Mr. Menko did his rescue work for the Jewish community. And in Hengelo, there was one more little girl from the Samuel clan. That was Truus, Abraham and Lewia's daughter, David's young cousin.

When Wiesje woke up in Hengelo that first morning, her young protector could not bring herself to send this little girl of not even five-years-old into the unknown.

In 1943, after all the Jews left in the province of Overijssel had received their feared letters of deportation and after their deportation had been carried out, E.D. Witschey, the mayor of Nijverdal-Hellendoorn was fired. The reason was that in his municipality too many of the Jews who had been ordered to present themselves with the key to their homes had disappeared without a trace. Among those missing Jews were small children, such as Louisie and Marianne, but the Germans did not care how old or young anyone was. They were merely Jews. The German administration in Arnhem and the head of police in Nijverdal wrote furious letters to the mayor about Jews and Jewesses who had not arrived at the train station to pick up their travel permits. Those Jews were now wanted criminals who sought to evade their fate and who refused to allow themselves to be murdered voluntarily. The Germans were relentless: they had to get their hands on every last Jew and in the post deportation era, a macabre dance between the occupation and the fleeing Jews began. The latter's crime was that they still breathed the air of Overijssel, while they should have left for Sobibor already where their oxygen would be cut off in the most efficient manner.

Letters were written back and forth; lists were checked by gray clerks in gray coats and uniforms. Everything had to tally. And it did not. Names could not be ticked off because those pesky Jews had not been on the train to Vught. Again, letters in German and in Dutch, again lists with names that could not be checked off, again comparing the numbers. The tally of death did not match that of the number of Jews on the list. There was an imbalance in the German murder machine. And yet, the Jews who had fallen off the face of the earth did not show up. They were not found. They were not rooted out. This is how it was in all of the Netherlands, because from the moment the northeast of the Netherlands (including Overijssel) had been made

Judenfrei, the action of sending the Dutch Jews to their death should have been completed. Officially there no longer were Jews in the Netherlands, except in the holding camps of Vught and Westerbork, but there they were already listed and ready for being checked off, and besides, they would stay there only for a short while. They were due to be pushed into cattle-cars and sent on to their deaths.

Gray officials desperately sought clarification, for the imbalance had to be addressed and corrected. However, the only conclusion drawn was that the list with the Jews who were called up was longer than the list of the Jews that actually showed up at their point of departure. Immediately, without delay, letters bearing black stamps arrived to announce that Jewish criminals had been left behind in Aryan society. As soon as possible they needed to be dragged out of their hiding places and offered up to the fiery maws of the Third Reich's Molech. These lists included the names of David and Betje, their children Louisie and Marianne, and also David's cousin, Truus. The five members of the De Lange family from Hellendoorn had also disappeared without a trace and their names too upset the German tally. Arnhem could not leave this situation without action. Jews had lost their right to their lives and should not stubbornly hang on to it. Even the Aryan citizens of the Netherlands would be exposed to Germany's iron fist to ensure no one dare lift a finger to help the fleeing Jews.

It was the same throughout all the provinces, and all those letters with their black stamps eventually ended up on the desk of Seiss Inquart, Hitler's representative in the Netherlands. After tallying up the numbers once again, he came to the disturbing conclusion that about 25,000 Jews had not answered the call for deportation. Those 25,000 Jews were not yet standing in the queue to the gas chambers of the East. They had managed to temporarily escape the otherwise well-oiled German murder machine.

In the next phase of the Final Solution to the Jewish Question, a hunt began. And this hunt would continue until the bitter end of WWII. It was a hunt orchestrated in the hell of Nazi philosophy. Men in uniform initiated house-to-house searches, and Jew hunters in neat, civilian suits, set out to ferret out a prey that might be hiding anywhere in the nooks and crannies of the occupied Netherlands. They dispersed north, south, east, and west, and turned over every stone. Hunters looking for a few guilders, the reward for betraying a Jew to the Gestapo, got busy and so did soldiers and policemen out of obedience or conviction. Opposite this phalanx stood the men and women of the resistance, mostly young but not always. Mostly poorly dressed but not always. Some acted out of a deep Christian belief in the sanctity of life, but there were also Jew hunters who quoted the Scriptures to justify their hatred of the Jews. The resistance had communists among its ranks who hated fascism and fought the occupation at every step of the way, including by a willingness to shelter Jews. The resistance was new, young, and naive; they learned by trial and error. For instance, it did not take the resistance long to realize that finding a hiding address for a Jew was not enough. One roof did not guarantee safety. The underground had to create a fallback option. To save a Jew there had to be more than one place where he or she could be moved to without advance warning.

The small remnant of those 140,000 Dutch Jews had to learn to live in deep secret. They continued living in cellars and attics, in small hollows dug into the floors under stables and pigsties or under ancient trees in the woods, and above haystacks in the countryside. In hidden annexes in the big cities. They had become shadow men and women. People struggling to survive without any protection of law. They were illegal oxygen users. And every day they had to hope that they would continue to survive that one too. And their protectors? They too were exposed to the same dangers, and yet, they spread their wings over the Jews in their care. Many did not survive the war because someone betrayed them, because they were discovered during a search. Because, because...

David and Betje Samuel and their two young daughters experienced those years of hiding in that way. There was no safe haven. Safety remained just beyond reach: a fata morgana in a desert of despair.

---

1. The German occupation appointed Jews to be the go-between between the German decisions concerning the Jews and the Jewish communities. In the Netherlands, there was really only one *Judenrat*, the one in Amsterdam, but there were satellite councils in the outlying areas which represented the Amsterdam council and passed on its decisions to the Jews in their community. Furthermore, the Germans appointed one person to pass on the new regulations to the Jews in the small communities. My father was the representative of the Jews of our village. He was forced into this role because he had always been an important member of the community and was active in public life from the time he was in his twenties.

2. The Netherlands had only one nation Jewish Council, but for every Jewish community there was a district representative. These representatives attended regular meetings in Amsterdam and were expected to follow its guidelines. Mr. Sigmund Menko opposed those guidelines, walked out of the meeting, and from that moment on, remained independent. Nijverdal-Hellendoorn followed the decisions made in Enschede.

3. https://europeanmemories.net/memorial-heritage/hollandsche-schouwburg-national-holocaust-memorial/

4. JOKOS is an organization founded in 1946. The acronym stands for Jewish Church Bonds and Social Organizations.

5. Since this book appeared in its Hebrew edition, in 2019, I learned that his first act as a free man was to search the village for Jewish people in hiding. He compiled a list of more than 120 names and aside from being the liaison for families looking for those hidden Jews, he also quickly became the "go-to" person for families with hidden Jewish children who wanted to give these young refugees a feeling of what might have been a Jewish vibe, perhaps a Shabbat meal. Hundred and twenty, mostly children, was tenfold the number of Jewish children who had lived in the village before the war. No wonder my father loved Nijverdal.

12

THE PERSECUTION: 1943-1945

Before 1940, about 140,000 Jews lived in the Netherlands, half of them in Amsterdam and the rest dispersed throughout the land. During the catastrophe now known as Shoah, 104,000 Jews were murdered, more than 75 percent of Dutch Jewry. Percentagewise, this was higher than anywhere else in western Europe. Just a few thousand returned from the concentration camps. This means, then, that the overwhelming majority of Dutch Jewry alive after 1945 was comprised of those who succeeded in evading their murder by going into hiding or by living under false identities out in the open. Some had managed to cross the border into neutral territory and returned after the liberation. Slowly, all surfaced from their secret lives and tried to make a new beginning. Eventually, they had to accept that their families had shrunk down to very few and that countless loved ones were no longer among the living. The destruction was so tremendous that it did not pass over any family. The survivors were a minority of what had been their prewar clans. This is an indisputable, historical fact. Now they had to deal with the aftermath of the war against the Jews. No graves were dug for parents, brothers, sisters, spouses, or children. The earth had swallowed those up as if they had never been. Such was the reality for the Jewish Netherlands in 1945. Humanity had never had to wrestle with such a situation. No learned theories existed to explain how that miserable remnant of 25,000 unmurdered Jews should take up the thread of their lives again.

In many cases, the prewar dwellings of the Jews had also been swallowed up. In Amsterdam, whole streets of the Jewish quarter had been stripped of their doors and window frames for firewood. Possessions that could be looted had disappeared and, in many cases, if the house remained standing and was livable, the German occupation offered it to Dutch Nazis who had no problems with fictitiously buying the homes of the deported Jews. The money they paid went to the German Reich. Thus, the Jews returned to a world that was no longer theirs. Help was not forthcoming, certainly not from the Dutch government.

Beyond all this, the returning Jews were burdened with what is now called survival guilt. They had survived the Shoah. They told themselves that they had been lucky. They were alive. And the dead?

The survival instinct, the need to earn a living, to raise children, and the everyday struggle to keep going, left little time for reflection and people tried, at least outwardly, to throw themselves into their prosaic daily occupations. Jews in the Netherlands did not organize large demonstrations if their homes were occupied by willing servants of the reign of German terror, and there was no authority to help the Jews to force the illegal tenants out. Whether consciously or otherwise, a collective decision was apparently made to put the war behind them. "We won't talk about this anymore. Draw a line under it. Nothing happened to us, we just went into hiding." They repressed their mourning, fury, and impotence over all that had been taken from them.

This is the world into which I was born. We were the only Jewish family left in a small village on the railway route to Zwolle, the provincial capital. It was clear to me that I was different from the children I played with, but I did not totally understand why. Inside our home were ghosts of the past, and my parents' whisperings were beyond me. I could neither explain them to myself nor ask to have them explained to me. The language in our home was different from that of the other neighborhood children, not only because Yiddish was woven into our Dutch, but also because my parents spoke in a code to which I lacked the key. I had no option but to draw my own conclusions, no matter how outlandish. I stopped asking for explanations. Words like concentration camps, gas chambers, deportations, arrests, fleeing and hiding, I associated with criminality. I constructed a fearful scenario and became afraid to ask my parents if I had it right: that I was the product of a criminal family, so criminal that many of our relatives had been condemned to die in the gas chamber. I carried this secret with me and hoped that my classmates would never know. The result was that just as my parents and older sisters, I kept silent and avoided bringing up topics that might release a storm. All that was left for me to do was to redeem myself by maturing into a solid citizen. I did try, but each time my mother sent me to the store, and I surreptitiously took a candy from the bin or enjoyed a few purloined raisins, I saw that my genes were stronger than me and I was already a criminal in my own right.

The historical truth came to the fore only after the Eichmann trial of the early 60s. He was on trial in Jerusalem for the murder of millions of Jews and the court proceedings were broadcast in the Netherlands. There he sat, a man with a crooked face, ensconced in a glass cage and behind him, a young Israeli soldier with a gun on his hip. I looked at that Eichmann, saw his misshapen, expressionless face. My father had a special definition for Eichmann's face that is untranslatable, he called it an ironed-out facade, but I knew that I was staring into the face of the devil. That non-human person had murdered Jews simply because they were Jews. This included my grandparents, uncle and aunts. This man had sent them to their deaths. We were not criminals. We were just as innocent as our non-Jewish neighbors. Perhaps I was 13 or 14 years old, but I had a powerful epiphany: like that soldier with the gun, like that judge in his black robes, I wanted to make sure that no man could ever again murder innocent people and I would live in that land where our executioners would not escape their punishment.

The thundering silence of our family existence started to rend a little.

Small cracks emerged just as it happened for the Jews in other lands. Here and there, my parents shared a few sentences about what their reality in the world before my birth had been. Among other things I learned that my parents were convinced that Hitler was not dead and even if he were, the evil that he had unleashed in the world was alive and well, and some other murderous individual would take up where he had left off to release a new wave of murder and mayhem against our people. We had to remain vigilant and be ready to flee at the first inkling of danger. We had to live from one day to the next, never letting down our guard. Now it also became clear to me why my mother was upset with my tomboy behavior, my chubby, dark-haired exterior. She worried that in time of danger, no one would be willing to rescue me because I did not listen!

The term *onderduiken* also became clear to me. My big sisters, Louisie and Marianne had found a home with courageous Dutchmen. There had been people who knowingly accepted the dangers inherent in rescuing two little Jewish girls and they had kept those children alive against all odds.

Louisie, almost five-years-old in 1943, arrived, once again in a narcotic sleep, at the Roelofs' family home in Hengelo. There too, the people thought that they needed to keep her only for one night, but that night grew into more than two years. The man of the house and his wife were no longer young; their children were all married, except for 18-year-old Trinie. During the day, she worked at the Ration Board's distribution office, where people came to collect their ration coupons. At night, Trinie was a courier for the resistance. She delivered illegal newspapers, transported false identification papers, or carried information from one group to the next. From the moment Trinie saw Louisie, she knew that this child was meant to be protected by her. Such a slender girl. Even in sleep, she looked traumatized. When she woke up, her eyes spoke volumes. Trinie could not let the child be passed on to another family. She had to keep her safe! "Mama," she said to her graying mother, "Sit down and listen to me, please, because we can easily keep her here! I can get a bigger food allotment through the resistance, and from now on, this little girl will be your granddaughter from Texel! She and I have the same color eyes, and even the same kind of hair. We can pull it off!" What could her parents do to stop their daughter? Yes, some difficult discussions ensued, but in the end Louisie stayed and became Wiesje Roelofs. A little girl they could send to kindergarten.

The cover story they spun around Wiesje was perfect. She was the daughter of one of their sons, the one who had moved his family to the island of Texel in the north of the Netherlands. All their other children lived in Hengelo, within walking distance. There were many grandchildren, and grandma and grandpa Roelofs enjoyed a close relationship with them all. The Roelofs were a highly respected, deeply religious, and conservative family, and everyone knew about Texel and Hitler's Atlantik wall, the German defenses against an invasion from the sea. Texel was a restricted military zone. No one entered, and no one left. And as it happened, Wiesje had been visiting her grandparents before the restriction on traffic to and from the island took effect, and she was stranded in Hengelo. They could not get her home. The child was absorbed into the Roelofs family and treated with love and care, as suits a little granddaughter separated from her parents. Still, when the Germans came too close to their street or when house-to-house searches took place in the neighborhood, Trinie simply left to spend the night by one of her siblings and took Wiesje along. One child more or less: no one paid any attention!

Louisie Samuel, then Wiesje Bemelaar, became Wiesje Roelofs for the final two years of the war; a child who grew up in the home of her Oma and Opa, and was deeply attached to her Auntie Trinie. And yet, at least 12 times she had to be hurriedly removed from her grandparents' home and taken to a different address within the family; during the final year of the war, she suffered the hunger Germany imposed on the Netherlands, and when it was all over, Wiesje/Louisie would always have a fragile constitution, malnourished during her formative years, and a child with severe asthma which stayed with her for the rest of her life. But in 1945 she was alive! Alive! Alive!

In 2014, while my daughter, Hani, and I were in the Netherlands to repair our bridges to the past, we sat for a while on a wooden bench across the home of my childhood, and almost hypnotically I started telling her how my big sister had been found, and how she returned to Nijverdal, not healthy but alive.

"Hani," I searched for a beginning. "My father was a person deeply aware of his status as a leading businessman and a maker and shaker who labored tirelessly to improve life for the local business community. He liked looking neat and always dressed with great care. He preferred gray, pinstriped, woolen suits, a white shirt, and a silk tie. When the weather got hot, he was willing to take off his jacket, although that revealed his suspenders, but he still always wore flannel underwear, summer and winter.

When he came to Israel, to see how Louisie, her husband, and two small sons had adjusted to their new home, he had prepared for the hot weather and arrived with a beautiful tailor-made tropical suit, short-sleeved shirt, and a khaki hat. But, his flannel long-johns and undershirt, that was something else. He did try to live without them. For an entire day he walked around in his tropical suit, jacket casually draped over his arm, his very visible suspenders holding up his pants, but he did not like how the clothes made him feel. The next day, it was 40 degrees in the shade, papa was still wearing his tropical suit with the short sleeves, but underneath he had his thermal underwear, sleeves rolled up, peeking out. He was dripping with sweat, but for that he had his huge red farmer handkerchief. Why else would he keep it in his pocket if not to wipe his forehead! One more day passed and he folded his tropical suit neatly, put it to sleep inside his suitcase, and with a sigh of relief, reverted to his well-known, trusted, woolen pinstripe. He accepted the heat with love, as long as he looked impeccably dressed, thermal underwear and all. "Ah, that was quite a story," I say with a sigh of pleasure, for I see him before me with that red bandana handkerchief in his hand, wiping his forehead, a huge smile on his face. Yes, my father loved routine. And yet, this interlude of an anecdote brings me back to the big story that was my father's life.

Papa kept to his routine throughout his life. Among other things, he always kept a roll of peppermints in his pocket. King peppermints, and now and then he rolled one of them into the palm of his hand and sucked it slowly. Till this day, if I have to describe my father, the aroma of peppermint and Old Spice are an indelible part of him. That, and the scent of our store, new fabrics and work clothing, linen, and blankets, are the cocktail of my father's essence.

It was always a special treat when papa allowed me to take two peppermints from the roll – one for me, and then one more for him. I was supposed to let it melt slowly in my mouth, make sure that I did not bite into the candy but to enjoy the lingering freshness of the peppermint on my tongue. He turned it into a game, "Want to see who keeps the candy the longest?" I always lost that bet, but it did not really matter.

Even something as innocent as two peppermints carry a story from that war, like everything in the world of my childhood.

I turn to Hani, but keep my inward gaze sharply focused on the story. "Well, it was like this, exactly like this, and this is how it has been written into our family annals: in April 1945, shortly after the end of the battle of Nijverdal, the liberation by the Canadian soldiers and the defeat of the Nazi regime, my parents set out to search for their children. With the assistance of the resistance, they found their first lead concerning the whereabouts of Louisie and Marianne. Someone in the village volunteered two bicycles without rubber tires, for like most natural resources, there was no rubber. They rode on the metal rims of the wheel, or perhaps the owner had succeeded in dressing the wheel in wood. Riding was hard and tiring, especially because they also had to battle against the wind. Hengelo was 40 kilometers away, and after their two years of sedentary life, they struggled on slowly. Now and then, David took hold of Betje's handlebars and pulled her along. Neither of them had the patience to rest along the way. They had to get where they were going as soon as possible. Was that little girl over there in Hengelo truly their daughter? No one knew for sure. And they rode on.

The Roelofs family had received notice that David and Betje were on their way to them, and Oma Roelofs stood at the window of the front room. The hand of her temporary granddaughter tightly held in hers. The girl wore a dress sewn for her by her mother, faded from the frequent washings, and stretched beyond normal use. Wiesje Roelofs, six-years-old already, stood at the window and looked outside, not sure what she was waiting for. She no longer really remembered her parents, but the moment she saw that man and woman get off their bikes, something moved in her. A distant memory floated up inside her dark head, and her huge blue eyes watched intensely as those people came into the house. For Betje and David there was no doubt: this was their child, the lost little girl, with David's eyes and her long, slender body. And she was alive. Yes, she was alive! Despite all the horror. She was pale, too thin, but there, before them, hiding behind her oma's skirts, was their first-born.

Very carefully, still hanging onto her grandmother, the girl took a few steps in Betje's direction, and the mother made a superhuman effort not to sweep the child up into her arms. For a second, she remained standing but then, suddenly knelt before the little girl, placed both her hands on that beloved small head with the silky hair, that big bow, and out loud she pronounced the blessing with which Jewish children are blessed every Friday night, before the Shabbat meal. *Veyesameach Elokim keSarah, Rivkah, Rachel, veLeah – May the L-rd make you like Sarah, Rebeccah, Rachel, and Leah – and then the priestly blessing Veyevarecheha HaShem Veyishmerecha; Yisah Hashem panav elecha vehhaneka; Yisah Hashem panav elecha veyasem leha shalom – May HaShem bless you and keep you, may He shine His countenance upon you and be gracious to you; May He lift up His countenance to you and grant you peace.*

The words come to Louisie from the fog of the long ago, and suddenly she knew. For the first time in more than two years, she was back in her own environment. She looked at the woman who had just spoken those words to her, "*Gut Shabbos*, mama," she said, triumphantly. And then her father approached and caressed her hair, touched that familiar head, and magically, produced a peppermint from his pocket. He had kept it carefully knotted up inside one of his huge, red handkerchiefs. He had two of them, hidden there like a miser, and had guarded them for over two years. For his children. A beacon of hope and faith, those candies. And now he handed the first one over to his first-born who immediately popped it into her mouth and sucked it with pleasure. Yes, she knew, and allowed the man to take her into his arms. The candy for Marianne will stay knotted up and hidden for a while yet, but even that candy will reach the right little girl, a little later, in a different province, a different town."

I remain seated on that wooden bench in front of our house, deep in thought, with my back toward number 30. Now Hani says something to me; she gently shakes my shoulder. I fall out of my time machine with a painful bang. The time is 2014 again. I have been telling this story to my beautiful Sabra-daughter, half in Hebrew, half in English.[1] "Do you want to leave?" I ask her, "Or shall we stay here a little while longer?" It is not too cold yet, and she gestures that she is ok with staying. "More stories, mama," she encourages me. And I obey. I have a story that I am allowed to release to the universe, the stars in the Milky Way, the planets, all the while seated in front of my father's house. In Nijverdal. And everything pales compared to this story. It will stop the world from turning and listen, resting on its axel for a heartbeat. Now there is only the story of two tortured parents and their lost children.

I know a great deal of Marianne's story, because her war-mother, Mother Dekker, saved detailed documentation of that time hidden in what I learned was called "Marianne's *onderduik* box". Shortly before Mother Dekker's death, she passed on the box to Marianne. "You are now old enough to understand and it is time that you learn how hard your parents fought to keep you safe," she said. At some point, my sister shared its contents with me, and she has given me permission to share it with all of you.

Marianne was that little girl who could carry a tune and loved to sing. After her beloved blankie had been returned to her tearful arms, Dr. Bakker succeeded in calming her down. She allowed herself to be lifted onto the luggage carrier of a young man's bike, threw her arms around him, and together they rode off down the street. Thus, started her journey to her new family. It was a long trek, and Marianne calmed herself by singing, sitting behind an absolute stranger. A two-year-old toddler escaping her murder, in the chilly spring of 1943. The rider loved how his little charge knew so many songs. It impressed him so, that after the war, after the liberation, after Marianne had already come home to Nijverdal, he went looking for her to make sure that his singing protegee had survived the war.

More than one rider was needed to finish this flight into uncertainty, and each time, Marianne was lifted onto another bike, behind a new courier. Perhaps the journey took more than one day, but eventually they arrived after she had sung "clap your hands" and "swinging high on my swing" over and over. Her riders had sung along with her and encouraged her to keep on singing in her high, clear soprano.

At the end of the first leg of her flight, Marianne arrived at Mother Dekker's across the Ijssel bridge, in the province of Friesland. The last rider lifted her down, hugged her for a moment, and together with her tiny valise, handed her over to the Dekker family. She waved goodbye to him but exhausted from the long trip, quickly fell asleep with her blankie in her arms. She was in Leeuwarden, the capital of Friesland, which only a short time ago had been the home of one of the Netherlands' largest Jewish communities. There had been a Jewish educational system, a beautiful synagogue, a rabbi, but all that had fallen silent. The Jews of Leeuwarden had been deported and only very few survived the war. Although the child knew nothing about this, she was one of the more than 100 hidden Jews of Leeuwarden.

The Dekker family ran a kind of emergency shelter for Jewish children. They came, spent one night at Mother Dekker's home, were fed, given a clean bed, and as soon as possible, perhaps the very next day, the children were sent on to what would hopefully be safe homes. A permanent diving address. The Dekker home remained that fallback haven, where, in time of need, the children could be sent if their location had been compromised. The Dekker family also took care of supplying the hidden children with ration coupons and other necessaries.

Marianne slept; Mrs. Dekker had put her own young children to bed, and now she finally had the time to read the letter that had arrived with the little girl. The letter from the child's mother. Betje related her daughter's history from conception. She neither glossed over the facts nor made excuses. She simply started with the moment she discovered that she was pregnant at the very moment their entire world came crumbling down. She related her attempts to convince her doctor to abort the unborn child. It was all there, up to the moment she returned home with her empty stroller, a loaf of bread and a few potatoes. She wrote how Dr. Bakker had promised to rescue her child and that he had kept his word. There were even a few words about Louisie.

Deeply moved, Mother Dekker folded the letter and returned it to its envelope. Her hands in her lap. In those few pages, a young mother had described the entire tragedy of the Jews. She nodded to herself in the halo of the one small reading lamp. She knew that she and her husband had made the right decision when they had joined the resistance in its efforts to rescue Jewish children. She also knew that the dangers to herself were irrelevant. In a world where innocent children could be torn from the arms of loving parents, she did not see how they had any choice but to "join in" as they had and she knew she would never have forgiven herself had she remained a bystander, perhaps clucking in sympathy but without lifting a finger. Children moving like driftwood through a stony river toward an unknown shore needed the protection of people like herself, those who had pushed aside their own comfort and safety for the sake of those innocent babies.

She hid Betje's letter deep inside one of her drawers. It must never be found. But that night, in bed with her husband, she whispered to him that they must do more. Help more children. Work harder in their rescue efforts.

The next day, she let her hands do the work for her. She woke up the little girl and gave her a bath after she had gently poured peroxide over Marianne's ink black curls. Black was a dangerous color there in the blond northern regions. From now on, someone would bleach the toddler's hair every week, before black roots could emerge and give her away. For the rest of the war, Marianne had hair that was almost orange in color. When it was dry, the woman dressed her in clean clothes, and shortly after, a young courier came to take Marianne on the next leg of her journey. Further into the northern country. A little girl just turned two in January, adrift in a world that had gone insane. And here and there some righteous people stumbled against the current to reach out to her. The little girl no longer objected to the bicycle rides and obediently put her arms around the biker in front of her, but she had stopped singing.

They had already left the city behind, entered the countryside far away from the urban clutter, into fields full of produce, farms dotting the tilled earth. They passed homes where blond people reside, and no one gave Marianne with her blue-green eyes and orange hair a second glance. Her light skin blended perfectly in the landscape, and her black curls had already gone into hiding. She might have looked more exotic before the peroxide, but her black hair would have drawn too much attention. She had become a Friesian child with carrot-hair.

Somewhere among the planted fields and orchards, a man and a woman in traditional dress stood on the path, waiting, tense, full of expectation. From far they saw the biker and impatiently they waited for what he was bringing to them: a child! A child! And what a lovely little girl. They embraced her tightly, took her inside with joy. And there, in the warm kitchen, they first fed her. Then they removed her city clothes and dressed her in red wooden shoes, pretty, traditional clothing with embroidered edges, and braided her hair. Now she was theirs! Marianne quickly learned the local language, so different from the queen's Dutch. Very soon she learned to call her protectors *hait* and *mem* (Friesian for father and mother). Her new parents took her everywhere. Their daughter, so small and so sweet, yet with that strange orangey hair. Till Marianne came, their farm had been so silent. There had been no children's voices, but now she had arrived and brought them new life. She was Marianne D. B., their new daughter. They spoiled her with all that the farm produced in abundance. She accompanied her parents to church, her father whittled toys for her while her mother sewed clothes for straw-stuffed dolls. They indulged her and surrounded her with love. *Hait* and *mem* had been promised that should the child's biological parents not survive the war; they would be allowed to raise her. This was not unusual in the occupied Netherlands. The resistance used every ruse to convince people to take in Jewish children. Sometimes the temporary foster families did not even know that the children in question were actually Jewish. In Friesland, Marianne learned to say her prayers before going to sleep. She was raised to be a devout Protestant, exactly like all the other children in the community. This was one more way to help the Jewish children to blend in, to keep them safe, and to integrate them into their new environment. The better adjusted they were, the safer they were. And so, Marianne walked to church, holding her *hait* and *mem*'s hands, dressed in the same bulky dresses with pinafores as the other little girls. Her mama and papa in Nijverdal became vague memories which slowly dissipated. Even Louisie was forgotten. Marianne spoke Friesian and drew no special attention. She was an easy-going child who loved to sit near her mem as she worked in the kitchen. And hait and mem? Their happiness knew no bounds. There was a child who lit up their world. A child, all of a sudden, who came to them like a miracle.

Even when Marianne had already returned to her Jewish household, and even when I had already learned to speak, she still said the prayer that she had learned when she lived in Friesland: "Dear Jesus, make me pious so that I may go to heaven." In Dutch, the prayer is a gentle rhyme, but the fact that I heard her recite it, and even wanted to say it with her, clearly shows how Marianne's years in hiding had marked her life. Unfortunately, while she may have been a beloved little Friesian girl during those war years, she was never safe. Her safety was an illusion that could implode at any second. Notwithstanding the remoteness of the village and the geographical distance from the seat of power, Jew hunters could arrive to hunt for prey, and it was always open season. Someone might let a few words slip about a little girl with strange hair who had come out of nowhere. So, when danger loomed close, Marianne was put into a narcotic sleep to be transported to a new place or returned to the Dekker home. To be rescued all over.

When Mother Dekker held Marianne in her arms for a second time, she was incapable of sending her away again. The Dekker family had two young sons, almost of the same age as the little Jewish refugee, but the girl was so tiny, they could pass her off as a precocious little sister. To realize this scenario, the Dekker family pulled up roots, left Leeuwarden and settled somewhere across the Ijssel bridge, not far from the Ijsselmeer Lake. Mr. Dekker, known as White Cees, because he turned gray at an early age, left all his other resistance work and the family focused on keeping Marianne safe. That is how she became their daughter, and Mrs. Dekker became Mother Dekker. When people asked about the girl's strange hair color, her "mother" explained that the carrot hair was something the child had inherited from her grandmother. "She had the same hair." "What a pity," people said, "otherwise a sweet child." And Mother Dekker nodded in commiseration. Every week, she bleached Marianne's hair, and still the child was not safe. The Dekkers kept to themselves, did not show up in town too often and the girl knew not to wander outside the garden. Sometimes, they would go to the lake together, but the moment strangers came to town Marianne was kept indoors. And when even that was too dangerous, she would be sent back to hait and mem. Until the danger had passed. Until she could return to Mother Dekker, to Ermelo, the town where the family now resided.

Nobility of soul does not stop with one single act. People like the Dekkers have a place in their heart that knows the suffering of others, and so they thought of David and Betje despite the dangerous lives they were living to save their child. They thought how horrible it was that the parents had no idea whether their daughter was alive. That is how in 1944, in a miraculous manner, via the resistance, a photo of a three-year-old girl arrived in Nijverdal. By way of the Overduin group, via *Dominee* Hijmans, and ended up in the Scheffer family's bakery at 18 Kerkstraat. There was Marianne, laughing and playing at the lake, together with her two foster brothers.

The child! She was alive! She was growing and looked healthy!"

———

"Mama," Hani says to me, "Do you know all of that from Mother Dekker's *onderduik* box?"

"No, well, actually, yes, but you are interrupting me. I am not done yet. May I continue?"

"Sorry," she answered with a shy smile and gestured for me to continue my story.

Not long after this photo arrived in Nijverdal, a new Jew hunter arrived in Ermelo, and Marianne had to disappear without warning. This time there was no time to send her to hait and mem and she was evacuated to a new address, a new family. I know that the man's name was Jan de Vries, and that there already was another little Jewish girl in that household. Marianne had learned long ago that it was not worth crying over her sudden sleepovers in a new place. She was here and then there, and then back to the first place. Tears would change nothing. She accepted her nomadic life the way many hidden children learned to do. Her blankie had disappeared many flights ago in the labyrinth of escaping danger. Marianne learned to self soothe by caressing her dress and face, until her tears were deeply suppressed.

She remained at the De Vries home for some time; she could not tell me how long exactly, but at some point, Father Dekker or perhaps a courier, came to pick her up again. Less than 24 hours later, the De Vries household was woken up by a loud banging on the door, and a Dutch policeman roughly entered and demanded a house search. His turning over of furniture, opening deep closets and moving sofas and beds unearthed a little girl a few days after her fourth birthday, sitting on a low stool behind the clothes in a deep wardrobe. She was arrested and deported to Westerbork. Her name was Hetty.

Perhaps there are even miracles in hell, and if so, then Hetty's story may be one of those. To begin with, she survived the war. A little toddler of about four, all alone. After the liberation she was even reunited with her biological mother, but from the moment she was torn away from her war foster parents, she walked a path of suffering that is almost impossible to describe, especially since she lived in spite of everything that happened to her.

She wound up in Westerbork, the final holding pen on Dutch soil. From there, Jews were shipped to their murder in the east. The year is 1944, the final year of the war. Hetty was housed in quarters for children who had arrived in Westerbork unaccompanied by any adult. Some of those children were so young that they did not even know their real name. This group of the so-called "unknown children" became the focus of a fierce battle between the Dutch resistance and the German occupation. There were about 50 such children in the camp and the resistance made valiant attempts to prove that this was a group of Aryan orphans, the offspring of resistance fighters who had been executed. The Germans were already losing the war, and somehow did not completely reject this claim. The unknown children were kept apart from the other prisoners and received slightly better food than the other children in Westerbork. After all, murdering Aryan children was not the objective. The camp authorities assigned caregivers to the children who were to make sure that the orphans were safe, and they stayed with the group until the liberation. They accompanied them to Auschwitz, for the Germans needed the space in Westerbork, but as their identity was still unclear, the "unknown children" were kept separately there too, and they were also kept off the lists for the gas chambers. One of the children died of disease, but the others survived. Alive but not necessarily healthy. Some of them, including Hetty, fell into the clutches of the notorious Dr. Mengele. Mengele pierced her ear drum and left her permanently hearing impaired.[2]

Marianne's miracle was timing. She had left the De Vries household one day before the disaster of Hetty's capture. Marianne, blissfully unaware what had happened in the wake of her departure, returned to Mother Dekker and remained there until her parents found her.

I remain seated without further comment. What else should I say? I know the rest of Hetty's story too. I know that she emigrated to Melbourne, Australia, together with her mother and an older sister. I tracked her down because I thought finding her might please my sister, Marianne, who had told me about her stay at the De Vries home. I thought perhaps they might share some of their stories if they could meet again, the child that was safe and the child that wasn't.

I had friends in Melbourne and based on the few details I had of Hetty's biography, someone realized that they knew her. It turned out that Hetty even had a third sister – a woman younger than her – who still lived in the Netherlands and whom Hetty visited regularly. I arranged a meeting after Marianne reluctantly agreed, but Hetty was enthusiastic and excited about meeting the girl she knew about, for she had maintained regular contact with De Vries, and less frequently, so had my sister, but the two women, while they knew of each other's existence, had never been in contact. My sister, Marianne, a tortured soul, and Hetty met over coffee somewhere near Amsterdam. Neither were young any longer, nor were they innocent children. For my sister, fragile and fearful from her years as a hidden child, this meeting was too traumatic. In my innocence I had assumed I was doing a good thing, but I had done the opposite. Perhaps for Hetty it was a better experience, for after this coffee get-together, Hetty and I corresponded for a while, and she told me more of her story. A brave woman, this Hetty, a fighter, who had built a life for herself, found love, had a family, and looked upon the world with compassion.

I cannot find the words to tell Hani how badly I had hurt her aunt, and so we simply continue to sit there in silence. My daughter waits patiently for my next utterance, but I choose to remain dumb. She touches my shoulder. The story has stagnated on the wrong side of the Ijssel, but she is not satisfied with that. "Mama, not fair! And then? Don't stop talking now! This is your time to tell me."

I take a deep breath. I accept the responsibility of doing my share in our joint search after knowledge. As long as her hand rests on my shoulder, I feel the courage to continue, but I let a few months flow silently down the river of our story.

"The day after my parents found Louisie, they were still at the Scheffer home and had yet to find Marianne. They hoped to pick up her trail by going back to where my mother had left her more than two years ago: at Dr. Bakker's villa. The reunion with the doctor was an emotional one. He was beside himself with joy to discover that the parents of his little protegee had survived the war, and he told David exactly how Marianne had been taken further and further into the warren of the resistance. Of course, the hope was that all the links of the underground were unbroken and could be traced. They had to get to Leeuwarden, but the city was much too far away to reach by bicycle. David and Betje needed a car. David, determined and creative as always, presented himself at the Canadian command post in Nijverdal. His story fell on sympathetic ears, and the commander offered his help by supplying an army jeep. That left only payment for fuel and although David had been stripped of all his worldly goods by the Germans, he still had friends and reached out to Van Aragon, one of the wealthiest residents of the village. The two men had been good friends before the war, and Van Aragon signed for the gas without hesitation. Betje did not come along on this trip. She would not leave her newly returned daughter. A Canadian soldier took the wheel, David slid into the passenger seat, and they drove towards Zwolle. Everything went smoothly until they reached the Ijssel. The bridge across the river had been blown up, and civilians could not cross into Friesland.

Allied soldiers moved back and forth across the river in dinghies, but David was not allowed to hitch a ride with them, and the far bank might as well have been a million miles away. Marianne was right there just on the other side, but there was no bridge. Friesland was still a closed military zone, and no matter how persuasive he was on the Overijssel side of the river, he was not allowed to cross. The soldiers saw his despair and took pity on him. They suggested that if he wrote a letter to the family where he believed his daughter to be, they would deliver it across the water.

Someone handed him a postcard, and David, faced with its limited space, wrote the most important note of his entire life. He wrote in tiny script, but his words filled the universe:

Greetings, my name is David Simon Samuel, and I have information that you have a Jewish girl in your home. I believe her to be my daughter. Her name is Marianne. She is almost four but was always small of stature. Her hair is curly. I am on my way to you but am stranded by the Ijssel... Please do not hand her over to anyone else, because I am on my way.

Sincerely, D. S. Samuel

The postcard travels across the river and is sent back. It is given a different trajectory and arrives at another address. There too, the postcard is returned but always just as far as the river crossing. It continues to wander around the area, sees the destruction of the war, but does not reach the Dekker family for quite some days. It could not find the Dekkers in Friesland because they were no longer there, after all, they had moved to Ermelo to keep a little Jewish child safe. In fact, David did not have to cross the Ijssel at all, but he did not know this. His message continued its search, but in Nijverdal, none of that was known, and the Samuel family waited for news from the people they hoped were the rescuers of their second child. Day after day, they waited, and after perhaps three weeks, a note arrived. Mother Dekker had received the postcard and hurried to respond. David and Betje opened the letter together, because neither had the courage to open it on their own. David brought his letter opener from somewhere in the house, but Betje pulled the envelope from his hands and tore it open. She pulled out a sheet of paper, written in tiny letters, but then lost her courage and handed the still folded letter to her husband. "Read it to yourself. Perhaps it is very bad news." David let his eyes fly over the lines and saw what it was all about. With a shaky voice, he read to her:

Dear Samuel family. We do not live in the far north. We live in Ermelo, south of the Ijssel, about one-and-a-half hours from Nijverdal. We wait for you with great joy and hope to meet you very soon. We hope that the adorable little girl who has been as our daughter for two years and more, is indeed your child. Please know that she is healthy and happy and that we love her very much. Best wishes, the Dekker family.

This time the jeep drove without hold-ups to the sleepy town where the Dekker family lived. In the house, they found not only Mother Dekker and White Cees, but also hait and mem, who were nervously waiting for the man who claimed to be the girl's father. They had wanted to raise her. They had wanted to be her parents, and they were ready to fight the Samuels for custody of the child. After all, from the day she came toward them on the path, it had been a given that the girl's parents would probably not survive the war!

From the moment he enters, David has eyes only for the little girl in the center of the "good" room. She is leaning against Mother Dekker's knee, but David has no doubt that she is his child. She is wearing an outfit that Betje sewed for her from some material from his store. The pants are too short on her. Marianne seems introverted, like always, but for a second, she raises her eyes to him. Those eyes! They are her mother's, Betje's beautiful eyes. His heart beats like a drum, and he only wants to scoop up the daughter he has not lost, a miracle, a miracle. He wants to run with her. Leave and bring her to her mother, but he knows that he cannot do so. Etiquette must be observed. He looks the little girl straight in her blue-green eyes, pulls a peppermint from his pocket and offers it to her with a smile. "Look what I saved for you!" She accepts the candy, examines it for a moment, and then pushes it happily into her mouth and sucks on it with pleasure. The taste is familiar somehow. She smiles at the kind man with the candy. And now what? The families talk among themselves, and it is decided that Marianne needs some time to adjust to the idea that she is about to leave Mother Dekker's home and return to Nijverdal to her biological family.

Hait and mem cannot let Marianne go, and David thinks that perhaps the best thing is to give them a little time, or at least to help them come to the realization that the situation is what it is. He agrees to let her stay in Ermelo a little longer. "We will all get used to the new realities. We will continue to visit here, also with Louisie." David sees the visits back and forth as a kind of statement, an acknowledgement of everything the rescuers of his younger daughter have done to keep her alive. He also wants to acknowledge the difficulty of the war-foster families to let his daughter go. Every time the Samuel family arrives, Mother Dekker shares with David that hait and mem are pressuring her to release Marianne into their custody, and while David tries to be sympathetic, he has no solution, aside from once again, to express his gratitude to them. In the end, he cuts this painful knot as gently as he can, and Marianne returns to Nijverdal. A few days later, his heart overflowing, David writes a second postcard to the Dekker family:

Dear Dekker family, now we are all home again, but Marianne asks us when we will let her go back to her mama and papa and her brothers. In spite of the difficulties, there was an immediate bond with our Louisie. Our house had been damaged in the bombardments, and part of it is uninhabitable but we are alive. We will never forget the amazing thing you and the D. B. family did for us. We will never forget your noble actions. I promise that Marianne will come to you for sleepovers. Meanwhile, many of our relatives are missing. We are searching for them. I would like to leave the village, but I must provide for my family. I have sent out some letters of solicitation and hope to get a job offer soon. As far as everything else is concerned, the Dutch government tells me to be patient, for they first have to take care of the war victims. Once again, our deep gratitude for everything you have done for us.

Sincerely, D. S. Samuel

I am going to ignore the sentence about war victims for a moment, except to say that it will haunt my father and other Jewish Shoah survivors for years to come. The shameful attitude of the Dutch government has become known by the term the little Shoah and I will return to this topic later. What is important now, is the fact that the Dutch Jewry had to experience and survive both the big and the little Shoah. They came back out in the open after years of secret survival in hidden nooks and crannies, from cellars to chicken coops, and now, while not a single German soldier remains on Dutch soil and the family has returned to 82 Rijssensestraat, life certainly has not returned to normal. Among other things, letters from the D. B. family continued to fall on the Samuel doormat with repeated discussions about Marianne's future. Hait and mem had not yet given up the hope to be allowed to raise her. "We have nothing, aside from that girl," they wrote, "And you already have one other," and to Betje, "And you are already pregnant again." The latter was like an accusation. In another letter they wrote, "We were the ones who rescued the child, and we are entitled to have her with us."

How is it possible to fight with the people who took in your baby and kept her safe, notwithstanding the dangers inherent in their actions? David and Betje have no idea how to bring this episode to a close, and one evening when they were visiting friends, they share their dilemma of who has the right to raise Marianne. She lived with the rescuers longer than with her biological parents. Does that, then, give those people the right to claim her as their own? Perhaps David and Betje have no choice but to relinquish her? The couple –need I add that they are not Jews? –across the living room does not even understand this question, and their answer is simple and direct, "Those good Dutchmen did indeed save your daughter. For her and for you. They kept her safe for her parents. Marianne is not a prize in some devilish lottery!"

David and Betje do their best to allow the D. B. family some quality time with their little girl, and over several years, she traveled to Friesland and stayed with her hait and mem for part of the summer vacation. Every time she arrived, they quickly got her out of her city clothes, put her in traditional clothing and put wooden shoes on her feet, just as they had done the first time. Again, she went to church with them, and for a short time, became their Marianne D. B. However, it was always made clear that the question of adoption was off the table, and slowly, the connection became less intense, and eventually ended. They did not come to Marianne's wedding, for they were busy that day, but Mother Dekker was there, and she, together with the bride and groom's mothers, accompanied her to the wedding canopy. Three mothers brought her to her bridegroom! Marianne's children had three grandmothers. Even her grandchildren met their super Oma. This was the woman who had given all of them life, even if not birth-life. And when Mother Dekker closed her eyes for the last time, Marianne was there to give the eulogy, together with this exceptional woman's biological children.

While no formal steps were ever taken to give her and her husband recognition as Righteous Gentiles, there is no doubt that their name belongs among its ranks. This book will serve to honor them. I add that people like Mother Dekker are but few in this world, and yet, they are the ones who keep this world from imploding into chaos.

---

1. A Sabra is a native Israeli.
2. https://www.youtube.com/watch?v=hMNxBmB1lE0. Very interesting documentary on the topic with English subtitles.

13

THE SCHEFFER FAMILY: 1943-2006

My father taught me all about life in the large macroworld outside and the microworld of our store. About the Scheffer family he simply said, "If you need shelter, just run to the Scheffers as fast as you can." In my child's eyes this was good advice, for the public school where I was a first-grade pupil was almost next door to their home. I knew the family quite well and referred to the baker and his wife as uncle and aunt. Yes, they lived in such a nice village house, and it always smelled of fresh bread. Yes, I loved going to see them, their farm-like home with the open central hall, the swept yard and vegetable patch. Of course, my father meant to teach me that the Scheffers would help me in time of emergency, but I did not know anything beyond the deep respect my father felt for the people. I did not really know they had rescued him and my mother. To me, my father encouraged me to run to their home when it rained. They lived much closer to school, and in the soggy Dutch countryside, it happened regularly that I ran to their house, jacket over my shoulders, hair in the wind, and wound up on Tante Henk's doormat like a wet cat. I announced that I had come for shelter, just as my father had told me to do. The entrance, called the *delle* in Dutch, was the central space of the home and housed the bakery, but I only had eyes for an amazingly beautiful grandfather clock that was decorated with copper ornaments, and on top, Atlas lifting the world. All that, my father had explained to me once when we visited together. I was also fascinated by the doors to the rooms off the *delle* which all had stained glass windows with red and blue panels. Tante Henk let me in, laughing a little because my father had already apologized for my misunderstanding of his admonition to seek shelter, and she let me stay until the sky cleared a little. She then helped me into my coat, pulled its hood over my damp hair, pushed a piece of fresh bread into my hand and sent me home with a reminder to say hello to my mother and father. And that is what I did, but after a few rainy weeks and my continued sheltering at the bakery, my father was afraid I might become a nuisance and explained something about different kinds of sheltering. Well, sometimes even the native language is confusing to a child! To the Scheffers he explained that I knew Hitler was not chasing me, and that I was simply running from the rain. "The child knows nothing of all that," he added to ensure that no one else would enlighten me.

Sometimes, however, after I came back from sheltering at the Scheffers, suddenly there was a story, assuming that papa was in a good mood. He invariably started with the same words, "When mama and I were in *onderduik* at the Scheffers... " and when he saw that I pricked up my ears, he would continue. "Suddenly there was nothing for me to do, and I did not know how to fill those empty hours. Doing nothing made time go even more slowly. The clock stood still, just as the hot air on sultry summer days. I felt that I was suffocating. I asked papa Scheffer to please let me help with something. Your mama and I sat in one room for an entire day and kept quiet. The room was at the front of the house, and we could only talk in whispers, because the younger children did not know we were there. We were so afraid! Only when the two youngest, Tony and Henny, had gone to bed, did mama and papa Scheffer invite us into the kitchen, to let us relax a little. They always saved food for us, which mama Scheffer kept warm at the back of the big stove, and we could talk a little with the adults in the household." I knew that story by now, but my father told it with great dramatic gestures, and I loved the way he told it. I did not understand all the nuances but that did not matter. For instance, my father never explained why they could not simply live in our house, but like the majority of his generation, he assumed that the children born in the "after era", simply knew everything through osmosis. Even the word "diving" was puzzling. That word made no sense. I had never heard it in any other figurative context and I needed to figure out what it meant by myself. Diving and under. Hmmm. So many of the stories in our home started with those words. Under and diving. I assumed that although the Scheffer house was not under water, there still had to be a possibility of diving there somehow, perhaps like Dagobert Duck, Donald's uncle, who dove into his mountain of coins. Adults knew to do so many things for which I was still too young. And despite all that, I never asked for explanations. I did not want papa to call me his Alte Bobelte, that child who misunderstood everything. If papa said they dove, then they did. They were diving at the Scheffers and that was a fact. Logic was less important. My father continued, "Papa Scheffer understood that doing nothing all day was difficult for me and gave me the task of gluing the ration coupons which people handed in to show their entitlement to their daily allotment of bread onto special cards. You see, everyone was given a certain number of those coupons based on the number of people in the family. Papa Scheffer would take all those used coupons, glued onto the cards, back to the Ration Board's distribution office and receive enough flour to bake more bread for all his customers. Everything was measured out carefully by the enemy – no more and no less than what he was entitled to. In this manner, the Germans were able to keep a close eye on what the population consumed, and the tally had to add up. That meant that illegals, such as those who were in hiding, did not have ration booklets and so could not buy any food. This made it harder for them to find shelter. The Scheffers received their allotment of flour and other ingredients needed for their business and with this they had to make do." "And then?" I asked, although I practically knew this story by heart. It was such a nice tale, funny even, and I loved to hear papa tell it again and again. He would pull a dramatic face and wave his hands around with theatrical gestures. "Shhh, keep quiet for a minute. You have no patience!" he said in a stern voice, but he was not angry. I saw that crooked smile of his in the corner of his mouth. "I wanted," papa continued, "to stretch out the gluing down of the coupons on the cards for as long as I could, for I was happy to have something to do with my hands, and besides, those coupons reminded me a little of my stamp collection." I nodded in agreement. I knew all about my father's stamps. He was an enthusiastic collector of Dutch stamps and owned an almost complete collection. He kept abreast of sales and attended auctions. He also read the stamp collector's monthly magazine, called *Het Stokpaardje* (The Hobby Horse), the collector's bible. I loved his albums almost as much as he did, and I also knew a great deal of patience is required to handle stamps without damaging them. And so, I imagined my father, carefully lifting and placing those bread coupons on the cards before gluing them down. "I handled them one by one and made sure that they all fitted together seamlessly in straight columns. When I was finally done, it was hard to say which were the new sheets of serrated, unused ration cards, and which the used ones. Papa Scheffer took the cards I had prepared and returned them to the Ration Board for his allotment of flour."

"And then?" I felt I needed to cheer him on to get him to continue this story. "And then," my father said, "Papa Scheffer handed those perfectly glued down coupons to the clerk behind his desk and asked for the permit for new ingredients for the bakery. That man picked up the cards and examined them. 'How in the world did you ever have the time to glue them down so neatly? Don't you have anything else to do?' he blurred out, rather perplexed. Papa Scheffer got so scared, that for a second, he did not know what to say. No one had even considered that handing over a coupon sheet looking like that might be a problem. He had to give a plausible answer. 'Ach,' he said with a shamefaced half smile, 'I had my children do it, and warned them to be careful and make sure the cards came out looking neat.' And he smiled again, although he thought everyone in the office could see his knees shaking with fear. 'Yes,' he admitted. 'They did go overboard a little.' As he walked away with the documents he needed to buy his supplies, Papa Scheffer realized how fragile and tenuous life had become, and how easily he might collapse the entire house of cards that had become their existence. And from that moment on," my father concluded, "I continued to take great care with the coupons, but now I made sure that the cards came out looking as if it had been done in a rush with the coupons stuck down helter-skelter."

The story of the gluing of the used ration coupon cards stayed with me until I was finally allowed to return it to the Scheffer family in Calgary, Canada, when I came as the emissary of my parents to honor theirs in 2007.

"Papa, tell me another story about the time you were in hiding at the Scheffer home?!" To my father's great sorrow, the Scheffers had left the Netherlands in 1952 and were living in Alberta, Canada. He had even taken me by the hand to go and see all their stored possessions in some huge shed in the village, ready for shipment. He only said, "The Scheffers are leaving," and could not hold back his tears. The day they actually left Nijverdal, we all stood on the sidewalk to wave them out. Marianne was worried because she did not believe that the ramshackle bus they were on would get them all the way to Canada. There was also talk in our home that we would join the Scheffers later on. To start a new life together with them. But, like so often before, we remained in Nijverdal.

Here and there, papa released some other stories about the years of *onderduiken*: "It was my task to listen to the BBC broadcasts. What we heard gave us courage to hold on one more day. We did not often turn on the radio because it was so dangerous. The Germans drove around in special vans equipped with sensors that could pick up whether anyone was receiving radio broadcasts. Radios were illegal and if one was discovered hiding one, there were dire consequences, but the Scheffers had so many forbidden things in their home that the radio was but a minor issue. I turned the receiver on, waited patiently till the lamps warmed up and I could hear something. To keep the room quiet and to make sure the little ones did not see us, mama Scheffer would place a chair in front of the door to the room with the radio and me, and the children knew not to open the door then. As soon as the radio was ready, I put on the headset and listened intently to the news. Afterwards, I passed on the information to the family."

This story, about my father listening to the English BBC broadcasts, returned to Canada to the Scheffers, where it found a crystal clear echo and more details surfaced. It started when my Dutch nephew handed me a hardbound notebook. This was the year 2004, when I had come to the Netherlands for my mother's funeral. She had died at the ripe old age of 94. I arrived with my brother-in-law, Ab, and we made it in time to say our goodbyes. He spoke to me as we walked into the nursing home where she had spent her final decade. "You need to sit down next to your mother, and you have to forgive her for everything that was wrong between you. And then you have to ask her to forgive you for everything you did to her." He had never been more serious. Ab was like a beloved big brother. I never considered arguing with him, so I did exactly as told.

Mama lay on her high bed and was deep in a morphine induced, narcotic sleep. The morphine pump sighed in sadness every few seconds, every time it dispensed some more drops of forgetfulness. She lay there, breathing laboriously. A blanket was pulled up high under her chin. The room was in semi-darkness. Close to death, her facial features had softened and she looked serene. I walked around the bed and gently touched her arms, legs, face, and breast, without turning down the duvet that covered her, and asked my mother to forgive me. "It is all good now, mama. You can rest. You can go to your papa and *moesje*, to your Bela and Louis. They have waited for you for so long." I could not kiss her. The bed was too high and I was afraid to lean over her fragile body. Instead, I took her hand in mine for just a moment and burst into tears. When that was over, I stood up, said the Hebrew prayers for a dying person, and just for certainty, also said the 91st psalm, the family psalm, and left her in peace. That night my mother closed her eyes forever, surrounded with gentle nursing care and the certainty that all her four children had come to release her. It was a Monday, and in keeping with the Jewish tradition, we wanted to bury her the very next day. We received the dispensation to do so, and on Wednesday, Ab and I flew back to Israel because I wanted to spend my days of mourning in the bosom of my family there.

Dave, my nephew, gave me the notebook after the funeral. "We found it in Opa's safe," he said. Yes, his grandfather, my father, thus. "Mama gave it to me because she thought I might be interested in its contents. And I did try to continue the collection I found there, but I am no longer interested in it now. Maybe you would like to have it," and he placed the dark notebook in my hands.

Still emotional from the funeral and without paying much attention, I accepted the notebook and glanced at its cover: POST CURIOSA, it said. On the first page, my father had glued an envelope mailed from Switzerland, but, according to the caption, the post stamps were German. Well, ok, I thought. If this was the level of my father's curious collection, I also would not be too interested in the notebook. Still, my father had been such an avid collector. He saved everything, organized matchbook covers, cigar bands, strange snippets of paper in notebooks, and liked to leaf through them on Sunday mornings, when the store was closed. I looked through the entire curiosa but did not see anything that drew my attention beyond a cursory glance. And yet, my father had saved that notebook for 30 years. In his safe, no less. And even Dave had kept it from 1975, when my father died, till now, 2004. He had even glued a generic Christmas card on the notebook's final page, his one and only contribution to the post curiosities. I took this collection of uniquely uncurious curiosa home, left it in the cabinet with other items from the past, and forgot all about it.

A few years before that, in the Netherlands, for my yearly visit with my mother in the nursing home, Krönnenzömer, I sat next to her bed and tried to fill my long, empty hours. After all, I was in Nijverdal, and perhaps people I had once known still lived there. I found a phone book. Yes, they still had them at the end of the 20th century and searched for familiar names. Herman Flim was listed, although the bakery was long gone. I called and he was pleased to have a member of the Samuel Prins family come to visit.

On the mantle above the hearth, Herman's wife had placed the medal from Yad Vashem, awarded to Herman and his parents in recognition for their rescue of almost 100 Jewish children.[1] It was during that visit that Herman told me how he had accompanied my grandfather Jacob on his horrible journey to Vught. "He was so afraid," he said. Then we turned to more neutral topics for a while, but my ulterior motive for the visit had been to find out if they were in contact with any of the Scheffer children and could give me an address. After all, Herman's mother and Tante Henk were sisters. Hennie Scheffer's Nanton address was quickly found. As soon as I got back to my hotel room, I started writing a letter to her which I finished only after I had returned to Haifa. A lively correspondence ensued. I started by writing how my sisters and I had never forgotten how the Scheffer family had helped our parents in spite of the danger to themselves. I once again expressed my feelings of respect and gratitude. Hennie responded with an enthusiastic letter of her own and described how my letter had moved her, and that she had immediately shared it with her siblings. Among other things, I wrote to her about my mother's deteriorating health, and that our families had flourished. While our letters flew back and forth across the ocean, I suddenly understood that perhaps Hennie knew some things about my parents' years in hiding that I might want to hear. Perhaps she could supply some pieces of the puzzle with what she knew of my parents' lives during the war.

Slowly the image of our existence clarified as Hennie lovingly shared whatever information she had. I asked questions and she answered with sheet upon sheet of closely handwritten words. Yes, her parents had been G-d fearing people, that I already knew, but I did not know that their rescue of my parents almost ended in tragedy the first day they were at 18 Kerkstraat. At school, Hennie told one of her classmates that she had seen a strange woman in their front room – a woman with black hair – who was cleaning. She had invited this friend to come to our house, but first needed her mother's permission. Asked why she wanted the girl to visit, she told her mother about the woman with the dark hair she wanted her friend to see.

My mother got furious and scolded me for telling lies. She said I was a bad girl. "What on earth are you talking about," she said in an angry voice. "We have no strangers here at all. Let that girl come over, and she can see for herself," she finally said. All that time I could see how angry she was.

Hennie told me the end of that story, and that eventually she understood that her mother had had no choice.

Even words were too dangerous, and my mother wanted to make sure that I was truly ashamed and would keep my mouth shut. And if I did tell more stories like that one, the children in school would not believe me.

The next day, Hennie and her friend came to the bakery, and the door to the front room was wide open. It was empty.

My mother punished both of us – me for telling lies and her for believing them. She sent us to clean the front room ourselves. And that was the end of talk about what might or might not be going on in our house. I had learned my lesson.

That was quite a tale and I felt that I needed to respond with something valuable of my own, so I wrote to her about my father's story about listening to the BBC. Hennie answered by return mail. She had something to add to this tale.

When my mother placed a chair in front of the door to that room, we were forbidden to open it. But I was a child – I opened the door anyway. Very quietly. I looked inside and saw a man I did not know. He wasn't very tall. He stood there with his back to the door and earphones on his head, listening intently. He was writing down things. I never breathed a word about it. I remembered my lesson all too well.

Hennie did not know the story about my father's attempt to glue the ration coupons so neatly that the cards looked like new ones. What she did tell me was that during those two years the whole family always had beautiful sweaters, and only after the liberation did she learn that my mother had knitted those. When people became curious about the origin of those lovely sweaters, cardigans, and even skirts for her, her mother explained that there was this spinster aunt who had enough time on her hands to unravel old sweaters and repurpose the wool to make new things. She, unlike the baker's wife with a house full of children, needed to find ways to keep her hands busy.

It did not take long for Hennie and I to understand that we were in a unique position to work together toward getting her parents recognition as Righteous Gentiles. Together we wrote a detailed letter to Yad Vashem. They responded with stacks of forms which we filled out patiently. Now it was up to the commission that dealt with these matters to make a decision regarding our request. Hennie took steps to strengthen our renewed bond and wrote to her family in Canada to let them know that if they were planning on taking a trip to Israel, they should contact me, for I had offered to put up anyone from the Scheffer clan. And sure enough, that summer someone came. She was the great-granddaughter of my Ome Cees and Tante Henk, granddaughter of their daughter Jo, who had also been active in the resistance. When she arrived, my entire family dressed in festive clothes, showered their children, and gathered in my home. Malinda, a girl of barely 20 was excited about visiting the Yad Vashem Holocaust Museum, and once there, even asked to see the file on her great-grandparents and to find out how the process for recognition was progressing. The file was found but it was empty. All our letters and documents were gone.

Undaunted, Hennie and I started over, but this time I no longer trusted the bureaucracy and kept a close eye on the paper trail. I knew the names of the decision makers as well as when the Dutch desk in charge of requests from Dutch survivors met. I kept vigilant, thinking that soon we would have our request granted. It was not to be: Yad Vashem refused to recognize the Scheffers as Righteous Gentiles. And why? That was of course my first question after I had swallowed my disappointment and anger. "You have no proof," they told me. "None of the parties in question are alive anymore."

For a while, I allowed my disappointment to spiral down into depression, but I could not stop thinking about this. The Scheffers were entitled to this recognition. And then I knew. In the early years after the war, when the Yad Vashem Holocaust Museum had not yet been built and there was no Righteous Gentiles program, Jews rescued and kept safe by good Dutchmen, still wanted to give public acknowledgement to those who had saved them. The most accepted way to do this was to plant a tree in Israel in a special forest, named for a Dutch resistance fighter.[2] It was certainly before 1953, for only then was the Yad Vashem museum established. The JNF (Jewish National Fund) was raising funds to plant trees in the Land of Israel, so planting a tree in honor of the rescuers was a popular choice. The latter received a nice certificate showing that a tree was planted in their honor and in gratitude for their help during the war. I knew my father had done this. I remembered such a certificate in the Bemelaar home, Louisie's first stop on her flight to safety. I had seen the framed certificate above Mr. Bemelaar's desk.

I write to Hennie and ask her about such a document. Does she remember it? We were talking about events that had taken place so many years ago; the Scheffer parents had died in the 60s, my father in the 70s, and my mother was alive, but her Alzheimer's had taken her away too. I did not feel very hopeful.

It turned out that the Scheffer family had saved everything from their parental home. Papers, documents, photo albums, heirlooms, everything had been passed from one child to the other for safekeeping, and now most things were in Hennie's home, neatly labeled and stored. She unearthed a manilla envelope marked Piet and Geertje, and she found an official-looking certificate but did not understand what it was – one side in Hebrew, the other in Dutch, and she knew neither language. She photocopied the document and sent it to me. And there it was: a phrase from the 92nd psalm – the righteous flourish like the palm tree and grow like a cedar in Lebanon- written around a drawing of a palm tree, and on the other side an inscription signed in my father's hand: "In memory of your help given to us in the dark years of the German occupation."

My heart beat so fast, I thought I might be fainting. We had found the key. The key to the recognition which I knew we could now bestow on the Scheffers in the name of my parents, my sisters and myself. I returned to the Dutch Desk of Yad Vashem, holding the certificate as a shield. Scheffer's name was clearly legible, written in my father's beautiful calligraphy, and then his name and the date. It was all kosher. I had no doubt. And then we were denied again. We had reached an impasse. What now?

In the digital era of the 21st century, secrets are almost obsolete. Everything lands in the realm of Google, and so, one day, Perry, my children's father, found a newspaper story about a Dutch family who had cleaned out their late mother's attic and stumbled upon a small valise. One of the items they found was a certificate of a tree planted in Israel in honor of their mother and father for rescuing a Jewish family. They decided to try and find this family, and after a search, they discovered their children in Israel. Neither family knew about the connection between their parents, nor did they know the significance of that certificate with the palm tree. Their parents had never spoken about their war experience, and the children in Israel did not know Dutch. Together, they set their sights for Yad Vashem and eventually, the Dutch family was given recognition as Righteous Gentiles. They were declared one of the righteous among the nations even though none of the parties were still living. The story made me want to go on the war path, so I put on my war paint and armed with everything Hennie and I had collected for the thick file on the Scheffer family's nobility, I made my way to Yad Vashem once again. I was quite prepared to turn over a few tables, make a long speech about geese and ganders and that if Amsterdam could get recognition, so should Canada. Our case was much stronger than that of the other families, for both the Scheffer children and my sisters and I remembered a great deal about the time Piet and Geertje hid David and Betje, and 18 Kerkstraat protected 82 Rijssensestraat.

I could have left my war paint in Haifa. The newspaper article apparently did the trick and the Dutch commission in charge of awarding recognition quickly concluded that all the documents, our stories, the letters, and then finally the tree certificate, were enough to give the Scheffers what they so richly deserved. The commission's decision meant that now there would be public recognition of the noble couple and their older children who had put their lives on the line for my parents, and without a doubt it was to their courage that the Samuel clan had already grown to number over 40 souls. All of them rescued directly or indirectly by the Scheffers!

The title *Righteous among the Nations* is like a knighthood in a monarchy and is bestowed by the government of Israel. Therefore, an official representative of the State of Israel must be present to preside over the ceremony and hand the family their certificate and medal proclaiming their heroism. For us, this meant that the Canadian consul would have to come to Calgary, and of course, I would be there as well. Wild horses could not have kept me at bay. All the Scheffer descendants had already promised to come as well, and they too were a large group. We settled on November, and I requested an unpaid leave of absence from the Ministry of Education so that I could take two weeks off from my job as a professor of literature to make this trip. I had an American passport so there was no red tape concerning travel and my suitcase was quickly packed. I was ready, standing in the gate, and foaming at the bit. I would stopover in the Netherlands for a few days to visit my parents' grave in Almelo and to tell them that I had finished what my father started. Hennie promised to pick me up at the Calgary airport.

There is a saying in Yiddish that man tries and G-d laughs, which essentially means that you never know what might go wrong. Life's path is strewn with banana peels, and yes, also here, so late in the game, we all slipped on a huge one. Two weeks before I was scheduled to fly out of Tel Aviv, Yad Vashem called, and shortly after that also the foreign ministry's department in charge of all the ambassadors around the world. They usually keep a watchful eye on their diplomatic service, but this time they did not do such a great job, for the consul scheduled to officiate at the Calgary ceremony had taken a ski vacation, slipped on a slope – no bananas – and broke a leg. They wanted to postpone. Perhaps for a year, for the current consul's term of duty was almost up and his replacement would need some time to get acclimatized. Blah blah blah. It was mostly a one-sided conversation, with the officials doing all the talking and me getting more and more upset, biting my tongue. I looked at my suitcase, thought of the almost eight years Hennie and I had fought our battle to get recognition for her parents and help give my father rest, and I stopped listening to the polite words in my ear. I suddenly heard my father whisper to me, "When you are right, you never step aside not even for the queen!" That was his motto and he had instilled this stubbornness in his children as well. I WAS in the right. I was not going to move. I was not going to move for the queen, but neither was I going to accommodate the consul with his broken leg. I planted my feet squarely on the cool marble floor of my home in my beloved Israel, and as gently as I could, I wished the consul a full recovery. I said that I was sorry he had had this accident, but everyone was already converging upon Calgary. I explained about my non-refundable ticket and the two week leave of absence from my college. I was not going to cancel. They were not going to cancel. Too much water under the bridge of all the bridges in the world, from the Ijssel to the Jordan. I even called the embassy in Toronto, made sure they too got the message and indicated that I did not care if they appointed their busboy as temporary consul, for the ceremony in Calgary was going to take place as planned. I put a huge, virtual exclamation mark after all of that. I could hear my father laughing deep in my soul. I had done it right. "You see, my girl, in the end, the queen can move." And in that snowbound corner of Canada, in that Jewish Community Center of Calgary, we had an unforgettable evening. All those present will remember it for years to come. It was heartwarming and filled with love and respect and gratitude. I was floating above myself. Something had been repaired in the universe. The story of the Scheffers' courage would survive after us! And that evening, I had the opportunity to tell the Scheffer saga. I was given ten minutes to make my speech. Ten minutes to tell the story of an entire generation. How could I possibly manage that?!

Impossible Missions is my middle name and as an experienced lecturer I hoped to be equal to the task. I thought I should paint the background by going back to everything I knew about the war from the papers in my workroom. I took everything out. Yes, including that Post Curiosa notebook Dave had given me after his mother gave it to him when she found it in our father's safe. For the first time I went through it with a fine-toothed comb. Every page was scrutinized. I did not skip a single entry. Nothing looked interesting, but I did notice a fairly large collection of postcards, neatly typed and addressed to the Scheffers at 18 Kerkstraat. The date stamps showed that those cards had arrived while my parents were there. What could possibly be curious about them? Papa saved so many things so carefully, but what was the importance of those nearly empty cards? They all had but a single line, perhaps two, "Sir, we received your letter dated April 24, but we are sorry to tell you that we cannot supply prewar articles as our stock was lost in the bombardments of May 1940. We are sorry to have to disappoint you, and remain, sincerely." The sender was a brush factory in Rotterdam, the postal stamp was dated 1944. It read "watching the front is a duty of honor". I found an advertisement for glue suitable for sticking the ration coupons onto cards. That one was dated 1943. I found nothing curious or interesting about any of it. Perhaps papa had liked the postal stamps because of their war related slogans? "Sand and water are the best materials to put out fires," and another one, "Save waste and raw materials," and on the obverse side an advertisement for Sinterklaas gifts, the Dutch holiday of December 5th. It was dated 1944. The postage stamps as such could not be valuable, for they were printed on.

Although the curiosa notebook was kept neatly, everything glued down and marked, one of the postcards was loose, as though it had simply been placed there for safekeeping. I picked it up without much enthusiasm. Probably another advertisement for some product needed in the bakery, or a polite regret that products were not available. It was, after all, war time.

The postcard opened, and inside was an order form for cards to glue the ration coupons onto, but on the side I could not have seen without picking it up, someone had drawn lines in black and red pencil which looked like a primitive map. And the names were familiar to me as well: Border of White Russia, Smolensk, Vitebsk, Dnieper. I knew those names. Somewhere in Russia. Ah, and the date stamp was 24 September 1943. My parents had already been with the Scheffers since May of that year. I knew those words were connected to the war, somehow. Red and black lines denoting troops of different armies, or something. And I knew that papa listened to the BBC. I did know that for he had told me, and Hennie had confirmed it. I turned to Dr. Google and discovered that in September 1943, a fierce battle had been fought between Russia and Germany. This was the battle for a bridgehead across the Dnieper River. It lasted for many weeks and was the beginning of the end of Hitler's military supremacy. I saw my father as through the closeup lens of a camera, listening with all his might, noting things down, coloring lines. Frugal as always. He would not waste new paper. He would collect some of the Scheffer's old correspondence, keep a few of the postcards next to him while he listened and scribbled to be able to report accurately. He understood full well that he was the ears of the residents of that home, and it was his responsibility to report accurately everything that he had heard. Everything my father had told me about their years of *onderduik* was true, and that postcard, addressed to the Scheffers, proved that he had indeed listened to the radio at their home.

Of course, I scanned that map and the Scheffer address on the other side as well as the date and took it with me to Canada. I was not the only one to bring things from the past: In Hennie Scheffer's home, there under the majestic peaks of the Canadian Rockies, I was given a big brown envelope. It bulged with letters my father had written to the family over the years, newspaper clippings with articles which mentioned the family, mostly written by my father, and a number of photographs of the Samuel family. Every year a photographer came to our home, but I never realized that those photos were taken to let the Scheffers know that we were doing well, that the children were growing, and that everyone was healthy. I found photos of our new home, at number 30, us posing in front of the store and in the back of the house. There were also photos of our make-believe eating in our new dining room and make-believe lounging in our new sitting room. Papa wanted the Scheffers to know everything about us. Once again, I knew how warm and embracing the connection with the Scheffers had been. While they learned everything about us, we were also kept informed about their new life in Canada. When my father heard that they were having a hard time, were living in a poorly insulated home, and worked as farmhands, he could not bear the thought that his beloved mama and papa Scheffer were suffering, that they were cold. They were old already! He was so upset, that within a few days he left his business behind, got on a plane and traveled to Canada, to freezing cold Alberta. He stayed in Canada for six weeks, and the photos in the envelope showed how all the family had rallied together to see him again. Later, things became a little easier for the Scheffers, and they started visiting their relatives living in Nijverdal. Especially the daughters, Jo, Ina, and Hennie came quite regularly, perhaps because they had a little more money than their parents, or because they were simply younger and healthier. A trip to the village included a visit to us as well, and mama would turn the house upside down, scrubbing and dusting and waxing furniture. "Jo and Hennie are coming," she would say, and heaven help us if we got in her way. She might as well have been expecting the queen. All that was lacking was a guard of honor and a flag. The connection between us held until the heads of both families died, my father shortly after Ome Cees...

In those years that my parents lived in hiding at the Scheffer family, no one was safe. The divers might be discovered any minute and too often Jews had to move on because their current situation had become untenable for the rescuers. People became too afraid to carry on and simply told their Jews to leave. Every day held the danger that someone might discover a hidden Jew. Every day there was the danger that the German Green Police, or a Dutch policeman would come banging on the door and search the house. For the Scheffer family, the church across the street and Pastor Hijmans remained the fallback address. In dire moments, David and Betje could always hide there and during those two years this happened more than once.

It cannot come as a surprise that in a village as small as Nijverdal, it is hard to keep a secret, and rumors about families hiding Jews were rife, and, of course, extremely dangerous. Stories about the Scheffers hiding Jews were already making the rounds, and they spread like wildfire. Those stories too often ended with a loud banging on the door. Papa Scheffer certainly wished he could put an end to those stories about who might be hidden inside his home and came up with a brilliant plan. He walked across the street to seek out the pastor. "My wife and I will shortly be married for 25 years, and I want to make a big celebration for our silver wedding. We will invite the entire village, open every room, and then they can all see that there is nothing going on in our home. In order to pull that off, I would like to send you Piet and Geertje for a short stay." *Dominee* Hijmans was receptive, and readily agreed. In the dark, long after curfew had gone into effect, and someone had looked up and down the street to ensure the coast was clear, Verger Smit's 10-year-old son knocked on the door of the bakery and escorted David and Betje back to the church. Now a safe hiding place had to be found for them inside the building. My father wrote about this moment in an article about the Scheffer home after he had helped them to sell it. They could trust him to get the best price possible. In the newspaper, my father writes, "This was a time when one half of the Dutch population hid the other half." About his stay in the church, he wrote, "We could not move into the attic because the verger was using it to dry his tobacco leaves," and with great emotion he wrote about the goodness and courage of all those people, "How has such nobility of heart disappeared from the world?" These are my father's exact words!

When the festivities of the silver wedding celebration were done, David and Betje were allowed to return to the bakery, and life went on.

In the final year of the war, Nijverdal was the target of heavy allied bombing. The village lay on the escape route back to Germany, and the Scheffer home was very close to the railroad tracks, so it was regularly hit by shrapnel. Windows shattered, especially those of the front room, where the Jewish *onderduikers* lived. Ome Cees insisted on repairing those windows time and again, but when someone asked him why he would bother, since he did not even use that room (that was the ruse to justify keeping it closed), he nailed the window opening shut with scrap wood and left it that way until the liberation. As a result, my parents lived in the dark, and even worse, perhaps, it was dangerous to talk, even in whispers, as they might be heard outside. It was also colder than before. The wind came into the room through the slats. The rain too.

During air raids, the entire street ran to the church cellar, but, of course, David and Betje could not. Everyone would have recognized them! My father told me that papa Scheffer refused to leave them by themselves, and mama Scheffer had to find a ruse to explain why her husband had not come with them. "Sometimes," my father told me once, "I went outside during a bombardment and let the bombs fall where they might. I screamed and screamed into the noise of the planes. Kill them, flatten them into the earth! Things like that. No danger that I might be heard; during the air raids the street was deserted. And sometimes I no longer cared what might happen to me. I needed a little fresh air. I pressed my body into the wall of the house and screamed."

---

1. Flim, Berend Jan & Gerardina Wilhelmina (van Leusen) & son Herman 2083.6 1981 https://www.yadvashem.org/yv/pdf-drupal/netherlands.pdf
2. https://www.tracesofwar.com/sights/67901/Remembrance-Forest-Joop-Westerweel.htm https://www.yadvashem.org/righteous/stories/westerweel.html

14

BELA (BETSIE MARGRIET) RUTH SAMUEL TENENHOLTZ: AND NOW ALSO ABOUT MYSELF, 1946-2017

Today, my name is Bela Ruth, but when I was born my parents named me Bela Betsie Margriet. I am a daughter, a sister, a mother, and a grandmother. I am even a great-grandmother. I am the matriarch of our tribe.

For a large part of my life, I lived as a pseudo hidden person. I heard words and sentences spoken near me and I learned to translate them into a language I could understand, and when I became an adult, I wanted to pass on those words and stories, but too often I felt that I did not really have the right, because I could only pass on fragments of my family's history. There were times when I left the storytelling to others who seemed better equipped than me to pass them on. Let them bear the burden of being the guardians of memory, and so, I found my existence in the shadows of their story telling. When now and then I released something of my childhood to my children, I first turned the stories into pink fairytales, until they bore but a vague resemblance to all that I had internalized, but the memory keeper inside me was overshadowed by my maternal instincts to protect my descendants. I felt that the truth of our history lay somewhere in the middle between storytelling and hard historical facts. I was a child born in the shadow of my parents' *onderduik*, and I had inherited my birthright to always hide parts of myself from the world. That is how life moved through time: part of it in the light, and part of it always in darkness like the other side of the moon.

To begin with, I can admit that the story of my life has brought me to the point where I need to give birth to it, and that it is now easier for me to speak of the fires that continue to smolder inside my soul. It is a fire that was lit well before I was even born and whose destructive heat did not die with the end of the war. Fire must be fought with fire and so, logically, words must be answered with words. Let me talk about that before I even get started – let me have a general rehearsal for all the things I would like to put aside, allow them to come outside and bask in the breeze of the Mediterranean Sea. My best weapon is time: chronological versus soul-time. In the latter, the impatient sand running through the hourglass will not let me grow old, and in that space between those different worlds of time I can approach all those who now live on white clouds, play harps, and smoke huge Cuban cigars while they cool each other with their ethereal wings. The result of that possibility is also that the timeline of my existence is capable of curling back upon itself or branching out, so that all, the family of my childhood and my present reality, can meet while all are young and full of energy. They live even though they are dead. Those are two concepts which to me do not appear as controversial in this unique universe of mine. And so, there is no struggle to fight against my existence in this wrinkle of time. Just the opposite: I am thrilled to be here. The confusion of time allows me to see myself dressed in the clothing of a little girl and that of an older woman, all at the same time. The fact that I can catch my father's eyes as he looks straight at me for a second, is a blessing in my eyes. There he is again, with those beautiful, clear blue eyes, looking a little mischievous. I can touch him and make good old injustices. I am deeply grateful for the soft stories my mother whispers in my ears, whisking me away to that wintery Shabbat around dusk, just before the end of our day of rest, and we are sitting on the ground in front of the hearth with only the soft light of the tiny flames behind the mica window of the fire. Mama sings sentimental songs from her own childhood, and we learn to sing along with her: "Grandma, what shall you give me when I start first grade?"

My daughter Hani and I traveled to the Netherlands together to discover the deep, pure roots of our family saga, and to pick up the thread of our story with those deep, undamaged roots. Papa's story had started there, long before that terrible war. Hani's grandfather had lived there as a normal child with normal parents and grandparents. We had to return to those people and to start anew in order to make our family whole. First, to a tiny cemetery in Raalte, sheltered by huge trees. There we built our first bridgehead and later we picked up the thread in the sad, hidden *keiver oves,* The Jewish cemetery of Almelo, cramped in between houses and offices, hiding, like those former hidden Jews who are now buried there, behind a high wall which reminds me a little of the walls of Jerusalem. The only thing that is missing here is a Roman soldier. For Hani and me this piece of earth was not only the end of the lives of the two people who gave me life, but also the beginning, for we had arrived with a kind of declaration of our intentions to set out on our search in honor of the people who had been laid to rest there. It was miraculous that my father and mother were able to tell us the story of their lives after their death, now that we had found the beginning, and they no longer had the ability to set off smokescreens around their stories or forbid us from unraveling the story of our families, starting at the moment they had carried out their *Vayibrach* plans to the end. I had permission. I was allowed to know everything I wanted to know. My parents no longer made excuses about their need to protect me from the history of our family. Everything was out in the open, and I was allowed to touch everything. Perhaps, that visit to their graves sharpened my memory a little. All the documents which had hung over our lives as a dark, threatening cloud, fell away; I was allowed to pick them up and read them. I was allowed to understand everything, and whatever was not clear I was allowed to check out with other documents, and then pass it on. Throughout this endless, slow journey, Hani, my beautiful, wonderful, loyal daughter, remained my rock and my strength.

It felt a little as if I too had been handed a diving-box like the one my sister Marianne was given. In part, thanks to my mischievous character, my stubborn insistence on knowledge, and the assistance of the good people in Nijverdal, I had been given access to information which had been molting in a dusty archive, wrinkled with old age, and yawning with boredom at the lack of visitors. The documents had been preserved by the caring, helpful hands of Johan Alferink, who shared with me everything he was guarding, and by now I truly was old enough, grown-up enough, to understand all that my parents had done for me!

In those ancient documents I discovered many of the missing pieces to the puzzle of my life, and with the knowledge hidden in them, I arrived at the point where half of my father's life that had been hidden for so long could come into the light. The documents were a study book for me which taught me about the courage and nobility of an unbending, introverted man. It revealed to me a story of the rescue of Jews, there, somewhere in a small village in a corner of the Netherlands. It had been waiting as a hidden treasure since 1943.

1946-2014

You might say that my mother bore me in an unbearable era. Although the fact that my parents had already returned to their home at 82 Rijssensestraat was a positive milestone, things were not so simple. They were not yet the owners of their home. Someone in the village had used the deportation of the Jews to his own advantage and had made a profit of the misfortune of those people. This was par for the course. After the German occupation confiscated Jewish property, they sold it to the highest bidder. Although my father locked the house and did not hand over the key, he was unable to prevent this desecration of his hard work. The buyer was a fellow villager, an ardent Nazi, and this person received two mortgages to finance the purchase, underwritten by German robber banks.[1] To be clear, the buyer knew my father and his family well, and also knew that the Germans did not have rights to the house, so the entire transaction was completely illegal and criminal.

A few days after it became clear that my father had not presented himself, his family and worldly goods at the Jewish Theatre in Amsterdam, the theft of his home went into high gear. My parents had disappeared into the warm protection of *Dominee* Hijmans' church, but the house was not left unmolested. The locked door at number 82 proved no obstacle. The new owner simply broke in and moved in with his family.

I always knew the name of the person who lived in our house, but I never saw it documented until I wrote this book. His name, the sum of money he borrowed, or the fact that he refused to relinquish the house when my parents returned, are all well-documented, bureaucratic facts, but I have no interest in naming names or pointing fingers at a Dutch collaborator who prospered at the expense of the misfortune of another. The guilty parties are long dead, and their descendants may know nothing of all this. I want to let it be. Let it suffice that "K" was forcefully removed by people who wanted to see the Samuel family back in their home. Unfortunately, that was not the end of the story. For a while justice seemed to have been done, but when my father started the process of rescinding the illegal sale of his house, and returning his name to the deed, the disenchanted collaborator who had physically broken into the house, had lived there for over two years knowing that he had no right to the property, now started a process as the injured party, deprived of this home by my father. Incredibly, this resulted in a drawn-out legal battle to determine who the legal owner should be. K. complained that he no longer had possession of the house, yet still had to pay the mortgage. Within a year after the end of the war, this person had even succeeded in getting himself appointed as the chairman of the commission which represented the victims of the war. This meant that my father had to appear before the man who had stolen his home and to convince the other members of this commission that he was the only one with rights to the house at number 82, since he had had the house built and he had neither sold it nor received any of the money K. claimed to have paid for the house. On top of that my father also had to assert his rights to inherit the homes of his murdered parents, uncles and aunts, and those of my mother's immediate family. All that, while seated at the head of the table was the man who had robbed him. Meanwhile, the most pressing problem was that the house had been hit in one of the bombardments of the final year of the war, and was in dire need of repair, but without a decision concerning ownership, the authorities refused to supply funding. We lived in a partially destroyed home behind a store that was unusable, for the front of the house had been hit the hardest.

My father was not the type to accept injustice easily and concepts of giving in, giving up, and letting go were not part of his vocabulary. He went to war. It was an exhausting, emotionally crushing trek to regain the family's rights to their prewar possessions. He would fight this battle without the help of the authorities, as he had done during the German occupation and the persecution of the Jews. Now, once again living out in the open, he sat himself down behind his trusted typewriter and fired off letter after letter to the various government institutions. The mayor of the village was once again the same person who had tried to be neutral during the occupation, while still trying to secretly aid the Jews a little here and there. He had been reinstated by the Dutch government shortly after the liberation.

During the war, my father had been forced to choose his words very carefully, because Jews were inferior *Untermenchen,* less than human, but now it was 1945-1946, the Germans were gone, and papa was a free man. He no longer needed to mince words. He named names, accused people who had acted against the Jews, such as members of the local police force who had collaborated with the Germans. This collaboration had almost cost him his life, he wrote. His fingers were the weapons that released his fury. He wanted only one thing: justice and the reinstatement of his prewar rights. He wanted to sue the guilty parties and refused to accept the given situation as unchangeable. Even the queen would not succeed in moving him from this position.

The resolution of ownership of his home reached an impasse, and meanwhile he had already become the father of a third child. Over and over, he turned to the mayor with a clear message, and I quote from his letter: "Only in our village does the nonchalant treatment of our rights continue, and only in our municipality do we get nowhere in our dealings with the authorities. All the obstructions in my path are the result of the indifference of the local authority."

He also reminded the mayor that he had to provide for his family and that this was still impossible: "I was forced to close my business as early as 1941-42 by order of the occupation, and now, ten months after the liberation, I have still not succeeded in getting it started again." His final sentence expresses his disillusion with the municipality: "I can no longer find the nobility to maintain a polite silence," he writes.

In the Netherlands, the post-war years have become known as the little Shoah, and it did not pass by the pastoral village of Nijverdal. My father had to go to war to reconquer his house and he fought the same battle for Truus, his young cousin.

I came into the world at the beginning of this battle and took my place next to my two older sisters and a few Canadian soldiers quartered with us. Because the store was damaged by the bombardments, and my father needed to make a living, he reluctantly moved his business to his parents' home at number 101. He also notified the municipality that if his demands to have his ownership reinstated came to naught, and if the surviving Jews were not recognized as the legal heirs to their family's property, he would find a different way to undo the terrible injustices of the war. In the end, he did indeed use the alternate road. All alone, papa faced the struggle to return Jewish property to Jewish hands, and he set out on his exhausting journey between our house and the red mailbox at the corner. He wrote reams of letters to the various official commissions, demanding explanations for the drawn-out process of finding justice and answers to his questions concerning the stolen property of the

Nijverdal-Hellendoorn Jews. After the 1943 deportation of the Jews, their possessions had become the property of the German occupation, through Omnia, the robber concern. After the war, everything under Omnia's ownership, although illegally acquired, became the property of the Dutch government. It was no longer certain that my father would ever be considered as the legal heir to the homes and other property that his aunts and uncles had owned. Most of them had left no direct descendants, and he and two cousins were the closest living relatives. Some of the disputed homes had been bombarded, sometimes completely destroyed, but the plots of land were still there. In principle, one might think that declaring ownership should have been simple, but this was not at all the case. My father put in a claim in the name of the survivors, whether it concerned an actual standing house or just a cratered plot of land, but he had no more rights than any other claimant. In the Nijverdal archive I found some official correspondence between local residents of the municipality and the mayor's office where the possibility of purchasing this so-called abandoned property was raised. All clothed in polite words and signed by lawyers in nice suits.

Papa's typewriter was busy. It creaked and squeaked and spit out letter after letter. Papa hired a lawyer and took advice from people who knew the law. Slowly but surely, he constructed a system that was bound to yield positive results. His motto remained the same as it had been during the war; nothing for the Krauts. But now he also added that he would not yield anything to the Dutch government either. "I'd rather burn it to the ground," he said time after time. But he was so alone in this struggle. He was like a child with his nose pressed against the shop window. He saw everything that should be his, but he could not touch it. It had all been pulled apart, sorted, distributed, sold and/or divided among those who had the money or the power to swallow up Jewish property. Nothing was holy or out of bounds, not even the grass behind Ome Abraham Samuel's house; even that was auctioned off by the German occupation, and in a region where farmers raised cows, a buyer was quickly found.

The battle for the house at 82 Rijssensestraat dragged on. It was now a struggle between the prosperous flower merchant with his beautiful greenhouses behind his shop and papa shorn of all his wealth, orphaned by the war, destitute but determined. The battle for his house continued for several years, and while he fought valiantly to have the family's possessions returned to the few living heirs, he had little to show for his efforts. For a long time, everything stagnated in the hands of the government and neither my father nor the two surviving cousins whom he represented inherited their family's confiscated properties.

Papa realized that he had to find a different tactic to rehabilitate his life and earn recognition of his rights of inheritance. He turned to the representatives of the Marshall Plan in the Netherlands. [2]

The American government had offered their assistance to the newly liberated countries of Europe to enable them to repair the destruction of the war as quickly as possible, and to kickstart the economy. In the Netherlands, this also included rebuilding homes destroyed in the bombing, and any Dutchman with the capital to build two houses was entitled to a generous mortgage to finance the work. I do not know how my father scraped together the money, but I remember the years of that building frenzy and his satisfaction with the process.

He started with a two-family home with a storefront, which he rented out upon completion. This gave him the seed money to apply for another plot of land. Next, he built a large dwelling with a store in the village center which was also rented out upon completion. This strategy allowed him to pay off the mortgage with the rent he received, and he was then free to apply for further parcels of land for building. He eventually succeeded in owning the dual family plot where his uncle and aunt had lived with their married daughter, and there too he built a very large house and an equally large store. This was 30 Rijssensestraat. By the time this house was finished it was already 1953, and we moved in. After my father finally won the fight for ownership of number 82, it was 1949. The war damage was repaired, and when we moved out, he rented it out. Our new home stood in the center of the village, and this was another economic advantage. In the final analysis, my father had succeeded in reclaiming his family's properties, not because he was recognized as the legal heir, but because he knew the law and used it to retrieve what had been stolen.

During the 1950s, the Netherlands was a beehive of construction, much of it with the assistance of Marshall Plan funds. Nijverdal was being rebuilt, as was our family's property. Papa always used the same architect, Mr. Bel. Every day that brick was laid upon brick, my father was deeply aware that with the progress in one of his projects, justice was at work, notwithstanding the government's resistance. Perhaps this knowledge comforted him just a little bit. Later on, it turned out that in those years there had been people who understood that my father's actions were a battle for his birthright, and they admired him for his inventiveness and tenacity. Proof for my statement here was found many years later, when it was too late for us to express our amazement at our father's cleverness.

It was like this: Marianne had driven to Nijverdal to help clean out our mother's house. Mama had already been hospitalized in a geriatric institution. When Marianne was done, she wrote to me about it and included a photo. Again, I am quoting: "Among mama's books, I found one that looked like a cheap love story. The cover showed a man and a woman in a steamy embrace. It seemed rather strange to find such a book in our mother's library. She never read those kinds of books. Ach, it did not seem a book I wanted to save, but for a moment I opened it, and imagine my surprise – inside the cover was a completely different book. It was old and far from frivolous. I was holding a history book written by Wolfgang (von) Weisl. The book was in German. Its title, **Der Kampf um das Heilige Land** (Berlin, 1925). Our mother did not know German and so I wondered what this book was doing in her house, and then I noticed that someone had glued a letter with a dedication on the inside of the cover. I am sending you a photo of that note."

"In gratitude to Mr. David Samuel of Nijverdal, in honor of the completion of the three buildings constructed under my supervision. I dedicate this book to you, as it also once lost its civil rights and had to be 'liberated' by me from Hitler's Germany by hiding it under a false identity, the so-called loose couple, in June 1943. Signed, Architect Bel, Nijverdal, 1958."

During the war, Mr. Bel had apparently been sent to Germany as a forced laborer. He found Von Weisl's book there and knew that under Hitler's regime it would be destroyed, for the author was both Jewish and an ardent Zionist who wrote a great deal about the development of The Holy Land. He had even gone to live in the land that was being reborn. Mr. Bel smuggled the book across the border when he was sent back to the Netherlands, hidden inside the innocuous jacket of the novel. After my father's death, my mother kept Von Weisl's *Struggle for the Holy Land* in her bookcase, apparently in recognition of its significance: Mr. Bel had understood full well how my father had succeeded in reinstating his birthright. His dealings had not escaped the eyes of his friends and I can only hope that those two men raised a glass in honor of my father's success in confusing the government a little bit, and how he managed to smuggle the possessions of the Samuel family across the hostile frontier of the bureaucracy, hidden inside the innocent cover of the Marshall Plan. His was a double victory and he had taken it on as a burden of honor to take back what belonged to the few survivors.

As a result of my father's experience with the authorities, he was thoroughly convinced that in general a man can only depend on himself, and that the government and the powers that be were not institutions that had his best interest at heart. The way he saw it, he had to consider all those government agencies as rivals and perhaps even enemies. This was a message instilled in us, his children: keep to yourself, know that you belong on some level, but always hide a part of yourself and be vigilant in your dealings with others. We existed as a group apart, surrounded by a narrow circle of good friends in the village, among them, of course, those who had helped the Jews. With those people my father and mother maintained a close relationship and we called them "aunt" and "uncle". The rest? Be careful. Who knows what they really have in mind!

Social studies and linguistics, 1952-1953

When I entered first grade I already knew to read. I had learned it effortlessly by leaning over my father as he read his newspaper and by playing with the books my older sisters brought home from the library. I loved school and was an outstanding pupil. That first year, our teacher was a young, pretty, blonde girl. All the children were mesmerized by her. She looked like an angel, slender and smartly dressed in fashionable skirts and blouses. She was beautiful! We hung on her every word, and when one day she told us that she liked drawing portraits and would be willing to draw us if we were good, the class became a disciplined unit. Each of us waited with bated breath for the day it would be our turn to be immortalized by Miss. I also put my name down on the list, and every Friday, at the end of the school day, one of us was allowed to stay behind to sit for our portrait. I waited for my turn impatiently, but the weeks went by, and she did not call my name. Some weeks I hung about and put on my coat slowly, for perhaps she had made a mistake and it was my turn after all? I was afraid to ask, out of fear that she might take my name off her list altogether. So, I lifted my things off the hook inside the classroom and went home. It was not yet my turn. When the school year was almost over, perhaps in that very last week before the summer vacation, Miss finally called my name and announced that it was my turn to have my portrait drawn. Oh, it was such a slow week, although a wonderful one, and I was looking forward to that Friday as if it were my birthday. That morning, I came to school wearing my Shabbat clothes, hair neatly combed, and hands carefully washed. I was ready. For the portrait.

"Sit in profile." I hardly dared to breathe. "Sit still." I could not see what Miss was drawing, but I could hear her pencil scratching the heavy paper. I forced myself to sit still, but I felt like dancing, so proud that this moment had come. My beloved Miss was drawing me, yes, the mischievous Bela! And she was drawing me in a real sketchbook. My cheeks were red with the excitement, and I succeeded in sitting quietly for the entire time. In profile. On a chair close to my teacher. When Miss was done and handed me the portrait, I pressed it to my heart, whispered my thanks, and ran out of the classroom without even glancing at the drawing. I only looked when I was by myself in the school yard. I looked again. In shock. Was that me? I did not understand what I was looking at. I definitely did not recognize myself. Who was that creature with the crooked nose, those thick lips, and the low protruding forehead? Was that really me? The image leaned forward with huge shoulders, exuding violence. That was no six-year-old child. It was a witch, a frightening figure. But I had heard the pencil scratch the paper and I knew this was a drawing of me. Deeply shocked, I slowly made my way home, the drawing burning in my hands.

I crept into the house, ashamed of how ugly I was. Papa ran into me in the hallway and asked what was wrong. Without a word, I held out the drawing to him, my eyes on the floor tiles. "Where did you get this antisemitic trash? Where did you find this?" my father asked in a stern voice. "But papa, that is me! Miss drew my portrait today." And I told him the whole story about waiting in anticipation, the fear of being passed over, the pretty dress I had put on in honor of the portrait. For a moment, my father stood without moving. He sighed, but then he shook his head very hard, as if chasing away an annoying fly. "Come with me child," and he opened the connecting door between the house and the store. He led me to the large mirror and placed me squarely in front of it. His hands on my shoulders. "Take a good look at yourself," and he raised up my chin gently and held up the drawing behind me so that I could see both my face and it. "You look nothing like this." And then, one by one, he pointed out the differences between me and that drawing. "You have a cute face and you have beautiful hair and a small little nose. I think you must be the prettiest little girl in the class. By far!" And he took that drawing, tore it in half and handed me one piece. "Go on, let's tear up this dirt together," and we did. The tiny snippets we threw into the wastepaper basket under the counter, and then we left the store hand in hand, back to the hallway into our house. Papa stroked my hair for a second and then rubbed his hands together in satisfaction. "Done!" he said with a smile. "That's been taken care of," and in the kitchen he scrubbed his hands with soap as if something unpleasant was stuck there and he had to rub it off.

I am breaking a vow of silence, which is the signature of my entire life, but no more. My story here is the result of a deep understanding for my parents, both mother and father. It cheers me up to feel that way, and these words fill my old age with a new energy. Yes, old age, what in Hebrew is called the years of gray hair and bent body. In Hebrew those two concepts are homophones, (seivah)and define the beginning deterioration that is old age. I am neither gray nor bent for the moment, and I want to give thanks for the fact that I have lived long enough to learn my family's history. I am grateful and feel the urge to say the Hebrew blessing reserved for such moments: shehecheyanu vekiymanu vehigi'anu lazman hazeh (Blessed are Thou Lord our G-d, Ruler of the Universe who has given us life, sustained us, and allowed us to reach this day). In my own words I add how grateful I am for the sudden flash of certainty that I can now have a great deal of sympathy for the home where I grew up, and for my father's struggle to prevent the persecution's goal: that that home would no longer exist. Consider for a moment the cold statistics of Hitler's success. Seventy-five percent of Dutch Jewry was murdered during the years of the German occupation, meaning that out of 100 Jews, 75 did not return. And how about Nijverdal? In the municipality of Hellendoorn? On April 9, 1943, 22 Jews resided there. All had received those letters with instructions to clean their home, pack a small bag, take themselves to the train station, hand over the keys to their house, and then take the train to Vught, the temporary holding camp, the converted punishment prison. They remained in Vught only until room opened up in Westerbork, and from there were shoved into cattle wagons and transported to Sobibor, the gas chamber and death, straight from the trains.

But in Nijverdal-Hellendoorn, almost half of the 22 Jews, 10 in total, did return. Their rescue was very much the result of the inside information my father had gained via the Jewish Council, and the help and training he had enjoyed under the tutelage of Sigmund Menko. The elderly among Nijverdal's Jews could not accept that they had to actively oppose the German plans by going into hiding. They placed themselves in G-d's hands, the G-d of Israel.

I was unable to trace the fate of two people whose names appeared on the German list for deportation on the same day as the Samuel brothers and their families. Their names do not appear on the digital monument for all the Dutch victims, nor are they engraved on the local monument in the Jewish cemetery in Hellendoorn. I want to hope that these people survived the Shoah, perhaps had succeeded in diving. Still, the fact remains that in our small village in a forgotten corner of Twente, my father was singled out by the Germans as the most well-known Jew in the village and ordered to be the representative of the Amsterdam Jewish Council in the area. That was their first mistake, for after the war, the tally showed that almost 50 percent of the local Jews had survived the war. This survival rate was similar to that of the Jews of Enschede, and nowhere in the Netherlands has this number been equaled.

I feel free to say that my father played an important role in the survival of at least six Jews, aside from his wife, his two daughters and himself. The relationship between those returned Jews and my father was a warm one, a bond of gratitude and a strong sense of unity and trust. Those people visited our home regularly, always bringing small gifts from their vegetable garden and chicken coop. With my father's young cousin Truus, who had survived the war with the help of the Overduin Group in Hengelo, the relationship was a paternal one. My parents stood in for her murdered parents when she got married, although there was another cousin who might have done the honors, and my two older sisters were her bridesmaids. To us she was a beloved aunt.

All the files with the correspondence between my father and the German occupation, and later the Dutch government institutions, are now at rest in my work room, but I never quite had the courage to read them thoroughly. One day I sat myself down and opened a letter, but soon enough blinded by tears of anger and loss, I had to stop. I felt such pity for my father and was ashamed of my lack of courage to keep on reading. He was able to write, read, respond, write again, all the time suffering humiliation after humiliation, but he never stopped. He held on to his typewriter for almost 20 years, firing off letter after letter. He could do this for 20 years. I barely succeeded for one day.

It was my heartfelt wish to write down my father's life seen through the eyes of a grown woman, and yet, also through the eyes of the child I once was. I wanted to draw his portrait in clear lines and honor his memory. Therefore, once again, I had to take myself back to the Jewish cemetery in Almelo, armed with a new attitude and a sense of liberation that came with the knowledge that I had finished my journey in his footsteps. Hani and I went together, the way she had been by my side throughout, for I knew that her pure presence allowed me to see everything in a clearer resolution. Everything that I had borne within for so many years, housed behind the seemingly shameful secrets of our family, had become clear to me. My father's pain for not having done enough. The belief that he was to blame for everything. That he had the death of all those people on his conscience. And yet, all that was absolutely not the case. The opposite was true. My father should not have been burdened by what he saw as his guilty secrets. He could have told us about his heroic efforts to try and save Jews.

I also need to ask my mother to forgive me. I should have immediately understood that if a woman argues with her husband, she does not really choose to accuse him of murder and killing her family. Out of the blue. A woman who argues with her husband may complain about the way he treats her, that he does not respect her. Perhaps she needs a new coat and he won't pay for it. Those are possible topics for domestic arguments. I should have understood that my mother's pain was unbearable. She could not encompass the loss of all those relatives. Perhaps the years of living in hiding had done something to her and she was no longer truly responsible for her actions. Who knows. It was a miracle that she was even capable of acting normally, kept a spotless home, fed us delicious meals, raised her children as good Jews. That was the miracle. Not the other things. They came from her broken heart. But all those years I spent in my parents' home, I silenced her voice. I refused to hear it. I turned away from her. A quick look at the circumstances of her married life should have made clear that she never really had the chance of a normal life. The threat from beyond the border started before they even got married, and as soon as her children were born, she no longer knew how to keep them safe. Her babies were marked for death by Hitler. As a child, I did not understand this. I looked at my mother through critical eyes, did not believe anything she told me and kept her outside my life as much as I could. Now I want to ask her to forgive me for this. I am sorry from the bottom of my heart, mama. Since I got my first look at that so-called *onderduik* box from the Nijverdal archives, I see everything in a different light. I have seen, heard, read, and understood. You married a man you thought was a hero capable of carrying out any task. He was undaunted and energetic. He always found an answer. But this time he couldn't. Of course, he told you, you'll see, I will save everyone. I will find hiding places for all of us. And that did not happen. I must even admit that my mother's accusations actually set me on the right path. Her cries of loss and anger led me to the key that solved the family secret. Her sharp words allowed me entry into our Shoah story.

I have already hinted that something happened in our home that caused me to change my attitude, especially toward my father. Up to that moment I was mama's little girl and like my sisters, I wanted her attention and love. When she had no time for me, I became my big sister Louisie's girl and sometimes when Marianne saw that I felt left out and lonely in our home, she took pity on me and let me belong to her. Our home was a camp divided and I did not quite know my place. My two older sisters were inseparable and acted as one. They always sat together, giggling and whispering. Most of the time they were hand in hand, and if Marianne and I had not shared a room, we might have never talked at all.

Louisie was my substitute mother and she taught me the practical things of life. She showed me how to tie my shoelaces, comb my hair with a straight part on the left, but she was also strict and often distant. Louisie was determined to excel in school and had no time for frivolities. That brought Marianne and I closer, and we sometimes found ourselves sitting together, giggling too. When that happened, my life was complete. Marianne was the peacekeeper of the home and she tried to convince Louisie to agree to let me come along when they went swimming or just for a walk, even when they rode their bikes to the theme park in Hellendoorn, and I begged to be allowed to join them and followed them around. I did my best not to complain when I was allowed to sit behind one of them on the luggage carrier of their bike. Mama was always happy when I disappeared for a while. She stroked my hair and with a half-smile said that it was nice to have a little peace in the home, without my noisy feet and voice. After all, she had a new baby who took up her time, and whose arrival had been a true blessing for her wounded maternal instincts. Danielle was the child whose presence worked as a balm on her deep war wounds.

If I have to define my position in the hierarchy of the family, I may be able to do so with the help of Dina Vardi's book about children whose parents were Shoah survivors.[3] She especially focused on those babies born shortly after the war, like me. According to Vardi, it was almost impossible for my mother to establish a normal bond with me while she was trying to deal with the unimaginable loss of her family, but when Danielle was born, the year was 1950 and things had somewhat changed. My mother turned to this baby as a flower to the sun. Her other children were moved to a secondary position. Although I no longer really found a comfortable place near my mother, I did not turn to my father because I was afraid of him. As a result, I kept on trying to catch my mother's attention and I was no doubt also jealous of the little girl who had usurped my place when I was just four years old. The change in our family constellation created a situation where I felt alone and lonely, belonging to no one.

The year we moved to 30 Rijssensestraat was also the first time that I felt how completely my mother had abandoned me. It was like the story of Hansel and Gretel, but I had neither pebbles nor a brother to guide me. I had come home from school for the midday meal and found the house locked. In those days, in the village, no one ever locked their doors, but the front door, the back door, the laundry room entrance, were all locked. Also, the store. Where had my family gone? I was about to burst into tears, the way a seven-year-old child might and held on to my bike not quite knowing what to do next. At that moment, my father appeared from behind the shed. He had waited for me. The family had moved – something I had momentarily forgotten – and we were now going to live just down the street. He walked me and my bike over to the new house. I looked at him from the corner of my eye. I was actually quite happy that he was there, and he did not look particularly scary. And he had been waiting for me, so that I had not truly cried for a long time. On the way, he explained that mama was fixing up the new house, and she was with Danielle, so he, after closing the store, had the time to wait for me. Perhaps my mother had forgotten me in the hassle of the move, but in my heart, I blamed her for leaving me all alone in the world! A tiny crack appeared in the blind trust of the child I was then.

The day everything changed in the balance of power in my family is an event that has been carved into the stone tablets of the painful memories of my childhood. It has been carved in words and images. I was an intelligent child with a good understanding of what was going on in my surroundings, and at school I learned effortlessly. On that fateful day we studied new words in Dutch. Pretty, fancy, high-class words which children would not need on the playground or in the garden behind our house. These were not words to use in a conversation with a friend, but words that made me grow. With those new words, I grew older and wiser, taller, and more erudite. With them, I felt a new respect for the Dutch language which had so many words that I, even at the ripe old age of seven, did not yet know them all. My vocabulary still had room for some new ones. The words defined rather adult concepts, and with one word I would now be able to say what might take a whole sentence in my immature, childish vocabulary. Oh, I loved those words, their length, high register, and music. I was one of the few children in my class who spoke proper Dutch. Most of the village children spoke the local dialect which was rather different from the queen's Dutch, but in our house, we were not allowed to use it. And now, rich with new words, I was ready to try them out at the first possible opportunity. I was going to speak Dutch like a professor!

The morning session ended at 12 o'clock and the children walked or biked home for their midday meal. We had to be back by half past one. The children from the outlying farms stayed over in school. They ate sandwiches their mothers had prepared for them, carried in a metal box whose sides folded down when it was empty. In winter, the headmaster allowed those children to make themselves hot tea in the staff room. I was often jealous of their daily picnics, but I lived nearby, and that day skipped home softly singing the new words to myself. They danced through my head and opened endless combinations of meaning. I thought up sentences and made stories with my new, fancy, important words at the center, strewn as they were throughout the tale like flowers in the meadow. I had to get home quickly to tell my mama. In the rush I forgot my bike, but never mind, it would be there in the afternoon. I had words to speed me on my way: compromise, dialogue, insight, understanding. Language poetry! Now I could give words to deep and wonderful thoughts and ideas. Language was a wonder!

When I came home, the food was already on the table, and mama, her beautiful clothes neatly covered in a short lace-trimmed apron, was waiting for me to serve the meal. My little sister sat in her highchair and my father was just locking the store. It was noon time, time to eat. We did, as usual, in silence. I was impatiently waiting for the opportunity to manifest my new linguistic skills but found no opening. The meal ended in a loud quarrel between my parents. This too was as usual. It was our dessert. Mama and papa disagreed about something, and words followed, tumbling down to the same old accusations. "Use some insight and understanding! Perhaps you might compromise a little," I yelled into the melee, but my words fell on deaf ears. They were too busy with their own argument to even notice my brand-new erudition. Finally, silence returned when my father turned on his heels in anger and fled to the store. But it was not yet over; mama sent me after him to say a few scathing words. "Tell him like this and this, and this, and then slam the door and come back to the kitchen and tell me exactly what papa said and did." She turned me in the direction of the store, gave me a gentle push on my behind and I went. I knew of no other routine. Entering the store was a little like an invasion. It was so completely my father's domain! That store was our bread and butter, and my father was a good provider. I carefully opened the connecting door between the house and the store and peeked in to see what he was doing. I was ready to carry out my mother's instructions and would also faithfully report to her what had taken place.

I was still standing on the threshold, half in the store and half in the hallway. My father was standing over the counter, leaning on his hands. His body sagged; his head hung low between his shaking shoulders. Was my father crying? I took a step closer. My father was crying! How then could he be a bad person without feelings? Something was not right. "Papa," I pulled him by his sleeve. "Why are you crying?" My father had never defended himself against my mother's accusations about his culpability in the death of the family. So, he was to blame, or he would have denied it. I did not think my father was shy, yet he did not answer me now and kept his silent back facing me, still letting the counter support him. Finally, he pulled his huge, red farmer's handkerchief from his pocket and noisily blew his nose. "But what could I have done?" he groaned, more to himself than me. It was such a strange sentence. What was he even talking about? But those were the words that echoed through our house in the orphaned hollows of the lost relatives. Suddenly, his words did not strike me as the utterance of a man without feelings or a vengeful person. My father did have emotions I had never seen before, and he definitely was not a bad man. He had tears. He was overflowing with sorrow.

I was incapable of carrying out the mission my mother had laid on my shoulders. My father's tears streamed on and on, while I was standing there, all confused. I realized that things in our house must change. I knew this as an axioma which is truth writ large and needs no explanation. This I knew in my seven-year-old soul. My parents would have to learn a new language, and I returned to my mother's kitchen, her territory, and placed myself facing her squarely, armed with the wonderful new vocabulary for which I had now found a perfect venue. I had beautiful Dutch phrases which would immediately change the atmosphere in our home. "Mama," I said in my best voice, "nothing is one-sided and perhaps you and papa can find your compromise, listen profoundly to each other and speak in heartfelt words. There is always room for a different kind of interaction!" I was sure that my mother would embrace me tightly, hold me close and say how smart I was. And thank me. That I had found words which had fallen on fertile soil. "How did you know to do this so well?" she would say. But that is not how it happened: my soft-hearted, sensitive mama, the one we had to protect, who knew how to make our house nice and clean and who made delicious food, that mama's face turned into a ferocious mask. It scared me and I took one step back. She did not even cry. I had not touched her heart with my wonderful words. "You are a very, very bad girl. Get out of my face. How dare you talk to me that way. I cannot even look at you." This outburst was so unexpected and so different from what I had imagined would occur that I froze on the spot in shock. "You are not my child anymore!" she shouted and pointed toward the kitchen door in dismissal. I did not wait for all the other words that continued raining down on me. I simply fled, far from my mother. What had I done wrong? I no longer understood anything. Completely undone, deeply hurt, I ran back to school, slipped into my chair, and sat there silently until school ended that day. My mother's outburst replayed inside my head like a stuck record. And the teacher punished me because he said I was daydreaming. He made me stand in the corner, facing the wall, hands behind my back. I did not cry.

The following day, when our midday meal ended in the usual quarrel and my father stood up from the table to escape into the store, I rose with him and followed him out. Like him, I faced the counter, my back to the connecting door, and like him, I laid my hands on the counter too. I stood close to my father and my small hands were close to his large, strong ones. We stood like that. He caressed my head gently, surprised by my behavior. After a while he pulled out a peppermint, handed it to me and then took one himself. He said we should see who could savor it the longest. He thought he would win that competition. And he was right. At 1:20 p.m., when I had to return to school, he opened the door to the store and let me out so that I did not have to go through the house and so I could avoid my mother.

A cooperation sprung up between us and that little girl that I was then discovered that doing things with my father was fun. The fact that my mother had not yet forgiven me smarted a little less although things between us remained tense.

When the grass seeds in our garden had sprouted into a green lawn and the roots had grown strong enough so that we were allowed to tread on it, my father bought a soccer ball and asked if I wanted to learn how to play. Of course, I did. For himself he marked goal posts between the hydrangeas, and for me between the elderberry bushes on the other side, near the clothesline. We ran hither and yon and kicked the ball from one goal to the other. It was a wonderful game, but while the lawn was quite large, it was not large enough to pick up speed, and mama hated our footballing in her beautiful garden. "You are killing the grass!" she yelled over and over, and when we ignored her, she brought home a young magnolia bush from the gardener's nursery and planted it in the middle of the lawn. Exactly between our two goals. For a while, this obstruction stymied us, but soon we devised a new rule: the magnolia might be a problem for a far kick, but we could easily jump over it and dribble with the ball. *Ach,* that poor magnolia. We jumped over it once too often and broke its crown. It remained a stumped little bush, sad, all alone in the center of our otherwise blooming garden, and barely managed to produce some tiny flowers.

Once in a while, my father took my hand and we walked to the soccer fields outside the village. Our local team was called the Nijverdalse Boys, and according to my father they were the worst team that had ever kicked a ball. They never won a single game, but they were tenacious, I will give them that. It was great. I understood absolutely nothing of the game, had no idea what the rules really were, but I was there, leaning against the fence post surrounding the playing field, my hand safely in my father's while he explained everything to me. We usually walked home in amical silence.

My mother could not find it in herself to change her attitude toward me. She remained angry and took my inspired speech as an insult. I was now in the same category as my father – persona non grata. "You are just like him," was one of her favorite sayings and I never forgot that line. As a child I thought about how I might learn from my father to grow up and be as strong as him, and not to allow myself to be pushed aside by life and people. I observed my father through my eyelashes and in time became his trusted apprentice.

The Yellow Danger

The year is 2014 and I am sitting on a nice wooden bench at the pedestrian mall, known as Keizerserf in Nijverdal, the former area of number 30 Rijssensestraat. I am in front of our house. Everything has changed so much but flashes of memories come rushing forward – we lived in that very big, very beautiful home on the narrow frontier between the catastrophe which almost destroyed our people and our family, and the normal life in a small village among green, pastoral meadows, trees, and farms. Suddenly, the physical changes here no longer block my inner eye, and as if a screen has been lifted, I have a glimpse of our existence there and I may hold on to it for a minute. The time tunnel has transported a few pieces of the puzzle of our lives. Then, like a flash of lightning, blinding and absolute, I know that just as the world is round, and I am cold in the pale November sun, my bench is exactly in the same place as where my father's Opel used to park. He called that car "The Yellow Danger."[4]

He kept his Opel in front of the store and for me, that little girl of then, our yellow car was a sign that my father was at home just as the flag above the Soestdijk Palace signified that the queen was in.

Our Opel Record played an important role in our lives. Every two years papa traded in his car, but he always wanted a yellow one. The car was papa's work car, used to deliver goods to the customers on the outlying farms, but it was also used for family outings. I am not sure what was more fascinating, my father's skill with the rope he used to tie the beds and mattresses to the roof of the car without benefit of a roof rack, or the way he made careful preparations before we took a drive on our free Sundays. My father did not expend energy on unnecessary movement and activity. Each gesture served a purpose; he was perfect in the performance of all his tasks, and delivered all big items sold in person. He carried all the pieces outside, and with a swing and a lift, he spread an old blanket over the roof of the car to protect its paint, and then arching up the bed frame quickly, he laid it across the roof, legs in the air. He was like an elegant dancer, arms raised high and balanced on the balls of his feet. He tied down the bed securely so that it formed a kind of roof rack. The rope turned into a solid weave, trapping the bed up there like a fly in a spiderweb. Once he had made sure that it was not going to move, he still pulled the cord once more and only then did he bring the three parts of the mattress up to the roof, laid the pieces down gently inside the upside-down bed and tied the sections to the legs of the bed frame. A hurricane would not have pried that delivery loose. My father used neither knife nor scissors to get the cord the length needed. Somehow, he tied it up without leaving loose ends. At the customer's house, he pulled on the cord once and it all let go. He rolled it up, using his bent arm as a guide, around the elbow into his open palm, until the cord was balled up and ready for its next use. The cardboard and blanket that had protected the roof were also dismantled, folded, and put inside the trunk. If he used thin or short rope, he wound it into a ball with the help of his thumb and pinky in neat figures of eight.

For family outings he also had a set routine. Papa took the map of the Netherlands from the glove compartment, unfolded it on the kitchen table and as he ran his index finger along the roads and byways, searched for the best route to take. He wanted more than just to arrive at our destination. He wanted his children to see interesting sites along the way. We were on a day trip and there was time to stop and break up the long drives. Sometimes he chose a converted mansion that had become a café to show us something about its architecture and treat us to our favorite drink: an ice-cold cherry soda. This was at a time when we did not have a fridge in our home and carbonated drinks were treats reserved for birthdays and weddings. Holding the frosty bottle and sipping slowly through the straw made us feel that we were on vacation. Danielle and I felt special and important, sitting at the small, square table, listening to the gentle flow of conversation around us. We were deeply impressed that in spite of our kosher lifestyle, it was still possible to sit there and have something, if not cooked food, then just a treat. Mama might order a sherbet with pink and green ice covered in whipped cream and papa usually settled for coffee with apple cake. Before every trip, my father took the car to Van Egmond's garage for a final inspection. Water, oil, air. Everything had to be perfect and only then were we ready to set out. There was no way our car would break down on the highway!

While papa occupied himself with the technical side of our trip, mama took care of food and put us to work to think of games to play on the way. For instance, looking for other Opels, other Yellow Dangers or cars with foreign license plates. Papa told stories; mama sang songs with us. These times have stayed with me as idyllic and welcome changes in our usually tense homelife. If it was cold, we had a plaid blanket to spread over our knees. The car had neither heat nor radio, but this was no problem. We had our games and we had the woolen plaid blanket. We were not cold. We were on an outing and were having a wonderful time.

Papa made sure that we did not skip any sites he had planned. He pointed to the left and to the right, with his typical theatrical, dramatic gestures, and we, his daughters in the backseat, were fascinated. We drove through the blossoming cherry orchards of the Betuwe when we went to visit our Ome Levi who had been engaged to our martyred Tante Bela, in his beautiful villa, and once, papa took us to see the flower farms of Lisse and Hillegom. There were rows and rows of tulips of every color, and other amazing flowers. We drove at walking pace, endless rows of bumper-to-bumper cars and looked around in amazement at the magical landscape that might have been painted by Van Gogh.

I am telling everything backwards because we had fun even when we stayed close to home. Papa took us to visit our aunts and uncles in Holten (who were actually mama's cousin and her aunt and uncle) and when he was in a good mood, he chose the scenic route through the tourist road through the heather and evergreens. He drove up to the top of the hill, turned off the motor, put the car in neutral, sometimes even passing the key to me before he let the Opel go. Danielle and I screamed with excitement and a little fear, for the car galloped like an out-of-control horse, but it always ended well. Papa waited till the car slowly came to a halt and held out his hand for the key which I handed over with hands still shaking from the dizzy ride down. For a second our eyes met in the rear-view mirror. He winked. Yes, we had been there together.

When our two big sisters, Louisie and Marianne, got married and lived in the west of the Netherlands, we often drove in that direction. It was far to the university city of Utrecht, where Louisie's husband studied veterinary medicine, or to Baarn, where Marianne's husband ran his import business. I always got carsick, but I would not have missed our trips for any treasure in the world! We had the best time when mama drove. Papa sat next to her, full of critique of the way she handled the wheel, but he was not mean, more gentle than normal, and mama did not argue with him. She hung on to the steering wheel like a drowning sailor to a piece of wreckage as if she were afraid to be thrown clear of the car. She bit her lip in concentration. Papa sat half turned toward her, his arm across her seat, his coat open, pockets overflowing with small treats for his big daughters. Things he had picked up at the last minute. My father's habit of filling his pockets has a long history and perhaps I should tell Hani about that. Later, maybe, when we are back home.

Anyway, there we were, driving, the entire family. Soon we reached a place near Amersfoort where the traffic light had been replaced with the first traffic circle we had ever seen, and mama simply did not know how to get off that turnabout and ended up missing the exit to the highway. So, she drove around the circle a second time. This was usually also the place where I gave back my breakfast, but who cared! We were on a road trip, going round and round. Later, when we came to that same spot, papa warned us in advance by saying that we were about to take a ride on mama's carousel.

Even now here in Israel, when I come to one of the numerous traffic circles, I would like to miss the turnoff and go around once again, and with my inner eye I suddenly see the Yellow Danger ahead of me, my mother at the wheel, desperately trying to take the right exit. And another memory, just as vivid and just as recurring, is when I get caught in a long traffic jam, cars slowing down and honking in frustration, yet the men at work on the road are unperturbed. I hear my father as clearly as I can hear the radio talking about the latest news, "Every time I show up, they see me coming and someone tears up the roadbed." My children are familiar with their grandfather's complaint and wait for me to say it time after time – in Dutch, no less. It is a piece of our family's history. And aside from that, it also proves beyond a doubt that road repairs are not a plague invented in the 21st century.

Of course, I have not remained frozen in time as a little girl of seven, but that day, when I learned that new vocabulary and my life changed, I did not forget. And neither did my mother. She was unable to forgive me for not doing her bidding and for choosing my father's side. And my father? He also never forgot that day that I launched my new vocabulary, and I warmed myself at his presence. I searched him out. Without words. Neither of us discussed what had actually happened in our household that day, and perhaps neither of us knew how to broach the topic, but something had changed. In the final analysis, it was the store that served as a bridge between my father and me. That huge space with the aroma of new clothing, pure sheep-wool blankets, and yard goods was the place where I could relax. The store, my father, they accepted me there without question. Of course, in the rainy climate of the Netherlands, the store also became my playground, something that my father did not quite appreciate as much as I did. All in all, my father's store was my first university, and I took the initiative, asked to be accepted and after I was in, took my studies seriously.

It started something like this: "Papa, I want to help in the store. Can I?" And with a sly smile I added, "Please?" On many levels, my father treated me as an adult, not as a child of not even 10 years old. He looked me over from head to toe and chose his words carefully. "Child, first you have to wash your hands and face and your shirt is full of stains. Go and put on something clean. The way you look is no way to serve our customers."

Everything that happened in the store was interesting in my child like eyes. I observed how my father stood behind the counter, always ready for the next customer and always with a friendly smile. The store made him whole; it was an organ of his body and that is how I wanted to fit in the store too. Papa's hands never rested. He also did not allow the help to sit around idly. Papa's rule was that no one was allowed to lounge in the entrance to the store, waiting almost desperately for the next customer. And personnel were not allowed to stand outside and smoke. Customers came as a steady stream. The store was profitable, and customers expected to find a prosperous, hardworking business, for that created trust. If business slowed down for a while, the girl could always dust the counter, make sure goods were neatly folded and returned to their proper places. She could also bring a bucket of soapy water to wash the big picture windows of the display cases. Doing nothing was bad for business!

To the left of my father's fixed spot, he had the cash register, a shiny, beautifully decorated monster with copper and silver ornaments and in the background numbers that popped up when you hit the right keys. When you had entered the right amount of the purchase, you turned the handle and the cash-drawer opened. To me, that cash register seemed enormous. It stood on a high shelf so that I had to grow a little before I could even use it and before I was allowed to do so. I learned to place the money in its proper places, each denomination in its own compartment, securely held in place by a spring. At the front there was room for coins. Every time the register opened, it sang a few notes like an accompaniment of our prosperity. Ching, ching, and the register displayed its hidden treasures. First, you put the money you had earned inside and then you gave change. Giving change was a trick I learned easily. It was not a matter of doing math, but simply a matter of counting. You just counted back until you reached the amount of money the customer had put in your hand. For instance, let's say that our neighbor, Mrs. Dikkers, had bought something that cost four guilders and 12 cents, and she gave me two coins of two-and-a-half guilders, meaning five guilders in total, then I handed her change as I counted back, starting with cents, "13, 14, 15, 20, 30, 40, 50, and one more coin of half a guilder." I triumphantly put down the coins on the counter. It was like magic. I loved giving change and was as proud as a peacock when I was promoted to stand by the cash register. I had to earn this task and papa did not give it to me before he was certain I was ready.

I started my training at the entrance to the store, "Bela, go stand over there and when someone comes in, hold the door and greet them. Then, after they buy something, open the door and see them out. Say, thank you and please come again soon." This seemed like an important job to me. I was the first face people saw. I made sure my hands were clean, my hair combed, and I checked my dress for stains and leftover food. I stood by the door with my back ramrod straight. A soldier on watch. Sometimes the customers greeted me by name, touched my head gently. Everyone knew me: after all, I was the daughter of Samuel Prins. Now and then I threw a glance at my father. We were providing for the family together. I helped him to sell the goods. And selling was the essence of our existence.

At precisely half past ten, my mother came into the store with a cup of scalding hot coffee for my father. Just the way he liked it. Whenever I was in the store too, mama played along with my presence there and asked if I would like a drink as well, as if I were just as important as my father. I always turned down her offer, for I was too focused on my father's coffee-drinking ritual. What I really wanted was to be allowed to bring my father his hot coffee, and in time, mama taught me how to do this the right way. The cup had to be balanced in the absolute center of the saucer and the spoon had to be inside the coffee, for its presence there reduced the liquid's movement and prevented it from sloshing over the top of the cup. At first, I made a mess of things, the cookie on the saucer was soaked through and half the coffee wound up there as well. But I was tenacious and kept on practicing. To keep the cookie dry, I devised a neat trick: I took it between my teeth and then, slowly, slowly, heel to toe, walked the endless length of the corridor between the kitchen and the store. By the time I made it, the cookie had disappeared, but even that problem was eventually solved. I succeeded in delivering coffee and cookie perfectly balanced and dry to my father. I placed the coffee on the shelf near the cash register and waited patiently for the coming event. At first, mama followed me to check and to make sure I had not spilled too much of the coffee, but soon that was no longer necessary. Papa inhaled the delicious aroma of freshly percolated coffee and embraced the cup with his hands. Very, very carefully, he poured a few sips onto the saucer and brought it to his lips. He blew on the steaming coffee and then emptied the saucer with great pleasure, sighed, and returned the coffee to its place next to the cash register where it languished the rest of the day. Now and then my father visited the cup, took a sip of the now cold coffee, but until he closed the store for lunch, no one was allowed to touch his coffee or heaven forbid, try to take the leftover drink back to the kitchen.

Today, in my home on the Mediterranean Sea, I drink my coffee in exactly the same way. I take one deliciously scalding sip and then drink the cooling coffee to make the pleasure last as long as possible.

The store had a man's department, where my father sold white dress shirts, flannel work shirts and work clothes of the Lonneker label, such as coveralls for the factory workers. All the articles were neatly stored on deep shelves, waiting for customers. Every time my father tried to sell a shirt, he unveiled it with ceremony to show it to the customer, all the while singing the article's praises. "Look at that quality and look how perfectly white this bleached cotton is. It is pure cotton! And yet, so cheap! You get two of them for the price you would pay if you went to the men's fashion shop!" Once the customer had made his choice, the unsold shirts had to be remounted on their cardboard spines, rewrapped in their cellophane covers and refolded so that they would look identical to the never-yet-unpacked items. Papa was going to teach me this art. I was given an old shirt to practice on and was reprimanded every time I did it wrong. He did not want messy looking shirts on his shelves. "Put the shirt down on the counter – no not here, where I serve my customers. Take it to the small glass-covered one, where we show stockings and girls' underwear. Good. Put it down with its buttons facing down. Fold the sides toward the center. Watch the crease! Now you can fold the sleeves inward as well, but make sure you bend them at the elbow, straight along the cardboard. Use a pin to secure the fabric in place. Good. Now put the cardboard back in the shirt's center, fold everything around it, turn it over... Bela, it is off kilter! Do it again." Until I mastered the art of shirt folding. I learned to fold the shirt's collar over the cardboard and push the shirt inside its cellophane prison. And I was done. I had done it right! "Customers like to feel that they are the first to get the shirt in hands. No one likes to buy things that have been unpacked too many times and rejected by others." Yes, my father was a strict task master, but he did explain.

In the yard goods department, I was not really allowed to do too much. Papa did not allow me to cut fabric. He did not even allow the store clerk to do this. He was the only one who knew to cut straight. He did let me try, but soon understood that my crooked scissor work would eat up the entire profit of the business, and so I had to be satisfied with being in charge of returning the fabrics to their shelves after he had made the sale. Folding back yard goods on their spine was a meticulous job and everything had to be exactly right. It was not enough to roll the fabric back carelessly. The edges had to match perfectly. It was more difficult than it looked, and I suffered a lot of my father's harsh comments before I mastered the task. Today, you might wake me in the night, push a bundle of yard goods into my hands and I will fold them back on their spines in perfect marching order. The technique is in my hands and arms: do not hurry too much, turn the fabric on its cardboard backbone with a gentle rhythm, smooth the fabric after every complete orbit, repeat until nothing protrudes. Then, return to its shelf, among other fabrics of the same family. Satin and other slippery materials are especially tricky, and papa taught me to use a pin to fold under the fraying edge. Doing so created the illusion that it was sewn under, while it prevented the fabric from slipping off its spine. It also kept the shelves looking neat and well maintained.

Once, when I was shopping for material in a small neighborhood store in Israel, I saw how the owner had discarded the piles of materials carelessly in a messy mountain of sagging fabrics. Yards and yards had slipped off their cardboard spines and the counter was a disaster area. The shelves behind the counter were half empty. It was obvious where the fabrics should be. Without a word, I slipped behind the counter and started returning the yard goods to their proper place, until I had restored the shelves and the counter to their former glory. As my hands were working, they stroked the soft materials, and I was transported to that other place. I was rudely shaken out of my sweet reminiscences when the owner touched my sleeve and in a stunned voice asked what I was doing. He raised his eyebrows at my trespass into his territory, but he was not angry. I had completely forgotten him, the Israeli heat and the Hebrew-speaking customers. I was back in Nijverdal and papa had put me to work. I ignored Yossi, the owner, until I had finished my job. When everything was done, the counter clear, fabrics sorted according to type and color, I rubbed my hands in satisfaction and half to myself, half to Yossi, I said, "Well, I am done. What's next?" My actions had created a respectful awe among the customers as well. Some of them even clapped. I apologized a little half-heartedly to the owner, "I grew up in a store and I learned this technique from my father," but Yossi said I was welcome to come every day, and part of me might have been happy to do this, but life still had some other plans for me.

In my father's store, the Firm of J. Samuel Prins, for a short time, the telephone was my domain. I had nudged my father to be allowed to answer it, but he hesitated. He believed that I should learn the art of speaking with an unseen party before he entrusted the store's office to me. He measured me with his eyes, decided I was old enough to take on a new responsibility and gave me the protocol: "When you answer the phone, you have to be polite and you must always say 'This is the Firm of Samuel Prins, how can I be of service?' and smile, even though the people cannot see you. A smile changes the intonation." The sentence was a long one, but the instructions were clear. I knew it was important to remember all the details. A phone was not a common instrument in those days and it was certainly not part of my daily routine. I did not need a phone. I had a bike and anyone I wanted to speak to lived within biking distance. Besides, almost none of the children in my class had phones; phone rates were high and calls had to be short and to the point. I had never spoken on the phone with anyone before. For people who lived beyond the range of my legs on the pedals, there were letters, such as Tante Klaar and Ome Bram in Holten. It is therefore not surprising that my father hesitated before giving me the job of operator. My repeated begging simply wore down his resistance.

I felt I had been given an important promotion and I was proud as a peacock. Of course, the phone decided to ring while I was still in the middle of opening the door for one of the neighbors who had bought a bit of flannel and some buttons. Now what? I wanted to answer the phone, but the store door was still open, and I was just saying goodbye to the client. That was important too! After endless minutes, or so it seemed to me, and the phone still ringing in the store's office, I was free to run and pick up the horn. I was out of breath but remembered to answer the way my father had taught me, "This is the Firm of Samuel Prins, how can I be of service?" and I smiled. I had a factory owner on the other side of the line. He was calling from Amsterdam. Amsterdam, a city I had never seen, and he knew to reach Nijverdal by phone. And I was the one talking to him. The manufacturer asked to speak to papa, but how was I going to get him to the phone? I certainly could not call out to him. That would have been rude. I had to leave the phone, get papa, and whisper in his ear that he was wanted on the phone. Papa's desk was covered with important papers, so I knew I should not put the horn there and make a mess. He might never find the orders, bills, letters waiting for his attention if I messed them up with the horn. In the end, I figured that the best way would be to do as my father had taught me, to put everything back in its place. I gently replaced the horn in its cradle, walked over to my father, pulled his gray dustcoat to draw his attention, and said that a manufacturer from Amsterdam needed him.

Of course, my actions had cut off the call! I had broken the connection all the way to Amsterdam, but papa was not angry. He laughed so much when I explained that I had wanted to leave the office neat and everything in its place so he would be proud of me. He smiled and gave me a peppermint.

The high point in my career as a businesswoman in partnership with my father came when he trusted me enough to pay the bills, deposit the daily intake of the store, and send off his orders to his suppliers throughout the Netherlands. During the day, my father kept the money in the huge office safe. It took up the entire width of the space there and was so heavy that when the house was built the office was constructed around it. The office had a concrete foundation that was much thicker than that of the rest of the house and the safe was placed there in its concrete shoes for safety. In the afternoon, my father took out the cash and counted it. He divided the money into several envelopes, added bills that needed to be paid. On each envelope he wrote in his beautiful calligraphy which bank it was intended for and what was to be done with the money. I learned new words such as receipts, invoices, plus 30, and other terms connected to the checks and balances of the daily running of our business. In those days, even a village as small as Nijverdal boasted a number of banks in its business center. Papa maintained business connections with all of them. In this way he got the best rates for his various payments and business accounts. When he was done, he handed me a small bundle of these envelopes, held together with a rubber band, put all of them inside a much bigger envelope and then watched as I hid everything inside my school bag. Papa made it clear that I was not to speak to anyone about what I was carrying and in fact, should not speak to anyone at all before I had carried out my task. Then he sent me on my way with my bike. I was to ride directly to each bank in turn, carefully save the stamped receipts that proved money had been transferred, paid, deposited, and bring all that paperwork to him. I carried out my mission to the best of my ability, blushing with pride that my father trusted me with our future, the fruits of his labor and mine in our store. I did not even say hello to classmates I saw outside, and never got off my bike to have a conversation with anyone. I rode, a serious frown on my face, from our store to the banks, following my father's instructions to the letter. For a short while I stopped being that mischievous tomboy I usually prided myself on being and became my father's partner. A child who had earned her father's trust and was not about to breach it.

Papa rewarded me for my help with a special prize: he was going to take me along to Amsterdam on one of his business trips. Mama made sandwiches with cheese, put a few apples in a paper bag, prepared lukewarm tea in a thermos flask and early in the morning, papa and I set out on our journey. By train. I was so full of my own importance that I forgot to bend his ear with questions and sat ramrod straight opposite my father in our second-class compartment. I was fascinated by the ride. We were on our way to Amsterdam where manufacturers walked the streets and made phone calls, and where they made things for my father's store. I was alone with my father. Everything was interesting: the steady noise of the diesel train that took us the first lap of the way; the sleek carriages of the electric train we took from Zwolle; the trees along the route which ran with us until the train outran them, and papa, sitting there, smiling at me, neatly dressed in his gray suit. We were on a trip together. In Amsterdam, we had to climb into a tram which stopped in the middle of the street. All around us were people who spoke Dutch in a strange singsong. I was perhaps eleven years old at the time and had never been in the capital.

At the factory, my father was greeted with strong handshakes and friendly shoulder clapping. I saw how important he was and felt proud that he introduced me to everyone, "This is my daughter, Bela." After a while I whispered in his ear that I needed to go to the bathroom, and the receptionist left her desk to show me the way. "Can you manage?" she asked, and when I nodded, a little embarrassed that everyone knew I had to pee, she walked away. I was left alone in a long, narrow space with on one side a number of stalls and on the opposite wall, the sinks and towels that peeked out from a strange contraption that supposedly sterilized the towel if you pulled on it. I found it strange that they had built so many toilets in this fashion, but I was in Amsterdam after all, so I was not going to question the wisdom of this construction. I chose the stall at the end of the row, walked in, and modestly pushed the bolt closed to lock the door. And that was it. I was stuck inside, for the bolt was a little rusty and when I was done, I could not open the door. I heard people coming and going when they came to use the toilets, but I was too ashamed of my predicament to call out. I sat. I stood. I pushed and pulled on the bolt and sat again. Children my age had no watches, and so it seemed that I was locked in that narrow, silent-as-the-grave box, for an eternity.

My father finished his dealings, and only then did he notice that I was not waiting in the reception area. No one knew where I was, and a search party set forth. Eventually they found a child, drowning in her tears with her neatly ironed dress all wrinkled and bunched up, the new bow in her hair sagging to one side. A child with the red cheeks of a country girl even redder because of all that crying and the sense of shame. I thought that my father had probably forgotten all about me in faraway Amsterdam and had already gone home, leaving me to live my life in the last stall of the toilets in the factory of that important man who had been so happy to see my father. I felt like Gretel of the fairy tale, except that I had no Hansel to help me. I told him. Perhaps the people who saw and heard me felt sorry enough for me not to laugh; I am not sure. I do remember that it was much too late to take a tour of the city. We still had a three-hour trip ahead of us and trains did not run very late in our area. We also had to walk home from the train and papa had to bring his Yellow Danger and put it to bed in Van Egmond's garage.

I saw the way home through my tears. Papa tried to comfort me. "Listen, child, you can tell everyone that you really spent a day in Amsterdam. You spent a whole day there and you also saw that very modern factory we did business with today. And you also learned something. Next time, you know that you should not lock the toilet stall."

Village life

Nijverdal was a village with many Christian denominations, varying from strict Calvinism to more liberal Lutheran groups, and a Catholic minority. There were at least six parochial elementary schools in the village and only one public one. The Catholic children were educated by the nuns. Every day they were taught about the church's sacred mission to bring the true religion to the sinners of the world. Every day a good Catholic put a penny in the mission box to support this work. The Jews were the most sinful of all and it was important to make them finally see the error of their ways and help them to embrace the true path. It was not unusual to be called names by those children as they rode past our house. All this was part of the deep-seated antisemitism of the church of those days. I realized that the Maria School pupils hated me but did not understand what they accused me of, and turned to my fountain of knowledge, my father. "Papa, why did we kill the Anointed? And what does that word mean?" My father sighed one of his sighs and explained, shaking his head in frustration, that those children meant Jesus. I knew that Jews did not believe in that Jesus, but I truly could not fathom why those children were so angry with me. I had no reason to want to kill anyone. I would not know how to kill anyone. Sometimes the explanations offered by adults only complicated my life. I shrugged my shoulders and went back to the sidewalk in front of the store to jump rope. Papa gave me some advice, "If those children keep calling you names, call back that it was not us at all, but the Jews from Haakselberg." This was a strange but common excuse in our house to shift blame for almost anything. There were no Jews in Haakselberg, so why say that? He was not helping, yet I did as told, and apparently the children I yelled back at were so surprised that their taunting cries stopped for a little while. When my father heard me yell back at one of those bikers, he came outside, pulled me close and said, "Child, it is impossible to fight such primitive hatred." Primitive hatred was an idea I had to research. It sounded interesting, but I was not sure of its meaning. "Papa, I do not want to play in front of the house anymore. They pass here all the time, and they always blame me for something I did not do. I hate it. It hurts and I do not really like yelling at them about those Haakselberg Jews. It is silly!" He answered after considering my words for a moment. "Beeltje," his nickname for me when things were bad. He lifted my chin, so I had to look him straight in the eye. "There is another way: you can fight." When I looked at him questioningly, wondering why he would tell me to use violence, I realized that I was dealing with something that he might have experienced himself. "If the child who curses you is on a bike, let them pass you, but then grab on to his luggage carrier, pull back on it with all your might so that he slows down, twist your arms to one side till he falls down with the bike on top of him. Tell him to leave you alone and for good measure, perhaps punch him once or twice and then run into the store." He winked. Perhaps my father did not intend this advice literally, but the next time some boy noticed me and screamed "*Jörre!*" I did exactly what my father had suggested. The cursing biker was alone, and as his bike had almost passed, I ran across the narrow street on chubby legs, planted my legs securely on the roadbed and pulled the back of his bike so suddenly and violently that he lost his balance. Then I pulled the bike sharply to the left, bringing it down on top of him. He was surprised, but not injured. I changed that a little, all the while screaming at him, "You are lying! I never killed anyone. And you are a *Jörre!*" I punched him once more and retreated to the safety of my father's store. The boy was left lying under his bike. The door to the store was open, and my father had witnessed the whole scene. "Good girl!" he said, laughing out loud.

Later in the day, a woman stormed into our store, pulling along her son. "Look what your girl did to my boy!" she yelled at my father. The boy had a few raw scratches on his arms, and he limped a little. My father gave the mother and her son a surprised look. "What? My daughter?" He spoke in the local dialect. "I am so sorry. I will fetch her right away." And he walked into the house to get me. Before I could even get scared, he whispered that he had been expecting this visit and that I should not worry. "You did a good job," he added, "That boy is even bigger than I thought." He added that I should play along now, not speak. "I will take care of everything," my father said. Then he took my ear but did not pull on it and we entered the store together. He placed me next to him, behind the counter. I looked at the furious woman and her crumpled child. He **was** much bigger than me. He gave me a furious glance, but he also grimaced in victory, certain that he was still going to win our little road-kill scuffle. I remained close to my father, hiding a little behind him for safety, but before my father even uttered one word, that woman looked at me, a chubby girl of some ten or eleven years old and her chunky teenager, about a year or so older than myself. "That one?" she asked, her voice rising in anger. The boy nodded and for emphasis pointed an accusing finger at me, hoping that now I would get a beating from my father and perhaps his mother too. But no, his mother turned to him, slapped his face, pulled his ear, and dragged him outside. "A little girl like that did that to you? For this you pulled me out of the kitchen? I left the laundry for this? Shame on you! A little girl like that!" She continued screaming profanities at him as they left the store, for wasting her time, for embarrassing her and for getting beaten up by the little *Jörre*. Papa waited silently until the bell over the door announced that she had left. He pulled me close. "A chip off the old block. Go get your roller skates and have fun or go play on the swing. You can jump your rope in front if you like," he said, fully satisfied that we had won this battle, if not the war. I used his good mood to ask for a peppermint and he immediately gave me one. It felt like a medal. That evening I wrote in my new diary that I had won, had not killed Jesus, and was not a *Jörre*.

Over time, the cooperation between my father and myself expanded a little. I was now old enough to be allowed to stand behind the counter with him and to serve the customers. I had already learned to write proper receipts and to write down purchases made on credit in a special long, narrow ledger. Papa signed off on everything I wrote down, just to make sure. Mistakes were out of the question. I also started accompanying him on a more regular basis when he took his merchandise to the customers. Papa continued the family tradition of peddling his wares to the outlying farms. Once a week on Monday afternoons, when the stores were closed in our village, papa delivered goods the farmers' wives had ordered the week before. Our Yellow Danger had room for everything, even for me. I would sit next to my father and together we went toward the planted fields and green meadows of the farms in the municipality. Papa told me that his father had peddled his goods with a three-wheeled cargo bike, and his grandfather had done it on foot, merchandise on his back. Our trips were a kind of journey into the past. We arrived at farms without running water, but a huge pump outside the kitchen, close to a large, smelly heap of leaky, fermenting cow pads mixed with straw to absorb the liquid – the dunghill. Sometimes the farmer had led a waterpipe from the well into the house, and above the zinc sink, installed a small pump. If I wanted a drink, the farmer's wife gave me a long ladle. With the ladle in one hand, I pumped with the other, working until water appeared. It was always cool and delicious. I loved that I could conjure up water from the well and I never stopped to consider that everyone used the same ladle to drink.

Papa was received with great hospitality and pleasure. He was all smiles, never forgot even the smallest of orders: needle and thread, elastic for underwear, or perhaps a yard of fabric for a small child. He also carried staples, such as those huge, red handkerchiefs the farmers liked, and my father also favored. (When I learned to sew, I fashioned summer blouses from two of them.) No order was too large or small for him. Just in case, he always brought some extras like wide brim farmer's caps for the men, towels, news from the commercial district, and if he did not bring goods, he came to sing the praises of all the things he could bring to make the farmer's life easier. The women liked the break in their hard work, bought a few items for their personal use, or chose pretty linen to update their bedroom. Papa sold red satin comforters, down pillows, work clothes, and aprons for the members of the family. Always something special at the Firm of J. Samuel Prins! That was our slogan.

Papa spoke the Nijverdal dialect with a flair that showed how much he felt at home in the village. I understood the language he used but did not speak it myself. My parents insisted that we speak proper Dutch, although we did so with a strong Twente accent. We swallowed the [e] at the end of verbs and emphasized the sharp nasal [n] instead. Still, here and there, the local dialect interfered with our queen's Dutch, making our utterances almost incomprehensible when we met people who lived in the west.

I understood that papa enjoyed my company and was proud to introduce me as his daughter. Sometimes, after he wrapped up his transactions, he asked if we might go into the stables, thinking I might enjoy seeing the animals and their offspring. I was deeply impressed by that huge sow who lay patiently on her side, allowing her piglets to nurse. They had arranged themselves in a perfectly straight line, each one latching on to their mother's teat. All, except for one. It had not conquered a spot at his mother's breast and tried, without success, to push aside one of his brothers or sisters. The farmer's wife pointed at this runt of the litter, "That one will be our Sunday meal," she said. I felt sorry for the little piglet, pulled my father's sleeve, and whispered that I wanted to leave. He took me to the fence around the meadow. There were babies everywhere. The filly was adorable, and the tiny lambs and calves were jumping and leaping all over the fresh grass. They were a little drunk with all those fresh minerals and vitamins, papa explained. Grass? Perhaps that is why cannabis is also called grass, I suddenly realize. Those animals were absolutely high!

Papa was not ready to drive away, and we once again entered the huge kitchen where he exchanged a few quiet words with the farmer's wife. He promised to return in a week's time and said his goodbyes. As we sat down in the car and he started the motor, he turned to me, "Bela, did you see that old man in the rocking chair near the stove?" Well, yes, I had noticed an old man but had hardly paid him close attention. An old man in a chair, what was so special about that? "Child, didn't you see how skinny he was, those thin, thin match-stick legs, but yet a huge belly?" I looked at my father questioningly. "Buying clothes for someone like that is not so simple, but his daughter loves him, and it hurts her to see her father in his pajamas day and night. And you know, I have an idea." He smiled, lifted one hand off the wheel for a second and I saw that typical crooked smile of his in the corner of his mouth. "Papa, what do you mean? Tell me? What idea?"

For my father, this moment signaled the beginning of his latest adventure and for the store it became a windfall. For the village it grew into a revolution in clothing for the sedentary elderly of the area. Papa realized that he had an idea that would profit him twice over. "I always have leftover yard goods that I simply have to write off as a loss. But what if I were to use those materials to sew perfectly fitting pants for the old people? I could leave extra space to fit their stomach, and I can sell the pants cheaply. How great would that be! Always something special by us, you know that! I have even thought of a label. We will call those pants stomach sizes, and we will sell them under our label, and that would also save us some more money. I will call that collection the SAPRINI collection, acronym for Samuel Prins, Nijverdal. It is perfect!" That is how the stomach sizes pants were born and so the name he had dreamt up during his early years became reality. The pants were a hit. And he made profit twofold: first, he wrote off the material that had not been sold by the end of the year and then he used it to make the pants. It was all perfectly legal. A roll of poison-green corduroy and one of radioactive dark purple, which should have been dark red, became the first collection. For the lining of the waist and pockets he had yards and yards of pink lace. He had bought that for the catholic families to sew first-communion dresses for their little girls, but no one wanted pink. They only wanted white. The factory that sewed the pants under our label used all the material my father supplied, and SAPRINI landed in our store. A half-page advertisement in the local paper brought in the buyers, and everything sold very quickly. No one complained about the strange color combinations. The women were grateful that their father could sit outside, dressed in neat corduroy which fit perfectly. And the men? None of them complained. The deep pockets easily contained their pipe and handkerchief and nothing else mattered. And papa? He was satisfied as well. Profit rolled in, the shelves had room for new fabrics, and when people started asking for SAPRINI pants by name, he was delighted.

One Monday afternoon, instead of going out to peddle his wares to the farms, my father announced that he was planning on visiting our uncle in Holten. Ome Louis was a beloved relative, son of my mother's aunt and uncle, our closest living relatives, and I loved them dearly. Tante Klaar and Ome Bram were brother and sister to my murdered grandparents and the closest thing to real grandparents for myself and my sisters. Of course, I wanted to come along, but feared that if I asked, he would say no, and so I decided to make sure I was there when he was ready to leave. I would be a stowaway in our

Yellow Danger. The car was already in front of the house, unlocked, which was common in those days, and of course there was no car alarm. Who had even heard of such a thing in the 50s! I looked around, saw the coast was clear, climbed into the back and pulled the red plaid over me. I must have fallen asleep while I waited. I had curled up in the footwell of the back seat, so I would not be so visible. I was only half awake when footsteps came near, and the door pulled open so hard that it nearly bounced back and closed again. I screamed and pulled myself up. The plaid fell away, and there was my father, as white as a sheet, the small nail hammer he used to attach the price cards to the wares displayed in our shop window raised high above his head. We both were in shock, but he found his voice first. "Bela," he screamed at me. "What are you doing here?! I nearly hit you with the hammer." And I burst into tears.

Papa allowed me to sit up front, next to him. We drove to Holten through the hills. It was wonderful.

Daydreaming

I learned to daydream when I was 14 years old, at the beginning of the '60s. Every day I took the bus to Almelo, to the Erasmus Lyceum High School. On that day it rained, and I had forgotten my gym clothes. Actually, I often preferred not to bring them, using some lame excuse. I had grown self-conscious about my body and hated my legs sticking out of the shorts and my arms out of the sleeveless shirt. I would tell my slender, energetic teacher that I had my period, felt ill or that my mother was washing the PE uniform. Anything to get me out of the embarrassing undressing in the open space of the gym. She frowned, wrote down a bad mark in her book, then pointed toward the side of the gym where she stored the horses. Jenny, another chubby teenager, had also succeeded in avoiding the gym uniform and was already sitting on one of them. I walked toward her, placed one hand on the horse and expected to pull myself up with the other so I could comfortably sit high up and kick my legs as I watched my classmates run around the gym. But things did not work out quite that way. The moment I put some pressure on my left arm I felt a sharp, searing pain, which was so intense that it overwhelmed me. I let go of the handle, fell down in a heap at Jenny's feet and stayed there, groaning and holding my arm. I tried not to scream. What was going on? I had not done anything out of the ordinary and had jumped up on the horse many times before. Where did that paralyzing pain come from? Jenny stared at me for a moment, but when she saw I was not faking, she ran to our teacher who rushed over to where I lay, groaning and trying to keep my arm still. The moment she tried to touch my arm, I forgot my determination not to scream and yelled, "No! No!" And protectively curled myself around my pain.

Someone brought the elderly amanuensis who also dispensed first aid, and he came running with his satchel. I refused to let him touch me. All I was willing to let him do was to help me walk back to the dressing room, and I sat down very slowly, all the time hiding my left arm from anyone trying to touch it. Because I was so uncooperative, it was decided that my parents should come and take me home. "Your arm is not broken!" said the EMT. "How could it be – you put no pressure on it."

After an eternity, my father showed up, huffing and puffing and a little annoyed. He gave me a penetrating look. He had left the store in the middle of the day, and only the clerk was there to handle things. He wanted to make sure he had not come for nothing. One look was enough. "I think you have dislocated your shoulder again," was his diagnosis. "Mama will put it back into place." After all, I had a history of dislocating my left shoulder, and over the years, my mother had learned to push it back into its socket. I did not respond. It did not feel like that. The pain was below the shoulder.

The trip back to the village was a horror. I felt every pebble on the road, every seam between the slabs of concrete of the roadbed. Pain shot through my upper arm, as if I had been shot. It was nearly unbearable. I held my arm as best I could, bit my tongue, but it was hard. Papa saw my silent tears, and finally decided that we should first make a stop at Dr. Bakker's clinic.

The visit was a fiasco. I refused to let the doctor touch my arm and hid the painful upper arm behind my right hand. Even my beloved family doctor could not convince me to let him examine my arm. He did notice its strange shape and after a moment said that I needed an X-ray.

The only place where that was possible was at the Princess Irene Hospital in Almelo, a few minutes away from the school. So, it was back to Almelo, over the pebbles and prefabricated slabs of the roadbed.

Papa filled in forms and we sat down to wait for our turn. I was not an emergency case. I was not bleeding, screaming, or dying, so we sat there, papa and I, waiting in anxious silence. My father was worried about the store, but also about me. He wanted to smoke his pipe or a cigar, but he had brought neither, so he just sat there, drumming his fingers. By the time they called my name, night had fallen. I had never had X-rays done and was worried about letting anyone touch me, but now no one paid any attention to my cries and objections. Someone straightened my arm, pushed it down, turned it this way and that, while the machine clicked and clicked. Finally, it was over, and papa and I were sent back to wait for someone to interpret the photos. "Don't worry," papa said, and then, suddenly everything moved into high gear. I was lifted onto a gurney, my father running along. There was an elevator, a long corridor, and I arrived at a semi-private room. "Private insurance," my father said. He did not want me in a crowded ward. My arm and I were lifted into a bed, and once there, someone hoisted it up and attached it to some contraption to immobilize it, still ignoring my cries of pain. Then everyone walked away. My father too. When he returned, he sat down on the edge of my high hospital bed. "Don't worry, child, you will be home tomorrow." He would repeat that sentence when the next day I was told I needed emergency surgery to fix my very broken arm. He still repeated it as I remained stuck in that bed, arm in traction, month after month. He visited every day after he had closed the store for the night, and I was always there, lying on my back, arm in traction. "Don't worry, child. You will be home tomorrow." He brought me summery baby doll pajamas from the store, pink, with tiny flowers. The top had to be cut open along the side seam, for I could not pull anything over my head because of the traction. My arm, held in place by weights to pull the bone straight, and I, attached to it, also almost motionless. Before all that took place, I was taken back to the enormous X-ray machines and every single bone in my body was photographed. Just to be sure, because there was a diagnosis, although no one really shared it with me. I was but a rag doll in a bed, tied to my immobilized arm. I had something called a UBC – a congenital bone cyst of over six centimeters – which meant that there were about six centimeters of bone missing in my upper arm. That is why the bone had weakened, for as I grew, the cyst had also grown. It was even the underlying cause of my dislocating shoulder.

I underwent a bone transplant, a surgical procedure that was almost experimental in the Europe of the early 1960s. Splinters of my hip bone were chipped off and implanted along the cyst of my upper arm, and all that was needed now was time. Time for the splinters to 'take,' grow, and span the space between the two parts of the bone. My arm was raised high from the elbow up, a steel pin had been inserted through the elbow, and to this pin, a weight was attached to keep the bone growing straight. It was all quite painful and tedious. The pin moved freely inside my flesh, causing the weights to shift the wrong way, and every three days a nurse came to straighten it again, pushing in back and forth through the elbow. At first, I screamed but learned to accept the torture. To avoid infection, I was pushed full of penicillin, given to me by injection, three times a day. After months of this, there was hardly any space on my arms and legs to push in the needle and even those injections became very painful.

I was a 14-year-old tomboy who suddenly found herself in a semi-private room where old women came to have their hemorrhoids, hernias, or other small problems surgically removed. They were not talkative. I was stuck, imprisoned in my hospital bed, and the truth is that after a few weeks my hip had healed itself from the surgery and I was as healthy as a fish. And yet, I remained bedridden because my body was attached to an arm that needed healing. I was stuck on my back, arm up in the air. The enormous sticky tape the surgeon had glued over the incision caused an allergic reaction and itched like the dickens. I scratched the itch with my right hand, and very slowly, carefully, tried to remove the sticky plaster. When I finally succeeded, and saw the huge, angry red scar, I was in shock. My arm was raw, from my scratching, and red, from the allergic reaction, but there was also a huge, slightly gaping wound, like two pouting lips, that ran from elbow to shoulder. The surgeon had closed the wound only loosely, running long stitches of catgut along the width of my arm, but leaving huge spaces between each stitch, for he was not sure that the one surgery would suffice. I would always have an ugly scar along the entire length of my upper arm. When I continued to scratch the area, the incision started to bleed. Only when my nurse threatened to immobilize my good arm too, did I leave the itch alone and suffered until my body finally accepted the smelly glue. I became a patient, docile and passive.

The fact remained that I had completely lost my freedom and autonomy. I lay there like a turtle on his back, legs in the air, in vain trying to turn over. I was attached to cables, pins, weights, and I could not even lift my head from the pillow, because of the angle of the traction. I could not turn over on my stomach, could barely turn to my left a little, but not for long, for this position cut off the blood supply to my broken arm. The only solution I found was to disappear a little. I turned inwards and learned to daydream. Now I could let the nurses do whatever they did for me or to me, without complaint or struggle. They kept me clean, took away my bodily waste, saw to the surgical incision, and gave me my daily injections. It was all the same to me. I had lost my body and now it was up to the nurses to see to it. For hours I lay there, alone with my vague thoughts. I could not really read because it was too difficult to hold a book. If I held it in my left hand, way up there, the text was too far away and soon my fingers would shake from the effort of holding the book. If I held the book in my right hand, I had to hold it flat somehow, but I could not turn the pages, one-handed as I had become. On top of it all, I was left-handed and missed my dominant arm sorely.

One morning, my favorite nurse made me a present of a radio set tuned to receive the hospital's broadcasts. It was mostly music to amuse the patients, and perhaps some talk shows about this or that. The radio was hidden inside a piece of foam rubber, like a small mattress, and covered by a tiny, white pillowcase. It blended in with my bed linen. The hospital broadcast stopped at nine in the evening, when patients were expected to go to sleep. I pushed the radio under my pillow and lay on top of it so that it would not fall off the bed, and no one could come and steal it. I kept my ears glued to the music, the long lectures in between and I completely tuned out the world around me. I started living inside the one part of my body that was in perfect working order: my head and ears. When people intruded into my space, they found me like that, silent and seemingly deep in thought. The nurses thought that I was depressed but I wasn't. I was living inside my daydreams and there everything was possible. I could make the hospital disappear, the strange smell of the camphor my body was rubbed down with to prevent bedsores, the useless groaning of the old woman in the bed next to mine. I wasn't there. I had entered a whole new dimension. I emptied my head so well, that even time itself disappeared. I floated elegantly above my head, opened the tall windows, and flew outside. I stared at a fly on the wall and followed its trajectory as an adventure. I could join it in its flight. In hindsight, I might have discovered a kind of meditation which rescued me from the frustration of being tethered to that bed, but then it was the only way to escape my humiliated, powerless, and imprisoned body while accepting the inevitable, and allowing it to heal.

Of course, my situation was quite complicated. I was not sick, and yet, I was forced to lie there for long days and weeks, more than eight months in total. Moreover, I was lonely because I was not in the children's ward where I might have had company, or in orthopedics, where I might have met people in similar predicaments. In the private ward I was the longest residing patient, and over time, perhaps because of all the above, the nurses spoiled me a little. They came to sit at my bedside for small talk and they brought me occupational therapy projects. I made trivets out of wooden beads which I put together slowly and laboriously, held high in my far away arm. There were also those who used my inability to flee to try and talk about Christianity. They thought they could save me from my Judaism and bring me close to that Savior I had once been accused of killing. So, yes, I knew about their Anointed and that Jews were still waiting for theirs. "Doesn't it bother you that you won't be saved?" This was a sentence that needed explaining, for I was not familiar with the concept "saving". I was told that my mistaken adherence to the faith of my ancestors would prevent me from going to heaven. There was no room there for me if I did not embrace Christianity. I did not know this. In my religious instruction, I had learned that after death our soul returns to G-d and that is paradise. I had never learned about a separate place for Jews and non-Jews. But who wanted to start a learned discussion?! For a moment I reflected back on those Haakselberg Jews and whether I might blame them for the Jewish oversight, but I did not find an opening to squeeze them in. I nodded and daydreamed on. Besides, my biggest problem was not so much what would happen to me after I died, but the fact that I was lying in that bed virtually devoid of clothing. The only thing covering me was the top of the baby doll my father had brought from the store, cut open and draped across my torso. My biggest fear was that it might move if I did not keep completely still. I truly wanted to hide my brand-new breasts behind the thin fabric and save my modesty. Having my soul saved and earning a place in paradise was not my first priority.

One day, a preacher came to visit the sick and paused at my bedside. He asked if I was "a believer". I nodded wordlessly, hoping he would move on to the old lady in the other bed, but he wanted to know what denomination I belonged to. "Dutch Israelite," I whispered, blushing all over and using the shameful euphemism that had replaced the word "Jewish" after the war. Hitler had turned the latter into a curse word. "Ah, I understand," said the pastor, but even then he did not move away. "Can I still pray for you?" What could I possibly say to that? I had just turned 15, was sitting on a bedpan and had been left that way by a nurse who was busy doing other things. I hoped I would not make unpleasant noises down there. I closed my eyes in despair, but that man who was trying to be nice to me, apparently thought I was going to join him in prayer and bowed his head. I kept my eyes closed and daydreamed that I could get rid of him without insulting him; it worked, for when I finally opened my eyes again, he stood up with a smile, tapped me lightly on my right shoulder, smiled again, and went on.

I consoled myself with the knowledge that it was already getting dark outside and soon papa would come with stories of the store. He would speak the only words he had to express his worries about my health and his sadness about my absence from the house, "Do not worry, child. You will be home tomorrow."

---

1. https://networks.h-net.org/node/35008/reviews/44187/foray-aalders-nazi-looting-plunder-dutch-jewry-during-second-world-war
2. https://nl.usembassy.gov/our-relationship/marshall-plan-1947-2017
3. Wardi, D. and Goldblum N. (1992) *Memorial Candles: Children of the Holocaust.* New York: Routledge. Translated from the Hebrew *Nos'e HaHotam.*
4. China was known as the Yellow Danger in those days.

EPILOGUE

Hani and I are almost finished with our journey, but we still have to make one more trip. It won't take long. Once more I will return to that small piece of hallowed ground where my parents have found their eternal rest. They lie side by side, in silent camaraderie, and I will bow down low over their headstones to touch something essential yet ethereal of their time on earth. If only I could, I would wake them up for a minute, but I console myself with the belief that the soul is always close and that it can hear me. I know that I have heard the ram's horn, the *shofar,* of their lives and that it has changed me. "You know, don't you? You know that I love you. Both of you." And I add that ancient accolade a child says when he asks G-d to protect his parents, "*avi mori, imi morati,*" my father my teacher, my mother my teacher, rest in peace. You have earned the right to that peace. I hope that you are together with all those people who were torn from your lives in the cruelest way imaginable. I hope you are there with your entire tribe, laughing and talking about us, the Samuel Prins-Pagrach daughters, our many children and grandchildren, and now even great-grandchildren, your descendants, all of them. I know you will tell them about the Jewish Homeland, the State of Israel, which came into existence too late, but it did come and now your children can live there in safety. Thanks to the Jewish State, your children in the Netherlands are also protected and safe.

I thank you, mama and papa, for all that you did for me and for all that I learned from you. Raise your glass out there in the Garden of Eden and drink to our health and to peace. Now there is a Jewish soldier behind every Jewish child, man, and woman, and that is your eternity! We will bundle up the memory of all the souls in the bundle of our lives and will carry it along with us into the future.

Bela Ruth Samuel Tenenholtz

Kiryat Shmuel, Haifa

ABOUT THE AUTHOR

Bela Ruth Samuel was born in the Netherlands, less than one year after WWII. Her parents and older sisters were Shoah survivors. She lives in Israel and is the proud matriarch of a large family, including children, grandchildren, and great-grandchildren. After many years as a professor of English literature, she is retired and has turned to writing. This is her third book.

FURTHER READING

The series **Holocaust Survivor Memoirs World War II** by Amsterdam Publishers consists of the following autobiographies of survivors:

Outcry. Holocaust Memoirs, by Manny Steinberg

Hank Brodt Holocaust Memoirs. A Candle and a Promise, by Deborah Donnelly

The Dead Years. Holocaust Memoirs, by Joseph Schupack

Rescued from the Ashes. The Diary of Leokadia Schmidt, Survivor of the Warsaw Ghetto, by Leokadia Schmidt

My Lvov. Holocaust Memoir of a twelve-year-old Girl, by Janina Hescheles

Remembering Ravensbrück. From Holocaust to Healing, by Natalie Hess

Wolf. A Story of Hate, by Zeev Scheinwald with Ella Scheinwald

Save my Children. An Astonishing Tale of Survival and its Unlikely Hero, by Leon Kleiner with Edwin Stepp

Holocaust Memoirs of a Bergen-Belsen Survivor & Classmate of Anne Frank, by Nanette Blitz Konig

Defiant German - Defiant Jew. A Holocaust Memoir from inside the Third Reich, by Walter Leopold with Les Leopold

In a Land of Forest and Darkness. The Holocaust Story of two Jewish Partisans, by Sara Lustigman Omelinski

Holocaust Memories. Annihilation and Survival in Slovakia, by Paul Davidovits

From Auschwitz with Love. The Inspiring Memoir of Two Sisters' Survival, Devotion and Triumph Told by Manci Grunberger Beran & Ruth Grunberger Mermelstein, by Daniel Seymour

Remetz. Resistance Fighter and Survivor of the Warsaw Ghetto, by Jan Yohay Remetz

The series **Holocaust Survivor True Stories WWII** by Amsterdam Publishers consists of the following biographies:

Among the Reeds. The true story of how a family survived the Holocaust, by Tammy Bottner

A Holocaust Memoir of Love & Resilience. Mama's Survival from Lithuania to America, by Ettie Zilber

Living among the Dead. My Grandmother's Holocaust Survival Story of Love and Strength, by Adena Bernstein Astrowsky

Heart Songs. A Holocaust Memoir, by Barbara Gilford

Shoes of the Shoah. The Tomorrow of Yesterday, by Dorothy Pierce

Hidden in Berlin. A Holocaust Memoir, by Evelyn Joseph Grossman

Separated Together. The Incredible True WWII Story of Soulmates Stranded an Ocean Apart, by Kenneth P. Price, Ph.D.

The Man Across the River. The incredible story of one man's will to survive the Holocaust, by Zvi Wiesenfeld

If Anyone Calls, Tell Them I Died. A Memoir, by Emanuel (Manu) Rosen

The House on Thrömerstrasse. A Story of Rebirth and Renewal in the Wake of the Holocaust, by Ron Vincent

Dancing with my Father. His hidden past. Her quest for truth. How Nazi Vienna shaped a family's identity, by Jo Sorochinsky

The Story Keeper. Weaving the Threads of Time and Memory - A Memoir, by Fred Feldman

Krisia's Silence. The Girl who was not on Schindler's List, by Ronny Hein

Defying Death on the Danube. A Holocaust Survival Story, by Debbie J. Callahan with Henry Stern

A Doorway to Heroism. A decorated German-Jewish Soldier who became an American Hero, by Rabbi W. Jack Romberg

The Shoemaker's Son. The Life of a Holocaust Resister, by Laura Beth Bakst

The Redhead of Auschwitz. A True Story, by Nechama Birnbaum

Land of Many Bridges. My Father's Story, by Bela Ruth Samuel Tenenholtz

Creating Beauty from the Abyss. The Amazing Story of Sam Herciger, Auschwitz Survivor and Artist, by Lesley Ann Richardson

On Sunny Days We Sang, by Jeannette Grunhaus de Gelman

Painful Joy. A Holocaust Family Memoir, by Max J. Friedman

I Give You My Heart. A True Story of Courage and Survival, by Wendy Holden

Flower of Vlora. Growing up Jewish in Communist Albania, by Anna Kohen

Zaidy's War, by Martin Bodek

In the Time of Madmen, by Mark A. Prelas

The series **Jewish Children in the Holocaust** by Amsterdam Publishers consists of the following autobiographies of Jewish children hidden during WWII in the Netherlands:

Searching for Home. The Impact of WWII on a Hidden Child, by Joseph Gosler

See You Tonight and Promise to be a Good Boy! War memories, by Salo Muller

Sounds from Silence. Reflections of a Child Holocaust Survivor, Psychiatrist and Teacher, by Robert Krell

Sabine's Odyssey. A Hidden Child and her Dutch Rescuers, by Agnes Schipper

The series **Holocaust Books for Young Adults** by Amsterdam Publishers consists of the following novels, based on true stories:

A Life in Shelter, by Suzette Sheft

The Boy behind the Door. How Salomon Kool Escaped the Nazis, by David Tabatsky

The Precious Few. An Inspirational Saga of Courage based on True Stories, by David Twain with Art Twain

The series **New Jewish Fiction** by Amsterdam Publishers consists of the following novels, written by Jewish authors. All novels are set in the time during or after the Holocaust.

Escaping the Whale. The Holocaust is over. But is it ever over for the next generation? by Ruth Rotkowitz

When the Music Stopped. Willy Rosen's Holocaust, by Casey Hayes

Hands of Gold. One Man's Quest to Find the Silver Lining in Misfortune, by Roni Robbins

The Corset Maker. A Novel, by Annette Libeskind Berkovits

There was a garden in Nuremberg. A Novel, by Navina Michal Clemerson

Aftermath: Coming-of-Age on Three Continents, by Annette Libeskind Berkovits

The Girl Who Counted Numbers, by Roslyn Bernstein

The Butterfly and the Axe, by Omer Bartov